Executive
Qualities

Congratulations on
Completing PSDP
— Sept. 19-22, 1989

Executive
Qualities

Joseph M. Fox

Addison-Wesley Publishing Company, Inc.
Reading, Massachusetts ■ Menlo Park, California ■ New York
Don Mills, Ontario ■ Wokingham, England ■ Amsterdam
Bonn ■ Sydney ■ Singapore ■ Tokyo
Madrid ■ San Juan

Ninth printing, February 1988

ISBN 0-201-02437-6
JKL-AL-898

To Mary Agnes Christie

Preface

In 1958 I was asked to present to my fellow salesmen some ideas on Executive Qualities; i.e., what qualities were needed for a person to be an executive. The subject has fascinated me ever since.

The list of qualities and abilities in this book is the result of 13 years of managing in the highly complex electronics industry. The last 6 of these years were spent as a general manager of a $100-million-per-year business.

This is a book about people—how to select and judge people; what to look for; what to beware of. It gives names to traits and qualities which all will recognize, but which perhaps all have not thought about as deeply as they should.

This book is for two different groups of people; first, those employees of large organizations that desire to 'get ahead,' to 'make it,' and become part of the management and particularly the upper management. Second, this book is for established managers who are trying to guide their employees and make them more effective and more capable. It gives words and structure with which to pinpoint strengths and weaknesses.

The book is a guide to be used by individuals to evaluate first themselves; second, their subordinates; third, their superiors, and last, all other individuals with whom they come into frequent contact. The title tells much about the book—*Executive Qualities*. The structure and content of the book is a naming and examination of those human qualities which are most necessary to success in today's large organizations.

There are, no doubt, qualities that are not on the list that should be, and some that may be on the list that should not be. Should the reader come to that conclusion, good. The idea is to have people think about the qualities; not to list them once and forever.

What are the qualities that enable one to become an executive? Are they inborn? Can they be developed?

"To name it is to know it" was a belief of many an ancient tribe and I have found it a great assist in managing people to be able to pinpoint in one word what areas a rising manager must improve to go further up in the organization.

I list 16 qualities, and 6 abilities. An ability is a talent an individual possesses, and it is a sum, a result, of several individual qualities. Too often these abilities, which are combinations of qualities, have been treated as though they are single qualities. The list is a result of the painful sting of failure. I would agonize over why a subordinate wasn't making it; he had all the qualities on my then current list. I would finally recognize the reason for the failure, and I would either add a 'new' quality to the list, or understand one already there to a deeper extent.

There are some who will argue that all of this focus on qualities and abilities is nonsense; "It's results that count," they'll state. This clarifies nothing! Of course, it's results that count. But how do you get results, today, in our large organizations? You get power, you become a boss, and hopefully, *the* boss. How you perform at each stop along the way determines to a great extent your next move—up, down, or sideways. How you appear to your superiors is very vital.

The understanding of what qualities are needed and desired assists a manager in picking the right subordinates, in getting results. Note that I state *large* organizations. The qualities needed to run small organizations differ significantly from those needed to progress in and run a large organization. This will be explained in the book.

Self-appraisal and self-improvement are the best kinds. You should use the list of qualities to check yourself. You should ask others (at the risk of being hurt by the answer), "Am I cheerful?", "Am I independent?", "Do I show empathy?" Such opinions must be sought, as most people will not openly comment on another's behavior, and some of the answers will hurt.

When you find a weakness, or the appearance of a weakness in yourself, you should then set out to change it.

A vice-president confided to me that early in his career he was once told that he was too argumentative. He didn't think he was, he said, but if his boss did, then he was going to go out of his way to be agreeable, or at least appear agreeable. Even if you cannot change yourself, you can change your image, how you impress others.

In this book I am reporting on the world of the executive as I find it, not necessarily on the way I'd like it to be. People have asked me why I accept some seemingly "bad" aspects of this environment. I accept them because that is the way it is, even if we'd all rather have it some other way.

About the quotes interspersed throughout the book: They crystal-lize ideas for me and set me thinking in new directions. The quotes were the stimulus of many of the ideas in the book. The quote by Pascal on page 141 stimulated the section on Judgment.

The quotes have been gathered from dozens of sources, but I must mention four. The *Forbes Magazine* and the *Forbes Scrapbook of Thoughts on the Business of Life* have been unending sources of dis-covery and interest. *Harpers Magazine* has a *wraparound* section which is a fascinating source of all kinds of quotes. Jess Lair's book *I Ain't Much Baby But I'm All I've Got* yielded beautiful comments written by some of his students who submitted them to him anony-mously.

And, finally, many of the ideas and quotes are from *The Practical Cogitator, or The Thinker's Anthology,* selected and arranged by Charles P. Curtis, Jr. and Ferris Greenslet, published by Dell. This gem of a book is crammed with the great writings of great thinkers over the centuries.

The quotes by Thomas Szasz are from *The Second Sin* published by Anchor Press/Doubleday.

I owe a debt of gratitude to many people for their help with this book; to Bob Lesko and Bob Porter, both chief executive officers, for their ideas and criticism of the text; to the hundreds of managers who have reacted in management schools to the ideas presented; to Jean Smith, my competent and supporting secretary for the past six years; to Donna Slovikosky, who typed most of the original manuscript; and to Donna Armfield, Debbie Wastler, Rene Williams, and Jo Ann Copeland, who took my handwritten early drafts and made sense of them.

Rockville, Maryland   J. M. F.
May 1976

Contents

An executive has nothing to do—that is except—to decide what is to be done—to tell somebody to do it—to listen to reasons why it should not be done—why it should be done by somebody else—or why it should be done in a different way—to prepare arguments in rebuttal that shall be convincing and conclusive—to follow up to see if the thing has been done—to discover that it has not been done—to inquire why it has not been done—to listen to excuses from the person who should have done it—and did not do it—to follow up a second time to see if the thing has been done—to discover—that it has been done but done incorrectly—to point out how it should have been done —to conclude that as long as it has been done—it may as well be left as it is—to wonder if it is not time to get rid of a person who cannot do a thing correctly—to reflect that the person in fault has a wife and seven children—and that certainly no other executive in the whole world would put up with him for another moment—and that in all probability—any successor would be just as bad—and probably worse —to consider how much simpler and better the thing would have been—had he done it himself—he would have been able to do it right —in twenty minutes—but that as things turn out—he himself spent two days trying to find out why it was that it had taken somebody else three weeks to do it wrong—and then realized that such an idea would strike at the very foundation of the belief that—An executive has nothing to do.

Author unknown

1
The What
and Why
of the Book

What is it that makes one individual rise to the top where another fails? Is it brains? or finesse? or astuteness? What?

Karl Von Clausewitz, in 1818 Director of the General War Academy in Germany and author of *On War,* commented that people could be divided into four categories, based on two qualities—energy and brightness.

1. Energetic and dull people. They should be driven out of the organization as soon as possible, as they can do great harm.

2. Lazy and dull people. You can take your time getting them out. They will not do much harm.

3. Energetic and bright people. They should be staff personnel because they enjoy working and are smart enough to do it.

4. Lazy and bright people should be executives. They are smart enough to know what to do and yet lazy enough to not want to do it. Therefore, they will send others to do what needs to be done.

Von Clausewitz was right, of course, but we cannot leave the subject of executive qualities with just brightness and energy.

We need a list of human qualities that are key to the executive role. Which qualities are important? I have compiled a list of these qualities and this book lists and explains them.

There are many lists of qualities and a great deal of interest in the subject. Some lists are short. I have chosen to make the list longer rather than shorter, because there are subtleties that may escape the quick reader. Some of the qualities are very similar to others, e.g., courage and independence, yet the differences between them are important. Many people will see the subtleties immediately, and others will not.

Some people have reacted to the list with the comment, "It's a *long* list." So it is, but to gain an executive role, you should have all (or most) of these qualities. The list is important because it provides a framework against which to evaluate yourself, your subordinates, your bosses. It provides many specific criteria to compare against as opposed to a few, vague, hard to specify attributes. It assists the putting into words what it is that "bothers me about that fellow."

I shall list and explore 16 qualities and 6 abilities in detail, explaining first what is meant by the label we use for the quality or ability. Then I will show the importance of the quality or ability by relating anecdotes of the quality or ability or the lack of it—in use in today's large organizations.

An ability is often erroneously treated as though it were a single quality, but it is really a combination of single qualities. Communications ability, for example, is not an indivisible quality, but a sum of intellect, knowledge, courage, and several more qualities.

There are many people who possess most of these qualities and abilities. Most people fail not because they lack many, but because they *lack one completely*. The lack of *one completely* can counteract the other qualities and abilities and make them liabilities.

Lacking one or two need not be fatal, if the individual recognizes the weaknesses and *acts* to prop them up. This fact—that the lacks can be managed—makes it all the more important that they be recognized and recognized early.

The qualities and abilities are needed for two quite different purposes: The first purpose is to attain power or position. The second is to be effective once power and position are attained.

Every individual on his or her way up is simultaneously a superior and an employee, a manager and a subordinate. This book is aimed at the individual *in both* roles. At one point in discussing a quality, I will address the readers in their roles as managers. "Look for this in your subordinate; emphasize such and such." And under the same quality heading I will address readers in their other roles, as subordinates.

Astute individuals never forget the duality of the roles they hold, and avoid confusing the roles. One of the most difficult situations that occurs every day is when the manager is in a meeting both with the boss and with subordinates. The manager's roles are confused and there is a danger of exhibiting the wrong qualities.

Indeed, this book is for *all* individuals who work in large organizations. Whether they are on their way up or down or standing still, it is still fascinating to watch others. This book, hopefully, makes sense of many of the seemingly incomprehensible actions.

THE QUALITIES

The qualities can be grouped under three headings:

> The Personality Qualities
>
> The Belief Qualities
>
> The Mental Qualities

If you are weak in any one of these three areas, your chances of success are lessened dramatically.

If your personality is such that you cannot work easily and effectively with other people in today's large people-oriented organizations, you are not going to go very high.

If your beliefs are out of step with those of your organization, you must beware. You are swimming against the tide.

If your mental abilities are inferior, you will probably lose out to sharper competition.

Everyone grows from infancy in the belief and mental qualities. These two in turn shape the personality qualities. This is, of course, oversimplified. All three groups interact and modify each other. But when individuals interact with other people in today's large organization activities, the important first impression is made by their personality qualities. This is the area that makes or breaks a person's chances to get to the top.

Therefore, we will start this book with the most important area—the personality qualities, even though in the development of the individual they are last.

This is not to say that the belief and mental qualities are not important. They are. And they are important in two ways: First, if persons lack one of them, their chances are hurt precisely because of that lack. And, second, their personalities are also hurt because of the lack. Two areas of competence suffer—the area itself, and personality.

The greatest portion of the book examines the qualities and abilities. Chapter Five reviews lists of executive qualities that others have selected as the key qualities and some qualities that did not make our list. Chapter Six is a short description of the "Executive Environment." "An Epilogue, Success," attempts to define success.

The 16 individual qualities that are important to achieving high managerial position in today's large organization are:

The *Personality* Qualities	Emotional maturity
	Independence
	Realism
	Courage and boldness
	Ambition
	Insistence
	Willpower
	Empathy
	Cheerfulness
	Resilience and Durability
The *Belief* Qualities	Beliefs
	Integrity
The *Mental* Qualities	Intellect
	Logic
	Nimble Mindedness
	Knowledge

Each quality contributes to the overall individual. A missing quality can mar a person's image badly. We shall examine each quality in detail.

The reader should discuss each quality with a friend or superior, using personal experiences to illustrate the possession or lack of a quality.

THE ABILITIES

The qualities are individual and singular, but there are combinations of them that add up to an "ability." These abilities are more like skills than traits; they are formed by a number of qualities and by the amounts or degree of each quality that the individual possesses.

Communications ability is a combination of several qualities. It is often treated, erroneously, as one item, but it is a sum, not a single capability. Communications ability is contributed to by independence, courage and boldness, empathy, knowledge, nimble-mindedness, cheerfulness, willpower, emotional maturity, resilience and durability, logic, knowledge, and intellect.

There are six abilities:

Judgment

Communications ability

Sales ability

Leadership

Political astuteness

Foresight

We will describe each in detail, with special emphasis on judgment, the most critical ability, and communications ability.

EDUCATION IS NOT THAT IMPORTANT

There is a fallout from the premise that personality is most important and that is that education is *not* as important as most people believe it is. What degree you have and from what university you received it doesn't make that much difference in the long run. Those items do not affect your personality that much.

A college degree will usually give the person beginning a career an edge over a co-worker who has no degree. And that advantage will last for the first few promotions. Someone reviewing the promotion will always ask, "Should we promote an employee who has no degree?"

But in the middle levels, after the employee has proven excellence by performance, the degree issue is usually dropped.

Which institution the degree is attained at will give one person a starting advantage over the next. A B.A. from Harvard gets you started in the management training program—a B.A. from Podunk gets you into sales, or accounting, or personnel! But in the long run the initial advantage is lost and personality most determines where a person fits in the hierarchy.

I do not mean to imply that the lack of a college degree is insignificant. Our large corporations are bureaucracies, and the lack of a degree will be a continuing source of annoyance and hindrance to the individual's career. The question will unfortunately come up. But it will not be a show-stopper, only a slight slowdown.

THE DOMINANT ROLE OF WEAKNESS

A man will please more on the whole by negative
qualities than by positive; by never offending, than by
giving a great deal of delight. In the first place, men
hate more steadily than they love; and if I have said
something to hurt a man once, I shall not get the better
of this, by saying many things to please him.

Samuel Johnson

What happens if you have 21 of the 22 abilities and qualities? That depends first on what level you have achieved. At the first level, the lack probably doesn't hurt you much. But if you are on your way up, the lack will hurt. How much it will hurt depends on which one of the 22 qualities and abilities is missing.

If judgment is missing, and it's missing altogether, your chances are slim. The same is true if you lack emotional maturity. "Not so," some will say. "Anyone who has 21 out of 22 will surely go far."

That is partially true, but only partially. If you as the 21-out-of-22 individual are competing against dozens of people who are 22 out of 22, then you will lose out to another. Yes, you'll get part way up the ladder, but unless you work on your weak areas, you will bog down.

Weaknesses at high levels distort the other strengths. They warp them and make them detriments rather than assets. For example, consider individuals who are habitually sarcastic or cynical (a lack of emotional maturity) and who also have fine vocabularies, voices, and good diction. Their positive attributes in communications make them more terrible to be with, because they distribute their venom effectively. Or, said another way, their cynicism warps the value of their communications skills.

Weakness becomes more critical as the persons go higher. As they go higher, they have less time to do things, and they become more visible to higher level management. Their weaknesses are easily spotted as they are constantly under pressure.

If they are indecisive, defensive, erratic, or cynical (indicating lack of emotional maturity) or timid (indicating a lack of boldness), their weaknesses *will be seen* by top management.

6

When it comes time to decide on the next step up for these individuals, top management will worry. "Can we trust this division to Jones? He's so defensive! He'll never let the corporation know anything if he can hide it. We've got to be able to see what is going on in that division."

If there is another candidate who is not as strong in several areas as Jones but who has *no obvious weaknesses,* he will get the job. This is not to say that Jones, with tight, close-watching management, can't do the job he's doing. But there comes a point in an organization where the boss doesn't have time to watch subordinates closely. And the boss will go far afield to find one that doesn't need to be watched.

What exceptional people do when they are missing a quality is to prop up the weakness with the strength of a subordinate. Of course, the first thing is to know what you don't know. To think you know when you don't means you won't be wary and propping up when you should be.

> An outstanding executive was very poor in marketing. His verbal skills were average. His method of operating was to have a "mouthpiece"—a representative—to do all the talking. If one were to observe this executive in a marketing situation, one would think he was the junior to the spokesman. This executive would take the time to rehearse the spokesman, to be sure they were thinking alike. Then he'd go along to the customer visit to get firsthand information. He propped up his weakness so well that few realized he had a weakness.

Any executive can do the same thing. One who is weak on details can get an assistant who excels at detail. One who is weak at results can have a fierce righthand aide who drives for results.

The Peter Principle by Dr. Lawrence J. Peter and Raymond Hull points out that one way to avoid being promoted, if that is your desire, is to be "creatively incompetent." They give several examples of people who are competent, yet who deliberately create an impression of incompetence in a single area *to avoid being promoted.*

They describe a person who deliberately exhibits sloppiness and one who displays eccentricity. These deliberate "weaknesses" effectively keep the individuals from being promoted. The authors suggest some weaknesses to adopt: being officiously economical, being eccentric in any one of many ways, e.g., constantly parking your car in the space reserved for the company president. They also point out that this creative incompetence should not be carried too far, or it will endanger one's present position.

Although many of the examples in *The Peter Principle* are hilarious, they are believable. The point is clear. Being incompetent (or eccentric) in any one area will in all likelihood result in your being passed over for promotion. In *The Peter Principle* the authors are suggesting, tongue-in-cheek, that this be done deliberately. In everyday work, it is done accidentally and often unknowingly.

STRENGTHS AND THE MANAGER'S JOB

A man's strength cannot always be judged by his strongest actions; in many instances he is judged by his weakness.

J. W. A. Henderson

Some argue that the ambitious person should concentrate on strengths, and not on weaknesses. Peter Drucker, in his fine book, *The Effective Executive,* published by Harper & Row, uses the following example to illustrate that a manager must use the strengths of subordinates, and avoid their weaknesses.

> Another story about General Robert E. Lee illustrates the meaning of making strength productive. One of his generals, the story goes, had disregarded orders and had thereby completely upset Lee's plans—and not for the first time either. Lee, who normally controlled his temper, blew up in a towering rage. When he had simmered down, one of his aides asked respectfully, "Why don't you relieve him of his command?" Lee, it is said, turned around in complete amazement, looked at the aide, and said, "What an absurd question—he performs."

Drucker is right, as far as he goes. But he doesn't go far enough. A manager has *two* jobs to do—first, to get the objective accomplished and, second, to train and grow subordinates.

In the first dimension, Drucker is right—the manager should deal with the strengths of subordinates. The manager does that to get the objective achieved, the job done. In the second area, the manager *must* point out to subordinates the weaknesses they possess so that they can take the necessary actions to correct the weaknesses, if possible, or to prop them up if it is not possible to correct them. If subordinates don't recognize in which area they are weak, they will not be attempting to fix them.

This second duty is critical because most people do not find their faults without some outside help. Most people are blind to their own faults.

> "I want to be a vice-president if I have the talents," is a comment frequently heard by managers. What managers should do is point out to their ambitious subordinates that they must do better at, say, communicating. This usually brings a comment

8

like, "Are you saying I'm no good at communicating? That I can't do my job?"

No, managers are not saying that. They probably just got through telling the subordinates that they're doing a fine job.

Managers are just pointing out areas of weakness that will hurt the subordinates' chances of becoming a vice-president.

The problem is that such conversations can be a little painful. Managers are pinpointing *weaknesses,* and subordinates may tend to become defensive. What happens is that all too often managers just avoid all possible unpleasantness and don't point out the weak areas. (This assumes that managers know which qualities are important.)

Strength Can Be a Hindrance

Strength can become a place of comfort and an individual often will not grow beyond that strength. The person keeps using it over and over. In *Management and Machiavelli,* published by Holt, Rinehart and Winston, Anthony Jay makes the very true but hard-to-perceive point that a person's strength can become a handicap:

> Richard Coeur de Lion was one of those managers who was first rate at his own job but never grew up into the wider responsibilities of managing the whole business. He was a marvelous soldier, but when he became king he could not give [soldiering] up. He went off to the crusades, which at that time had a fairly low priority, and left England to get into deeper and deeper trouble. Moreover the capital appropriations he made to the crusades were ridiculously high and desperately needed for other parts of the enterprise. He was a great warrior hero, but a disastrous king. There are many Coeur de Lions in industry. They are the ones who cannot let go, like the sales managers who cannot make the transition to management. They still go out and sell to all the big customers themselves, instead of creating a context and formulating a policy within which others can sell more effectively. If they become chief executive their professional craftpride blinds them to the real faults in the organization—they just think it is because the salesmen are not as good as they were in the old days. It is, after all, a difficult transition from skilled production engineer or process planner to production manager, from salesman to sales director: It means abandoning the craft skill on which all your security and self-esteem and reputation have rested, or at least reducing its importance compared to the unknown demands of managing others who possess them. The higher that skill, the harder it is to abandon. The sign of a potential manager in a craftsman,

in fact, is not craft excellence; it is the willingness to see his craft as only part of the whole problem, and not to blame other departments for what is beyond their control. As a production man he may justly blame sales for faulty estimating or insufficient information at the design stage, but not for wanting things in a hurry if the competitive situation clearly demands it. But the budding Coeur de Lion will not see it that way: Wisdom and folly in others are judged only by the criterion of how easy or difficult they make his job.

Strength can be too comfortable, and it also can be *too* strong. An individual who is always fierce, or demanding, can hurt any chance of personal progress. Each quality should be exhibited, used, to the right degree. The choice of degree—it should be choice, not just an accident or habit—is one of the functions of judgment.

THE EXECUTIVE POTENTIAL SCORECARD

Figure 1.1 is a listing of all the qualities and abilities. The scorecard should be used by filling in a minus sign for those qualities a person lacks and a question mark for those in question. Put a plus sign where a person has the quality.

This should be used by two sets of people. It should be used by all managers. It's difficult, but essential.

Subordinates should use this list to evaluate themselves.

You know yourself better than anyone else does. You can seek the views of others if you are mature enough to solicit true feedback.

Many will not tell you the things that may help you because they don't want to hurt your feelings. They are not up to truly criticizing.

The scorecard helps focus on the areas that need improvement. To isolate that area and name it is a start toward improvement.

The scorecard can also be used to score your superiors. You may find that when you list their qualities, you may understand them better as a result. You will be better able to work with them, if you understand them better.

> ... when at some future date the high court of history sits in judgment on each one of us—recording whether in our brief span of service we fulfilled our responsibilities ... our success or failure, in whatever office we may hold, will be measured by the answers to four questions—were we truly men of courage? were we truly men of judgment? were we truly men of integrity? were we truly men of dedication?
>
> *John F. Kennedy*

Qualities	Yes	No	Possesses ?
Emotional maturity			
Independence			
Realism			
Courage and Boldness			
Ambition			
Insistence			
Willpower			
Empathy			
Cheerfulness			
Resilience and durability			
Beliefs			
Integrity			
Intellect			
Logic			
Nimble-mindedness			
Knowledge			

Abilities

	Yes	No	Possesses ?
Judgment			
Communications ability			
Sales ability			
Leadership			
Political astuteness			
Foresight			

+ means the person possesses the quality or ability
− means the person lacks the quality
? means not clearly a + or −

Fig. 1.1   An executive potential scorecard.

11

In War: Resolution
In Defeat: Defiance
In Victory: Magnanimity
In Peace: Good Will

Winston S. Churchill

Try not to be a man of success;
but rather try to be a man of value.

Albert Einstein

I have three precious things which I hold fast and prize. The first is gentleness; the second is frugality; the third is humility, which keeps me from putting myself before others. Be gentle and you can be bold; be frugal and you can be liberal; avoid putting yourself before others and you can become a leader among men.

Lao–Tse

To be great, to be a person of stature, a man must have character, judgment, high intelligence, a special aptitude for seeing his problems whole and true—for seeing things as they are, without exaggeration or emotion.

Field Marshal Montgomery

When a top executive is selecting his key associates, there are only two qualities for which he should be willing to pay almost any price— taste and judgment. (Almost everything else can be bought by the yard.)

John W. Gardner

The four greatest virtues are
moderation
wisdom
justice
fortitude

Marcus Aurelius

2
The Personality Qualities

The set of qualities most critical to gaining high position are those we call the personality qualities. Specifically they are:

Emotional maturity	Insistence
Independence	Cheerfulness
Realism	Willpower
Courage/Boldness	Empathy
Ambition	Resilience/Durability

Some of the personality qualities are very close to each other. Independence and courage are very similar. Ambition and willpower overlap. Emotional maturity is present to some extent in independence, courage and resilience and durability.

Some examples of managers in action, exhibiting a quality, could be listed under more than one quality.

I have deliberately made the list longer rather than shorter because I believe that the overlaps are not complete and the subject is worthy of the longer exposition.

Many authors and executives believe that personality should not enter into the evaluation process. Some even argue that there is no such thing as personality. Both views are erroneous. How can anyone doubt that a person has an overall effect or impression on others, that this impression is a total of the effects of individual abilities and characteristics, mental, spiritual and physical?

The following definition of personality is abstracted from *The Oxford Dictionary of the English Language,* 1973:

Personality *n.*, 1. the visible aspect of one's character, as it impresses others. 2. a person as an embodiment of a collection of qualities. 3. psychology a. the sum total of the physical, mental, emotional, and social characteristics of the individual, b. the organized pattern of behavioral characteristics of the individual. . . .

Some of the personality qualities are internal, some are external, some are both. The external ones are seen almost immediately by the observer. The internal ones are those that shape one's decision process. The internal ones will not be as obvious as the external, but over time they will be seen. Some individual qualities are both internal and external.

Internal	*External*
How I make up my mind	How I impress others
Emotional maturity	Willpower
Independence	Empathy
Willpower	Insistence
Courage	Boldness
Ambition	Resilience

14

Internal (cont.)	*External* (cont.)
How I make up my mind	How I impress others
Resilience	Independence
Realism	Cheerfulness
Empathy	

Personality can be managed and changed. Persons cannot change their intellect at all, try as they might.

Persons can decide to be more cheerful, less argumentative, or more patient. And with effort they can change their actions, and in time their mannerisms, their personalities. Those persons who can't change their personalities can manage their images. They can *appear* more cheerful, even if they're not. This takes great strength, of course, but it can be done.

Personality shapes all. Look at the following from *The Money Game* by "Adam Smith" published by Holt, Rinehart and Winston. The author is talking about the money managers who make the big investment decisions.

> If you are not automatically applying a mechanical formula, then you are operating in this area of intuition, and if you are going to operate with intuition—or judgment—then it follows that the first thing you have to know is yourself. You are—face it—a bunch of emotions, prejudices, and twitches and this is all very well as long as you know it. Successful speculators do not necessarily have a complete portrait of themselves, warts and all, in their own minds, but they do have the ability to stop abruptly when their own intuition and what is happening Out There are suddenly out of kilter. A couple of mistakes crop up, and they say, simply, "This is not my kind of market," or "I don't know what the hell's going on, do you?" and return to established lines of defense. A series of market decisions does add up, believe it or not, to a kind of personality portrait. It is, in one small way, a method of finding out who you are, but it can be very expensive. That is one of the cryptograms which are my own, and this is the first Irregular Rule: If you don't know who you are, this is an expensive place to find out.

> It may seem a little silly to think that a portfolio of stocks can give you a portrait of the man who picked them, but any tuned-in stock-picker will swear to it. I know a private fund where there are four managers, each with one section—$30 million or so— to run. Every three months they switch chairs. "In three months," says my friend, "Carl's portfolio will have little Carlisms creeping in. Maybe Carl is skirting the high fliers too much—he never has liked them. Maybe there are a couple of real Carl-y ones in

there that he gives too long to ripen. So when I move into his chair, I have no trouble dialing out the stuff that is too Carl-y. Meanwhile Teddy is doing the same thing in my chair."

EMOTIONAL MATURITY

We examine emotional maturity here because it colors all the other qualities. Without emotional maturity, success is largely a matter of chance. With it, a person's other qualities are enhanced.

Emotional maturity means being at peace with yourself, accepting your capabilities and limitations, blessings and failings, and your situation in life. It means that you can strive for higher positions, yet accept failure.

Emotional maturity enables you to avoid the negative attitudes of despair, of anger, of guilt. It is an acceptance of events and their consequences. It is recognizing that all you can do is your best, and if it doesn't work then, so be it. It enables you to put your energies into positive endeavors.

Emotional maturity makes you dependable and largely predictable. You will not—in a fit of anger, despair, revenge, euphoria, gratitude or whatever—throw away a valuable secret, plan, relationship or information.

If you have a healthy view of yourself, like yourself and are able to withstand the lack of appreciation or reward, the censure and attacks of peers or superiors, and can live with your failures, you have emotional maturity. You are durable.

If you wish to travel far and fast, travel light. Take off all your envies, jealousies, unforgiveness, selfishness, and fears.
Glenn Clark

Emotional maturity is inner strength and security. It allows you to separate yourself from the problem and make a dispassionate decision. It allows you to be a "big" person in the sense that "big" is opposed to small, meaning petty. You are your own person. Emotional maturity carries you and allows you to never lose your head, despite disasters, of which there are many. If you are an emotionally mature person, you are predictable and steady. Once the boss knows your strengths and weaknesses, the boss can judge whether to let you go to see the higher ups alone.

Life is too short to be little.
Benjamin Disraeli

The middle manager doesn't let too many subordinates see the vice-president without being along. If, however, someone who is "safe"

16

needs to see the vice-president and it is not convenient for the manager to go along, the manager will allow the subordinate to make the visit. One way to tell if your boss thinks highly of you is to observe whether you are allowed to see the "big guns" without your boss—or whether your boss is always along. Once is not enough; the boss must continue to let you go in order for you to decide that you haven't mangled things.

> The first time the division president let me carry a project to the group vice-president alone, I knew I had reached a new plateau.
>
> But I also knew that to stay on that plateau I had to do the thing right. The test was whether the *group vice-president* thought I was adequate to do the job of briefing him.
>
> If I "turned him off" for any reason—too defensive, too nervous, too quick, too deferential—all he needed to do was raise an eyebrow when asked by the division president how the briefing went. Or say "Well, I don't know, really."
>
> When I was allowed to go again within a month I knew I was doing okay.

If you are mature, you know that only you can judge your own performance. Only you know the pressures for your time and talents. You should regard both praise and criticism as signposts, not to be trusted entirely. Many times praise will come undeserved. Many times, even if deserved, you could have done better. You must be your own standard setter, your own goal setter, your own judge.

> **It is only the young who can receive much reward from men's praise; the old, when they are great, they get too far beyond and above you to care what you think of them.**
> **John Ruskin**

Emotionally mature executives know when to make a decision and when not to. They are not afraid to make the decision or to not make the decision. Decisiveness is neither good nor bad in itself. To be *always* decisive can be as bad as being never decisive. It may mean a person is making decisions when decisions shouldn't be made. If one is emotionally mature, one can *choose* to decide or not to decide.

> **Deliberate with caution, but act with decision; yield with graciousness, or oppose with firmness.**
> **Charles Hole**

Peter F. Drucker, in his fine book, *The Effective Executive*, states, "... there is no inherent reason why decisions should be distasteful—

17

most effective ones are." This burden can become unbearable, and the effective executive must either have the maturity to handle this before he becomes an executive, or must gradually develop those characteristics as he climbs the executive ladder.

Some questions can be decided even if not answered.
Harry S Truman

To be frozen into not deciding—for any reason; fear, confusion, carefulness, etc.,—is debilitating to an organization. There are times, of course, when *"no decision"* is the right action, but such a situation is rare. Many executives like to "muddle thru," to let "time work its way."

'decision' comes from: 'de'–meaning off and 'cision'–to cut—to cut off (as debate).
Ronald Olsen

Mature persons handle uncertainty two very different ways. First, they should fiercely drive it back and out of all situations that they can. Secondly, they must live with it as a constant, ever-present companion. It cannot be driven out of many situations.

Some fine project managers are excellent because of the fierceness with which they attack uncertainty. They seem to loathe it. But, when put into a marketing role when uncertainty is a part of the everyday job, they come apart. They *do* loathe uncertainty and this positive drive to rid oneself of all uncertainty destroys their equanimity when uncertainty becomes a constant companion. The "positive" trait gets out of control; the man lacks emotional maturity.

An outstanding scientist who had several patents and inventions told me that one of the great attributes of the systems engineer or systems designer was this same quality—the ability to live comfortably with uncertainty!

The really competent guy doesn't rush things, doesn't push things before they need to be pushed. He's confident that he'll get a system working and therefore he doesn't make rushed mistakes. He takes enough time, and it pays.

An example of handling uncertainty correctly:

A young executive, Mr. Foss, was working on a very large order, approximately $40 million worth of computers for a national insurance company. The computing company he worked for was very anxious to see the equipment installed.

18

He found out early in his assignment that the key manager of the insurance company was not competent.

Foss began to apply pressure to both the computer company management and the insurance company management to force them to realize that their plans were ill-founded .

The key manager in the insurance company grew resentful. One day he informed Foss that he was going to call the vice-president in charge of the computer sales division and talk to him in general. Foss did not object. He said that it was all right with him.

The meeting took place on a Monday afternoon about four. At about three the phone rang, and it was the vice-president of the computer company to find out from Foss why the customer was coming to see him.

"Probably, he wants to tell you about the fact that I am putting pressure on to get these decisions remade. I am telling him these decisions are not technically well-founded, and that we are beginning to miss our schedule because no one can tell us what the use of the computers will be. He probably, frankly, wants to complain about me."

"OK," said the vice-president, "I'll let you know what happens."

Foss heard nothing on Tuesday, Wednesday, or Thursday, and was sorely tempted to call the vice-president to ask what had gone on. He would have had every reason for doing so since he was pretty sure that the insurance manager was going to complain about him, and he had to work with him daily.

Finally on Friday, the vice-president called. "I am sorry I forgot to call you. I meant to call you and tell you about our meeting."

"What happened?"

"Nothing. I couldn't understand why he had come to see me. We talked for about an hour and I could not make head nor tail of why he was there or what he wanted."

"Now you are beginning to see some of the problems I am wrestling with."

"Yes, I do. Just keep on trying to get it resolved. See you later."

> Do little things now; so shall big things come to thee by and by asking to be done.
>
> *Persian proverb*

That's not quite the end of the story. Several months later when the vice-president was appraising Foss, he mentioned the incident. He praised him for not being nervous and worried about the interview, for not calling up and asking what happened. He stated that it showed a remarkable amount of maturity. Of such small things are careers made. The appraisal was a very high one.

The emotionally mature manager delegates.

Delegation is giving a subordinate one of your responsibilities. It is often pointed out that one must check on the task and its progress. "Delegate, not abdicate." But it is not often pointed out that delegation is an emotional problem more than it is an intellectual or communications problem.

> A fast-rising, brilliant performer went to pieces on the new contract. When we investigated, we found that it was the first time in his fifteen-year career that he had held a job that he could not completely keep on top of. He *had* to delegate.

> Yet he had never delegated (in the true sense of the word) before this. He had always, because of his brilliance, been able to hold all the extraordinary parameters and options in his own mind. Not being able to do this on this job unnerved him.

Every act of conscious learning requires the willingness to suffer an injury to one's self-esteem.
Thomas Szasz

A manager who can do 80 percent of his job (100 percent is perfection) in nine hours per day may be able to do 90 percent in fifteen hours. At twenty-four hours per day—if that were possible—a manager still could not do 100 percent. There is always a way to do more, to improve. The emotional decision is: At what point do you say, "That's it."?

Very, very few people can sustain 90 percent/15 hours per day very long! Yet the boss wants the thing done right. This trade-off is often very difficult to make.

When Emotional Maturity Is Lacking

Bear failure without self-pity, success without self-admiration. What matter what others judge.
Dag Hammarskjöld

The last thing a manager wants to hear continuously from a subordinate in response to questions is, "Why? Why do you want to know?" Audits, reviews, and simple understanding demand that superiors *know* what is going on. Subordinates who view these valid managerial inquiries as threats or "invasions of their area" are simply not being realistic or emotionally mature. They are a chore to manage.

Some people view valid inquiry as an insult and consider it a personal affront that someone would question them. Their attitude should be: "Here is what I did. If it's wrong, tell me so I'll learn. If it's right, tell me I did a good job."

20

A high-level manager was being audited on his handling of a sticky personnel decision. A headquarter's personnel man was visiting the division to make inquiries. The high-level manager was so nervous that he almost ruined his own case. He kept constant track of where the headquarter's man was at all times. He repeatedly asked, "Can we do more for you? Can we do more for you?"

The headquarter's man found that the case had been handled properly but went out of his way to tell the general manager that the high-level manager was so nervous that his capacity to make decisions looked impaired. "That man followed me all over the building. I felt like a spy," he complained.

The high-level manager was insecure, dependent, scared. He feared making a mistake so much that he made few real decisions.

> All men's miseries derive from not being able to sit quiet in a room alone.
>
> **Blaise Pascal**

Some people must win all the time. They must be superior to everyone else, all the time. They quickly become unbearable and unlikeable.

I know of three high-level managers whose careers have stopped rising because they must win. Two must win by showing you constantly that they know more than you—about everything! The third just wants to win—even if it means high-pressure tactics. He asked his boss once if the boss were interested in his ideas about a reorganization. When told yes, he said he'd share them with the boss if he were promised a good job in the new organization. The boss threw him out.

The other two will insist that their views on a small, minor point be judged right before the discussion proceeds. When told by the other party that they don't see it the same way, these individuals will become indignant and strident.

Telling them that the point is not worth discussing will not end the discussion. They *must* be shown to be right.

The tragedy is that some of these individuals are very, very talented. They are very intelligent and knowledgeable, but they are immature. And immature only in this respect. It is their Achilles heel. Some high-level people get so uptight at a possible failure that they begin to act in such a way that even if they win, they have hurt their careers. They start to whine, to make excuses. They "look bad."

What they should do is to tell the boss, "I don't think we can win without A and B, but I'll do my best," and then stop worrying. Some managers need almost constant reassurance that they are valuable. They are so insecure that if the boss is out of town for a week or more, they begin to panic. They'll call the boss, ask trivial questions, and reassure themselves that they are still valuable employees.

Some persons are unable to disappoint people. They can't say no. They will try to reconcile opposing views, but will agree to both when pressed. They will then try feverishly to bring the opponents to a mutual agreement. This is fine, but they have not told the opponents that conflict exists. Indeed, they have led the opponents to believe that they are in agreement. They then must try to reconcile the disagreement before the opponents know the difference exists. Often they will succeed.

If they are not very capable, this method of operation will not carry them far. If they are, they usually will climb to positions of importance. In these positions they are very dangerous. The better their communications skills and sales ability, the more they will be able to practice this method of operation.

The danger of such persons is that when the conflict finally gets recognized, months have usually gone by, work has proceeded. Now that the basic difference is unearthed, each opponent feels betrayed and is justifiably angered. Even at this point, the bright 'avoid-conflict' persons can usually survive by seeming not to be the key to the situation. Either someone else gets the blame or everyone agrees that the job is just so complicated that such occurrences are "part of the job."

J. F. Kennedy and Charles DeGaulle got along because they shared a preference for a crisply worded difference of opinion over a vaguely worded agreement.

One doesn't hear an executive tell a high-level manager, "You're immature." But one hears very often, "You're defensive." "You're too cynical." "You're too dependent." These are but nicer ways to say immature.

From what I have seen of genuinely powerful people, people of authentic integrity; the sum existence of their assurance in themselves ... allows them, because they are no longer aggressively competing, to be tolerantly charitable.

Catilin Thomas

Applause waits on success. The fickle multitude, like the light straw that floats on the stream, glide with the current still, and follow fortune.

Benjamin Franklin

Do not trust to the cheering, for those very persons would shout as much if you and I were going to be hanged.

Oliver Cromwell

To accuse others for one's own misfortunes is a sign of want of education; to accuse one's self shows that one's education has begun; to accuse neither one's self nor others shows that one's education is complete.

Epictetus

Great men suffer hours of depression through introspection and self-doubt. That is why they are great. That is why you will find modesty and humility the characteristics of such men.

Bruce Barton

To fight aloud is very brave
but gallanter I know,
who charge within the bosom
the cavalry of woe.

Emily Dickinson

The mind of Caesar. It is the reverse of most men's. It rejoices in committing itself. To us arrive each day a score of challenges; we must say yes or no to decisions that will set off chains of consequences. Some of us deliberate; some of us refuse the decision, which is itself a decision; some of us leap gradually into the decision, setting our jaws and closing our minds, which is sort of a decision of despair.
Caesar embraces decision. It is as though he felt his mind to be operating only when interlocking itself with significant consequences.

Caesar's Doctor

Dignity does not consist in possessing honors, but in deserving them.

Aristotle

But, if I tell you who I am,
You may not like who I am,
And it is all that I have.

John Powell

The dice of the Lord are always loaded. For everything you have missed, you have gained something else ... The world looks like ... an equation, which, turn it how you will, balances itself ... Every secret is told, every crime is punished, every virtue rewarded, every wrong redressed, in silence and certainty.

Ralph W. Emerson

A really great man is known by three signs—generosity in the design, humanity in the execution, moderation in success.

Otto von Bismarck

Great occasions do not make heroes or cowards; they simply reveal them to the eyes of men. Silently and imperceptibly, as we work or sleep, we grow strong or we grow weak, and at last some crisis shows us what we have become.

Brooke Foss Westcott

Half of the harm that is done in this world is due to people who want to feel important . . . they do not mean to do harm . . . they are absorbed in the endless struggle to think well of themselves.

T. S. Eliot

O God, give us the serenity to accept what cannot be changed, the courage to change what should be changed, and wisdom to distinguish the one from the other.

Reinhold Niebuhr

One thing the effective executive will not do at this point. He will not give in to the cry, "Let's make another study." This is the coward's way.

Peter Drucker

You may be deceived if you trust too much, but you will live in torment if you do not trust enough.

Frank Crane

He that has never known adversity is but half acquainted with others, or with himself. Constant success shows us but one side of the world. For, as it surrounds us with friends, who will tell us only our merits, so it silences those enemies from whom alone we can learn our defects.

C. C. Colton

If you can meet with Triumph and Disaster, and treat those two imposters just the same. . . .

Rudyard Kipling

Equanimity
In this thing one man is superior to another, that he is better able to bear prosperity or adversity.

Philemon

Bullfight critics ranked in rows,
Crowd the enormous plaza full,
But only one is there who knows,
And he's the man who fights the bull.

Dominiga Ortega

> This, above all, to thine own self be true, and it must follow as the night the day, thou canst not then be false to any man.
>
> *William Shakespeare*

Independence means an inclination not to agree with the standard answer, with the majority, or with established policy just because it is there. It is a quality of mind that forces the individual to constantly rethink the why of the question and/or policy. It is the unwillingness to follow the boss for the only reason that he *is* the boss. It is a quality of mind as opposed to a willingness to endure risk, i.e., courage.

Independence is valuing your opinion of yourself more than other opinions of you. Only you can judge you—but others will. They will praise you unjustly, when a "bluebird" has landed on your shoulder through no particular effort of your own. And they will censure you when your heroic, brilliant efforts do not meet with success! Others' opinions of you are meaningful only in your pursuit of power—*not* in the long run of your view of yourself! Independence is self-confidence!

> Let all your views in life be directed to a solid, however moderate, independence, without it no man can be happy, nor even honest.
>
> *Junius*

An example of independence at its best is shown in this excerpt from Peter Drucker's *The Effective Executive* published by Harper & Row. He is discussing Theodore Vail, president and later chairman of the board of AT&T in the 1890 time frame.

> Vail had actually been fired by the board of the Bell System when he first was president. His concept of service as the business of the company seemed almost insane to people who "knew" that the only purpose of a business is to make a profit. His belief that regulation was in the best interest of the company, was indeed a necessity for survival, appeared harebrained if not immoral to people who "knew" that regulation was "creeping socialism" to be fought tooth and nail. It was only years later, after 1900, when they had become alarmed—and with good reason—by the rising tide of demand for the nationalization of the telephone, that the board called Vail back. But his decision to spend money on obsoleting current processes and techniques just when they made the greatest profits for the company and to build a large research laboratory designed to this end, as well as his refusal to follow the fashion in finance and build a speculative capital structure, were equally resisted by his board as worse than eccentricity.

What another would have done as well as you, do not
do it. What another would have said as well as you, do
not say it. Be faithful to that which exists nowhere but
in yourself, and then make yourself indispensable.
André Gide

There is a perversity to life. At times, the harder you try and the
more you care, the further away the goal seems to get. Often great
strides are made when one seems not to care. Often the approach and
the quality expressed should be the exact opposite of the one that all
your training has taught you to bring to bear. Sometimes it is good to
not give a damn, to be relaxed when everyone else is uptight. Sometimes it is good to get angry when a situation seems to call for patience.
This seeming contradiction is very difficult to explain. An example:

A young salesman was calling on a customer in a small town 50
miles away from his office. It was a snowy day, and the roads
were slippery. He arrived there after an arduous trip through the
mountain passes late in the day. He had called for an appointment. After saying hello, the vice-president immediately launched
into a tirade against the salesman's company, explaining to him
that years ago he had been disappointed by the company and
that he would never do business with the company.

Now all the salesman's training had told him that at this point
he should apologize for the corporation's errors in the past and try
to steer the conversation gently around to a more amenable
subject.

But the day was late, the salesman was tired, and the vice-president
was being rude. With a flash of true, but controlled, anger, the
salesman fixed the vice-president with a glare and stated, "You've
wasted a lot of my time allowing me to come up here through
the pass on such a miserable snowy day only to tell me that you
don't want to discuss anything. Thank you, sir, and good day."

"Wait, wait," yelled the vice-president, "Please, please, I was just
venting off steam."

They went on to have a very amicable friendship.

Now clearly what the salesman had done was very human, very real,
very spontaneous and, upon reflection, very just. Sometimes just sheer
justice and common sense outweight all the structured rules.

So remarkably perverse is the nature of man, that he
despises those that court him, and admires whoever will
not bend before him.
Thucydides

26

A similar example can be seen in the idea of caring but not caring. The age-old advice given to the young suitor by his older sister was to "play hard to get." "What does that mean?" he asked. "Make believe you don't care anything about her," she said. "Make believe she doesn't exist. Ignore her. In fact, if you can, insult her." This advice seemed so strange that it was almost incomprehensible to the young man. It was only years later that he began to see that the advice was good not only for the situation given, but it was good in many respects in the business world.

For to care too much is to be dependent. To not care, or to seem not to care, is to exhibit strength, independence, and maturity. I have seen elaborate games played by high-level executives to try to seem not to care.

> The president of the corporation was quite angry. Jones, one of the vice-presidents, had done something unauthorized in a critical sales situation. The president had let a third party know that he was upset. Independently Jones called at 5 P.M. for an appointment at 6 P.M. with the president on another matter. He and I arrived to see the president in the late afternoon. When we arrived, the president's secretary said "You're here on time, Mr. Jones. By the way, the president knew early this afternoon that you were coming." This statement took the vice-president aback and, after further inquiries, he found that indeed the president had expected him to come up and see him. Yet the vice-president had made this decision only an hour before. How had the president come to the conclusion that the vice-president would come to see him?

> Several judicious phone calls uncovered the fact that the president had made known to the third party his ire over Jones's action. Now ensued a fascinating game. If Jones now saw the president immediately, he would look weak. It would look as though he had gotten the indirect message of disapproval and had rushed to headquarters in order to square himself with the president. For a half hour from 6:00 to 6:30 we sat in an outside office doing nothing. Jones made a few inconsequential phone calls. I, of course, understood what was happening only later. Finally, the president came out of his office and into the small outer office we were sitting in.

> "Well, Ralph," he said, "I understand you've come to see me."

> "I don't really have to see you," replied the vice-president. "It's not really that important and could wait until tomorrow if you want to go home."

> "I thought you wanted to see me."

> The vice-president replied that it really wasn't important and if the

president wished to go home—it was getting late—that he could catch up with him at a later time.

"Well," said the president, "I thought perhaps we'd talk about the sales situation that's come to my attention."

"Oh, sure," said the vice-president, "I'd be happy to do that."

We went in and had a very stormy meeting during which many heated words were used. But the vice-president effectively avoided appearing panicked.

To this day I believe that the president did not realize that the vice-president had played a game. He had deliberately wanted the president to understand that he did not care, that he was not "running scared," and that he was his own man—a firm, strong executive.

This episode was a rare glimpse at high-level executives in action, and one was effectively playing the "hard to get" game. The lesson was not lost on me.

I call that mind free which is not passively framed by
outward circumstances, which is not swept away by the
torrent of events, which is not the creature of accidental impulse, but which bends events to its own improvement, and acts from an inward spring, from
immutable principles which it has deliberately espoused.
William Ellery Channing

Some organizations foster independence.

T. J. Watson, Jr., Chairman of the Board of IBM for many years, often spoke to large audiences about the "Wild Duck." He exhorted his employees to buck the system, to fight the establishment, to cut the red tape.

And IBM benefits from the policy. It tolerates a great deal of dissention.

Another way of saying independent or bold is perhaps to use the word *irreverent*. A suspicion of the established wisdom is very healthy. The established wisdom has been wrong many, many times.

One reviewer of this book felt that to "review your boss" was too radical, too imprudent. But one *should* examine everything—*including* one's bosses.

Even if the organization you belong to does not foster or tolerate boldness, you may evaluate without anyone's knowledge. Knowing where you and your boss differ helps you alter your beliefs (if you want to) or your style.

Too Little Independence

There is a natural tendency to believe that as one climbs the ladder of success and is paid more and more money per year, that one will become more and more independent. The reverse is true. First the natural inclination is to live up to one's income. Executives buy bigger cars, bigger houses, take long, more expensive trips and invest their money into money-making schemes. If all of a sudden they had to live on a sharply reduced income, they would be in serious financial trouble. Their net worth is certainly enough but their liquidity, their ability to get cash and to dispose of accumulated investments and ownings, would take at least several months, perhaps as much as a few years.

In addition, age has made them less saleable. At this point, they are probably 45–55 and past their most saleable years. It would be most difficult for them to switch companies and arrive at the same income level.

Therefore, they are far less independent, based on their external circumstances, than when they were 25 to 30-year-old young firebrands. Although their children were smaller at that age, they had more energy, were more saleable, were not heavily invested and committed. One could argue that having now been executives, they are easily saleable. Perhaps.

The problem is that individuals must make the judgment for themselves and in many cases 45-year-old executives will make a trade-off in favor of pleasing a boss that they would never have made as a young, 25-year-old, up-and-coming manager.

> Whatever crushes individuality is despotism, by whatever name it may be called.
>
> *John Stuart Mill*

All managers, except *the* boss, have a boss. I have seen many managers trembling with fear before going in to see the chairman of the board.

One confided to his assistant that he could not sleep at night because he worried about what the chairman thought about him.

The following dialogue is too common:

"Joe, we want you to spend two weeks every month on the West Coast. Times are bad, and we really need you out there."

"But my wife isn't too well, Al. I think it will be very hard to do."

"Joe, we need you there. You must do it. The market here is off, as you yourself state. We don't need you here."

"Yes sir, Al."

Why do executives put up with this? Look at the following by

James Morgan in the *TWA Ambassador*, November, 1975, in an article called "The Executive Family":

> Why is there a conflict between business and family life, anyway? Why do successful executives compusively work 12, 14, 16 hours a day? Why do they accept promotions or moves that are certain to wreak turmoil in the lives of their family members? Why do they seemingly prefer nights out entertaining clients to nights at home with the family? Why do they spend weekends at the office or else golfing with business associates? Why, when they're finally alone with the members of their families, is there so much silence?

> "Because business offers an executive the kind of strokes he can't get anywhere else," says the insistently anonymous Midwestern executive . . . (who, by the way, is back with his wife for "one more try"). "Success becomes a ladder: once you get to that first rung, you just have to try for the second."

Surely the "strokes" mentioned in the article are a reason. There are "strokes" at work and they are different from the "home strokes." Sometimes there are no home "strokes."

How many chairmen of the boards, great lawyers, or doctors, or artists, are "great" because they can't stand to go home? David Olgivy, in *Confessions of an Advertising Man,* points out that one of the best advertising agencies was good because its founder was so unhappy with his wife that he usually worked till midnight.

But the more frequent reason for this kind of behavior is simply fear. It is hard, perhaps, to accept this but most of the work-work-work syndrome comes from the fear that unless high-level managers know what is happening everywhere in their purview, they may not remain high-level managers for long. Or they won't get this year's bonus (which they need), or they won't get the next promotion. Or they can be fired! They have not made it to the inside circle of the proprietorship! They are hired hands, subject to dismissal, despite high salaries. And dismissal is harsh.

Upward-moving executives may well be storing up great equity in real estate or other ventures, but they need their high salaries to fuel their investments. On paper, they may be worth one-half million—in real estate, stocks, annuities—but in reality they need maybe $20,000 per year in cash to keep up the mortgage payments on their investments. Five- or ten-year periods occur during which it is not advantageous to liquidate back to cash—or not even possible.

Now they are trapped. They are getting older and need the income. Perhaps they can get another employer to pay them the same amount —but maybe they can't. Perhaps they'll have to take a job at two-thirds the salary—or one-half!

Disaster!

What choice do they have? Let the bank foreclose on their 700-acre farm. The loss of money would be great, but the ego-shock may be greater!

So they refuse to leave—if they *can* refuse. They get to be more and more timid—more and more "yes-men."

Guarding Independence

People have known for centuries that independence must be vigilantly guarded.

> John Curran, an Irish patriot, said: "The conditions upon which God hath given liberty to man is eternal vigilance, which condition, if he break, servitude is at once the consequence of his crime and punishment of his guilt."

Curran is talking in 1790 about the subjugation of Ireland by England. He speaks of countries. And he states that servitude is the price for not vigilantly guarding their liberty. The same holds for the employee of a corporation.

Compare Curran's comments to what Anthony Jay has to say about power and freedom in *Management and Machiavelli* published by Holt, Rinehart and Winston:

> Most people who aspire to power within organizations will tell you that they want it so as to achieve objects they believe in, but even that does not go to the heart of the matter. The real pleasure of power is the pleasure of freedom, and it goes right back to one of man's most primitive needs, the need to control his environment. You get no great sense of freedom if you are liable at any time to starve or freeze or be devoured by wolves or speared by a neighboring tribe, and so you set about securing a supply of food, shelter, warmth, and defensive weapons.
>
> ... However, if you become a respected and successful person within the organization, you may begin to be involved in the control of it. You taste what some people call power, but to you it tastes of freedom. Your life is still partly regulated by the actions and decisions of others, but now a part of it is regulated according to your own choice and by your own decisions. You are regaining control of your new environment.

To think of the company as an oppressor is difficult for several reasons. First, we want to think of our employer as paternal, friendly, and committed to our welfare. That is a much more comfortable situation than viewing the employer as cold-blooded, profit-oriented and "willing to get rid of me at any time I cease to be an asset." After all, we are all getting older.

Second, the company wants us to think that our long-term future is with it. This generates loyalty and spirit and commitment.

The point is simple: to protect one's freedom one must keep from being tyrannized by anyone, including one's employer. It requires constant vigilance.

No one starts out viewing the employer as a slave owner. But slowly and imperceptibly two things are happening—employees are aging and 9 out of 10 times becoming less valuable as their drive and wits decline, and the employees are beginning to live up to their salaries as they grow and to count on retirement benefits, etc. At 45 employees are not likely to be very bold or willing to challenge the system. They need that system to sustain life! It is that simple.

How few when they are earning $60,000 per year gear their lives to $30,000 per year! Yet they are entrapping themselves; their vigilance is down because they do not see the employer as a potential tyrant.

Unique individuals who keep their life-styles *well below* their incomes will be willing to go find other jobs. They are going to fight when they are told to do something that is offensive or wrong. They are *free* because they are vigilant. And they are more valuable because they are independent. And the *employer* profits.

Yes-Men

Yes-men is a term used to designate all those employees who will say "yes, sir" to anything the boss says. Never will they say, "No sir, I don't agree." Yes-men exhibit no independence.

I once stated in a speech that yes-men don't succeed. I was corrected by a member of the audience and he was right. Yes-men get pretty high up and very powerful at times.

We sometimes imagine we hate flattery, but we only hate the way we are flattered.
La Rochefoucauld

What I should have said was the yes-men are not good, effective executives. They are, instead, parasites on the power of someone else. They represent a failure of emotional maturity on the part of their sponsor. They are usually destructive to any organization and lack beliefs, independence, courage, and emotional maturity.

Two types of organizations promote yes-men. First there is the very rich organization. It can afford this type of sickness in the organization. Only when *performance* is *required* will the yes-men be forced to produce. And if the company is very rich, this may take 20 years!

The second type of organization that fosters yes-men is the one that is run by the autocrat. It may or may not be doing well, but the autocrat's got the wheel and is steering, and that's all there is to it. The fact that he wants and promotes yes-men should be a sure sign of *his* lack of emotional maturity.

Many organizations are run by absolute autocrats, and the yes-men syndrome is very obvious. The fact that there is a 35-year-old director of long-range planning for a billion-dollar company is a sure sign that either he is a genius *or* he's a protégé of the autocrat. Damned few 35-year-olds should be directors of long-range planning for a billion dollar giant.

Yes-men are often very adept at communications. They are extremely good at finding out what the other person really wants. Unwary executives will tip them off by facial or verbal expression as to what they think. The yes-men can almost imperceptibly change their own previously stated position to make it agree with that of the executive.

I have seen this manner of yesmanship practiced so adroitly that, even though I was aware that the individual players in the meeting were primarily yes-men, I didn't notice them change their positions until the meeting was over, and I reflected on it. This skill is superb even though ultimately detrimental to the company!

Fast Readers

Another failure of independence is often seen in people I will label "Fast Readers." Some upward climbers are very adept at presenting all the facts, outlining several possible alternatives, watching the boss's reaction very carefully, and then selecting the one that the boss wants. This is fine, as long as the boss realizes that the subordinate is not making any decisions!

Some fast readers are even more open; they ask their boss what option the boss wants. The unwise boss tells them, and the fast readers then point out the pitfalls of that approach (every approach has pitfalls) and allow themselves to be persuaded or ordered by the boss to select an option. Then, if it doesn't work out, well, it was the boss's decision. Fast readers can even point to the fact that they had advised caution and that the boss said go. Such individuals are not independent. They will be good number-two employees, but don't count on them as number-one types.

> The people to fear are not those who disagree with you, but those who disagree with you and are too cowardly to let you know.
>
> *Napoleon*

Too Much Independence

Independence is not a quality that can be exercised indiscriminately. Too much independence can be arrogance.

Too much independence may frighten your superiors. The following is from Anthony Jay's *Management and Machiavelli* published by Holt, Rinehart and Winston:

> And regrettable as it may seem, the potential leader is often an uncomfortable, and sometimes a disagreeable, subordinate. It is possible that he is of higher caliber than the men he works under, which in itself is hard enough to bear; but he is also unlikely to conceal his perception of this truth, which they find almost unforgivable. When they describe him in formal reports or informal conversations as insolent, egocentric, and argumentative, they are likely to be speaking no less than the truth. They will probably add that he is conceited or arrogant (the difference apparently being that if he thinks he is cleverer than you are, he is conceited, and if he knows he is, he is arrogant). Moreover, if he is already starting to see the corporation as a whole he is likely to question and criticize policies and decisions which have nothing to do with him or indeed with his immediate superiors, and this can be even more irritating since they find it harder to argue on unfamiliar territory. He is also likely to have extreme confidence in his own judgment, and this, while invaluable in a creative leader who needs to stimulate morale and enthusiasm among his team, is not a quality that superiors find endearing.

Independence Test

Test yourself to see if you are independent. You have been overruled by your boss on a project. You tell your people:

1. I've changed my mind. We're going to do it this way.
2. The boss insists we do it this way. I still don't agree but let's make it work.
3. We're going to do it this way.
4. The boss says we are going to do it this way. Let's go through the motions again.

This is a question that gets a lot of debate started in advanced management schools. The managers that pick option 1 argue that to say you disagree with the boss is disloyal, sour grapes, and bad for morale. Those that pick option 2 state that the subordinates deserve to know the issues so that they can grow in understanding. Usually all reject options 3 and 4. Option 2 is right.

The key points here are the growth of the subordinates, the manner in which the explanation is given, and the frequency of its occurrence. If it occurs every week, then the two managers are out of step and this will hurt morale and effectiveness severely. If the disagreement is explained dispassionately and the "let's make it work" is sincere, then there should be no impact upon morale. If it doesn't happen often, and it is handled right, this openness of disagreement is a very effective teacher. The subordinates learn a lot in a hurry! There is drama, conflict, and interest. Who was right? And why? It is *not disloyalty* if it is handled with humility and maturity.

He is great who is what he is from Nature, and who never reminds us of others.

Ralph Waldo Emerson

To be a philosopher is not merely to have subtle thoughts, nor even to found a school, but so to love wisdom as to live, according to its dictates, a life of simplicity, independence, magnanimity, and trust.

Henry David Thoreau

Each time a man stands up for an ideal, or acts to improve the lot of others, or strikes out against injustice, he sends forth a tiny ripple of hope, and crossing each other from a million different centers of energy and daring, those ripples build a current that can sweep down the mightiest walls of oppression and resistance.

Few are willing to brave the disapproval of their fellows, the censure of their colleagues, the wrath of their society. Moral courage is a rarer commodity than bravery in battle or great intelligence. Yet it is the one essential, vital quality for those who seek to change a world that yields most painfully to change. And I believe that in this generation those with the courage to enter the moral conflict will find themselves with companions in every corner of the globe.

Robert Kennedy

Mistrust the man who finds everything good; the man who finds everything evil; and still more the man who is indifferent to everything.

Johann Kaspar Lavater

REALISM

Delusions, errors, and lies are like huge, gaudy vessels, the rafters of which are rotten and worm-eaten, and those who embark in them are fated to be shipwrecked.

Buddha

A realistic person sees the world the way it is, not as an idealized, fantasized, or feared world. This quality is closely tied to one's emotions. When you are not being realistic, it is more often for an emotional rather than intellectual reason. You want to believe something, so you do.

Emotions mislead you in two opposite directions. First, they lead you to believe things are better than they are, that a certain subordinate will succeed (when it is clear to everyone else the subordinate will not). Second, they lead you to fear things that should not worry you.

Realism applies to both a short-term and long-term outlook. A short-term outlook requires you to realistically appraise the chances of selling your favorite diversification project to the boss. A long-term outlook requires you to assess your chances of becoming a vice-president in five to eight years.

Realism usually involves some hard knocks to your ego. Reality is often difficult to handle. It takes stability to admit your failings.

The easiest thing of all is to deceive one's self; for what
a man wishes he generally believes to be true.

Demosthenes

Realism does not mean having a negative or pessimistic outlook. However, if you are openly realistic with superiors (or subordinates) who may not have a healthy amount of emotional maturity, you run the risk of being judged "negative." Some people think that realism is negative thinking. They are usually foolishly optimistic. But if they happen to be in power, be careful how you state your realism. You may even have to conceal your views and work out your plans privately.

Realism should not be interpreted to mean that you should not think highly of yourself. If you err in judging yourself, you should err in the direction of expecting more of yourself rather than less. This stretches you and makes you grow.

The realist knows that bosses want subordinates who are compatible with them. This is sometimes called "cliquishness" or "cronyism" but, call it what you may, it is a very human trait.

Hope is generally a wrong guide, though it is very good
company by the way.

George Savile

If an individual is capable *and* compatible, then that individual will be selected over someone who is capable and incompatible.

The trouble with most people is that they think with
their hopes or fears or wishes rather than with their
minds.

Walter Duranty

The realistic manager knows that people from different divisions will not necessarily work together just because they are in the same company. The jealousies and struggles are often much more ferocious between divisions of a company than between competitors. Whoever coined the word "divisions" was prophetic for many companies.

The realist knows that many high-level managers are not interested in moving the company forward, but only in making sure their own positions are not jeopardized. The realist also knows that because a person is an executive doesn't mean that that person will use executive power. Some executives are basically "administrators." They keep huge organizations running well. They have the intellect, knowledge, skills, and personality to keep vast, complex operations moving effectively. But they do not change things. They do not create new entities, processes, or methods. Executives who change things are entrepreneurs. They build new products, organizations, processes, or businesses.

> Neutrality, as a lasting principle, is an evidence of weakness.
>
> *Louis Kossuth*

It is useless to try to get administrators to initiate a bold new plan. The key is to recognize that they *are* administrators, to know that they will never say yes and will always be looking for ways to say no. You must neutralize them before they can say no. Get around them quick and find an entrepreneur. Otherwise your project won't get far.

You probably will not even get a *quick* no from administrators because to them a quick no is a risk. So you'll be asked for more data, more studies—and more—and more . . . until *you* wear out, thinking that *you* aren't smart enough, tough enough, or clever enough to sell this great idea. You aren't. You haven't recognized you are with administrators, or even that there *are* executives who are administrators only.

Don't take this as a condemnation of administrators. They are very valuable to organizations in their own way. An organization consisting of entrepreneurs only would be chaos!

> We were going to see the senior-vice president with the new factory proposal. One of the new managers was excited, "Hey, this should bring some action, no?"
>
> "No," said the general manager, "This is a necessary but not sufficient visit. He won't say yes. He's an administrator. But we've got to get him to say he won't say no."

Administrators are always playing defense; entrepreneurs are always playing offense. A good player plays both.

The realist recognizes two devices that an "executive" uses to avoid a decision. First, there is the "need more study" theme. The executive will say, "Obviously we cannot make a decision of this magnitude without knowing the effect of gamma. Please do a study of the gamma effect and get back to me in three weeks."

Sounds impressive, doesn't it? But hidden in there is the fact that the gamma effect lies largely in the future and is unknown. Three weeks more work will add little or nothing to the decision.

If you want to kill any idea in the world today, get a
committee working on it.
Charles F. Kettering

The second way to avoid making the decision and yet "look effective" is to appoint the "task force," the committee. Committees are not bad, per se, and if an aggressive executive is waiting for the committee report in order to take action, then the committee is a powerful instrument.

Unfortunately, too often the "task force" is a dodge by the weak executive to gain more time. As such it is a waste. Cecil Woodhan Smith writes in *The Great Hunger*, published by Harper & Row:

> There were, however, voices crying in the wilderness, and contrary to the usual course of history the voices were official. The Devon Commission reported in 1845, on the eve of the famine, giving warning in grave terms of the dangerous state of Ireland. The report was dismissed on the grounds that "it did not contain anything of striking novelty" and "there was nothing in it that everyone did not know already," and a timid bill based on its recommendations giving Irish tenants a right to compensation for improvements in certain restricted circumstances was denounced as "a violation of the rights of property" and withdrawn.
>
> The Devon Commission moreover was only one of many. In the 45 years since the Union no fewer than 114 Commissions and 61 Special Committees were instructed to report on the state of Ireland, and without exception their findings prophesied disaster; Ireland was on the verge of starvation, her population rapidly increasing, three-quarters of her laborers unemployed, housing conditions appalling and the standard of living unbelievably low.

A decision is the action an executive must take when he
has information so incomplete that the answer does not
suggest itself.
Admiral Arthur William Radford

When Realism Is Lacking

Many do not realize that power is rarely absolute. Few people ever can direct others and be obeyed without fuss. Look at the Presidents of the United States. Surely one would think that they have power at its utmost. Yet listen to some comments on presidential powers:

> Truman, commenting on the incoming President-elect Eisenhower: He'll sit here and he'll say, "Do this! Do that!" And nothing will happen. Poor Ike—it won't be a bit like the Army. He'll find it very frustrating.

> An Eisenhower aide in 1958: The President still feels that when he's decided something, that *ought* to be the end of it . . . and when it bounces back undone or done wrong, he tends to react with shocked surprise.

> President Truman: I sit here all day trying to persuade people to do the things they ought to have sense enough to do without my persuading them . . . that's all the powers of the President amount to.

These quotes are from *Presidential Power* by Richard E. Neustadt published by John Wiley & Sons. In this fine book, he details three failures of presidential power to work. When it doesn't, the embarrassment is on a scale with the power.

The realistic manager knows that people will not do what they are told just because they are told.

> A new manager was quitting the company and joining a new engineering firm. He was good, and I tried to talk him into staying.

> After an hour, he blurted out: "I am a bad manager. I'm not good at it."

> "Why do you say that?"

> "Because I tell people to do things and they don't do them! And I don't know how to make them do what I say."

> I told the young man that *all* managers had that problem. (I failed to keep him in the business.)

> **Compromise is odious to passionate natures because it seems a surrender; and to intellectual natures because it seems a confusion.**
>
> *George Santayana*

Refusal to compromise when it is necessary is being unrealistic. When one's superior must always enter the situation and effect a solution via compromise, the rising executive cannot look good.

The realist knows that there are at least two sides to every problem, and that often compromise is necessary in order to get action or to gain support.

A very wise government official who signed off on billions of dollars of contract awards once told his subordinates: "First decide what is right; then decide what is possible. If you let the possible confuse what is right, you will never run a good organization. What is right may not be possible, but you should know what you missed, what you gave up, and what you settled for."

The realistic know that praise is not an end, but merely an accident; is not permanent, but transitory.

Charles Parnell was a great Irish leader in the 1890s. He struggled through an adoring crowd in Dublin one night. The scene was wild turbulent emotion.

He and his followers at last entered a building. He immediately got down to business, giving directions, unmoved by the wild adulation.

"Are you not excited?" he was asked.

"Why should I be? A year from now they may be demanding my resignation."

They were!

Realism is not fooling yourself. Merle Miller in *Plain Speaking* quotes Harry S Truman as stating that his Secretary of State Jimmy Byrnes would often quote Truman as saying things that he, Truman, never said. When asked if Byrnes were lying, Truman answered, no, that Byrnes probably believed what he was saying, that he was "fooling himself."

It is useless for the sheep to pass resolutions in favor of vegetarianism while the wolf remains of a different opinion.
Anonymous

Joyous distrust is a sign of health. Everything absolute belongs to pathology.
Friedrich Nietzsche

Fortune, when she caresses a man too much, makes him a fool.
Publius Syrus

On his first day as President, Richard Nixon ordered removed from his office the three color television sets and the wire service teletype machines that President Johnson always had had on.
R. Buckminster Fuller

The facts of life do not penetrate to the sphere in which our beliefs are cherished, as it was not they that engendered those beliefs, so they are powerless to destroy them; they can aim at them continual blows of contradiction and disprove them without weakening them; and an avalanche of miseries and maladies coming one after another, without interruption into the bosom of family will not make it lose faith either in the clemency of its God or the capacity of its physician.
Marcel Proust

Success has a great tendency to conceal and throw a veil over the evil deeds of men.
Demosthenes

Those who mistake their good luck for their merit are inevitably bound for disaster.
J. Christopher Herold

Success is a rare paint; it hides all the ugliness.
Sir John Suckling

Everything seems possible when we are absolutely helpless or absolutely powerful—and both states stimulate our credulity.
Eric Hoffer

Prejudice, which sees what it pleases, cannot see what is plain.
A. DeVere

A lie has always a certain amount of weight with those who wish to believe it.
E. W. Rice

For the most part I do the thing which my own nature drives me to do. It is embarrassing to earn so much respect and love for it . . . I live in that solitude which is painful in youth but delicious in the years of maturity.
Albert Einstein

COURAGE

Springing from basic beliefs comes courage. You as the leader/executive are willing to take risks because you are willing to fail and to be judged by your co-workers. You are more interested in how you judge yourself. You are not afraid of taking an unpopular or hazardous approach. Good judgment keeps you from going too far, past courage to foolhardiness.

Courage is the willingness to fail, to get in trouble, to be thought
less of, to risk your next raise or next promotion. When you never fail,
you are probably not stretching, reaching, pushing. You are probably
playing it safe.

Everything looks fine in an organization that has hit the right
market at the right time with a unique product or advantage. All the
indicators are up, Up, UP. Everyone is a hero. Happiness reigns.

Good executives look for upcoming managers who are pushing
and innovating. The manager who always plays it safe, never gambles
and never fails may not be of much use when the hard times come.

Tom Watson, Sr., the founder of IBM, said that he judged people
by their failures, not by their successes.

A prominent physician had become a knowledgeable and
influential force for reform of the United States Medical System.
He worked closely with a government agency and had some
sponsorship from them. He was due to testify to the United
States Congress about his ideas on a certain bill. Some people at
the agency told him that they would give him a tough time if he
testified in a certain direction. He asked a friend what to do.

"Do you believe in your idea?"

"Yes."

"Well, tell them what you think."

He did.

(And the agency did not retaliate)

It's courage like this that makes a leader a leader.

A few years ago, a vice-president of an insurance company
found the best candidate for an underwriter's job was a female
employee. He decided to give her the job and wanted to pay
her what the job was rated at.

He found he'd run headlong into the bureaucracy. "We don't
pay females that much." "She might leave." "She doesn't have a
family to support." "Why pay her as much as a man?" "You're
setting a *precedent.*

42

He fought it through and he won, but he made a lot of enemies. He was a "radical." He was bucking the system. He won and was happy he won. Then he went on and repaired his image. As a young, relatively unknown executive, he had been daring indeed.

> **The fearful unbelief is unbelief in yourself.**
> *Thomas Carlyle*

Conflict

> **In prosperous times I have sometimes felt my fancy and powers of language flag, but adversity is to me at least a tonic and bracer.**
> *Sir Walter Scott*

As in all walks of life, organization life is filled with conflict. Indeed, many organizations deliberately organize to create conflict. To always seek, or always avoid, conflict is wrong. One must accept it as a normal part of life. Conflict has a way of boiling out the impurities, of bubbling to the top problems that otherwise may remain imbedded in a new venture until they destroy it.

Robert F. Kennedy, in his book on the Cuban Missile Crisis, states that he often took the opposite side of an argument in the National Security Council simply because no one else did. He believed that the dissidents had been "shouted down," intimidated, during the Bay of Pigs fiasco, and he didn't want that happening again.

Charles Sloan in his book *My Years with General Motors* makes the same point. If there were quick unanimous agreement, he would recess the meeting stating "We'll reconvene when we can generate some opposing views."

> **Crises refine life. In them you discover what you are.**
> *Allan K. Chalmers*

Not all conflict is constructive.

I had been trying to get a new coordinator for the proposal from the engineering division. They had one who was not experienced enough to carry the load.

I asked the vice-president. To a gruff "Why?", I explained the inexperience.

"Write me a letter," was his reaction.

A week later, late in the afternoon, I was meeting with several of the vice-president's subordinates. He came in and asked what was going on.

His top man explained that I was complaining about the lack of progress, which I was.

"Have you met our new coordinator, the one you wanted?" the vice-president asked.

"No," I said, pleased to hear that one had been appointed. "Thank you for naming him."

"Well, you should meet him fast," the vice-president said, "because he's going to get you. He's going to put your neck in the wringer and squeeze." He twisted the neck of an imaginary chicken as he said this.

I was crushed. I did meet the new coordinator, and he did try to get me.

This is not a typical example, but it is unique only in its intensity. Business is filled with such conflict, and the executive must be mature enough to take it and not crumble.

I had told the senior vice-president that things were not going well. He told me to call the division president, which I did. The division president asked what Mr. Maslow, his man in this area, thought.

"I don't know," I answered. "He hasn't returned my last four calls."

"I'll fix that," said the president. And he did. Within a half hour, Mr. Maslow called me. "What's the problem?" he asked.

Pleased that things were finally moving, I began to tell him the problem that needed to be solved. He cut me off in midsentence. "No, I mean this jazz about me not calling you."

"Well, you haven't returned the calls."

"Baloney. I have too! You'd better shut up and stop telling the president this stuff. . . ." Now I cut him off. "Knock off this tough guy role, will you? You're not returning calls and you know it and when you don't, I'll call the president and tell him. Now do you want to talk about the problems?"

"No."

"Fine, I'll tell the president that." We both hung up.

Mr. Maslow never did make an effort to work with me.

The difference between iron and steel is fire, but steel is worth all it costs.
Maltbie Babcock

Willingness to engage in conflict is critical. The person who tries to avoid conflict all the time may be well liked, but that person will not accomplish as much as the one who has the courage to engage in conflict when it arises.

> The chairman of the board of a large company had a favorite tactic to test the depth of conviction, independence, and courage of his subordinates. He often opened any session with a newcomer by attacking a fact stated on the briefing charts. It didn't matter what fact; indeed, it seemed he picked them at random.
>
> If the presenter was awed by this attack and lost his self-confidence and composure, then the chairman put much less credence in the presentation (and spent a great deal less time on the matter).

People who had excellent ideas and good knowledge and most of the other traits did not last very long with the chairman unless they also had courage.

People have argued that this kind of attack was unfair, that it was "bullying." I think not. I think the chairman had the right to put subordinates to his own test, and the test is a fair one. If persons have the courage of their convictions, they should be able to defend their facts. Anyone briefing the chairman of the board should have the needed qualities.

Merle Miller in *Plain Speaking* quotes Harry Truman's physician, Dr. Graham Wallace, saying that President Truman used to play poker with someone he was considering for some position in order to test the individual. Truman would "ply him with champagne," and get an associate to rib the candidate. If the candidate got flustered, Dr. Wallace believed that Mr. Truman would feel he shouldn't get the appointment. President Truman's testing is close to a Japanese custom. The Japanese took a group of Americans they were doing business with to a geisha house for dinner. The Americans soon found that the elaborately dressed geisha girls kept filling the glasses, filling the glasses. Then they started playing chug-a-lug games. The person who lost had to chug-a-lug (drink his drink without stopping to take a breath). One of the Americans noticed that only the Americans were being entwined in the games. All the Japanese were observing carefully.

Some of these examples show courage as the needed trait. Some also show that emotional maturity is needed, too.

You must live with conflict, and with stress. If the short, intense stress of conflict immobilizes you, you are unlikely to rise very high. You lack courage.

If, on the other hand, conflict "turns you on," energizes you, gets all your powers into high gear, then you are far more likely to succeed.

Some people work much better under stress than others, and since conflict is ever-present in the large organization, how one does under stress has a very substantial effect on how high one goes.

Never to have experienced misfortune is a misfortune in itself.

Arnold Glasow

Make conflict ideological, not personal. With all this conflict, do not become a brawler. When you have a disagreement with peers, make it a business problem. Tell them that there are times when people judge things differently and that they may be right, but that you cannot accept their position. You must either overrule, if you have the power, or you must appeal to a higher authority. If you win, be gracious. If you lose, be cheerful. Don't make the difference of opinion become a personal breach.

Sarcasm is the language of the devil; for which reason I have long since as good as renounced it.

Thomas Carlyle

I have seen fierce struggles between peers, who then go out and have a beer together. The organization is stronger for their emotional maturity.

Courage can get you into trouble.

Joe Johnson was a first-line sales manager working a 30-million-dollar proposal. His team lived in Washington, D.C., but were spending five days a week at the engineering location in Boston with the engineers. It was a tough assignment both technically and in the amount of time spent away from home.

Sam, Johnson's boss, told him in early October that because their sales division was behind quota for the year, all sales personnel not "at quota" would work Saturdays until they were at their assigned quota. Johnson was on "special assignment," working just the 30-million-dollar proposal.

"I assume this doesn't include me and my team."

"Oh, yes," said Sam. "Everyone is included."

Johnson protested, pointing out that the team couldn't make quota that year unless they dropped the big proposal, which everyone agreed could not be done. Sam was adamant. They had to work.

The team worked that Saturday; morale was very low.

The next week Johnson and Sam were driving through Boston with Steve Fisher, the sales vice-president. "How are the men reacting to the Saturday work, Sam?" asked Fisher.

"Oh, they understand, Steve," said Sam. Johnson expected Sam to continue and point out the special problem of his team, but a long silence ensued.

Johnson spoke up. "My people are very unhappy, Steve. They are away all week and there is really nothing for them to do in the office on Saturday. They should be excused from this." Steve was visibly angry.

"Joe, they have to understand that the company is in trouble. They have to soldier, to help."

Johnson was getting frustrated by dominance of emotion over logic.

"Well, Steve, the company has to understand that these *people* are in trouble. They are working 60 hours a week away from home all week, and they need time off. Besides, it doesn't help the company for them to come in on Saturday."

"You don't understand, Joe," was the way the vice-president closed the conversation.

A long, cold silence ensued.

> Some people mistake weakness for tact. If they are silent when they ought to speak and so feign an agreement they do not feel, they call it being tactful. Cowardice would be a much better name. Tact is an active quality that is not exercised by merely making a dash for cover. Be sure, when you think you are being extremely tactful, that you are not in reality running away from something you ought to face.
>
> *Sir Frank Medlicott*

Sam was a company man. He did what the boss said—period. Joe was courageous. He did or tried to do what was logical. Joe "lost" the encounter with the vice-president, who was angry with Joe for being "difficult." Courage can be resented.

> Sometimes a noble failure serves the world as faithfully as a distinguished success.
>
> *Dowden*

Lack of Courage

Let's look at what the lack of courage can do.

The vice-president of sales of a major corporation was meeting with his lieutenants. They convinced him that the project X was in big trouble. The planned announcement was in bad shape.

After discussing the matter at great length, the vice-president informed his lieutenants that indeed the problem was serious and severe. "However," he said, "we cannot bring it to the president because we do not have a solution."

One of the subordinates protested, "But the solution is beyond us. It should stem from the engineering department and they should solve it. We should ask the president to direct the engineering department to solve the problem."

"No," said the vice-president, "you cannot bring problems to the president unless you also have the solutions."

This problem waited three more months before it was brought to the presidential level that could effectively address it.

The vice-president of sales did not have the courage to risk "looking bad" in the eyes of the president.

None love the messenger who brings bad news.
Sophocles

Bad news must get to the top. In the process of superior talking to subordinate, there are two qualities that are crucial in the subordinate—independence and courage. The subordinate must tell the boss the bad news.

Some companies operate on the basis that if your superior calls you and asks a question about any area under your command, you should be able to respond to that inquiry immediately, and knowledgeably. This is a fine idea at the lower levels of management where people have frequent contact with all areas under their direction. However, at the higher levels of management it is an absurd practice.

I have seen high-level executives work consistently 16 hours a day so that they can be ready to answer *any* inquiries that come to them from higher management. This obsession to always know the answer and be one step ahead of your superiors is not a strength, but a weakness. It is demoralizing for the subordinates of such an executive to be constantly at work at 10 o'clock at night giving briefings for no apparent reason. To be there at late hours during a crisis is exhilarating. One feels wanted and feels one is making a contribution. To be there consistently at those hours simply because the boss wants to know everything is the opposite of exhilarating.

Fear is not in the habit of speaking truth; when perfect sincerity is expected, perfect freedom must be allowed; nor has anyone who is apt to be angry when he hears the truth any cause to wonder that he does not hear it.
Tacitus

Of course, if the boss is immature and *so fierce* as to "kill" those who bring bad news, the subordinate must have a large helping of courage.

"How's it going down there?" barked the big walrus from his perch on the highest rock near the shore. He waited for the good word.

Down below, the smaller walruses conferred hastily among themselves. Things weren't going well at all, but none of them wanted to break the news to the Old Man. He was the biggest and wisest walrus in the herd, and he knew his business—but he did hate to hear bad news. And he had such a terrible temper that every walrus in the herd was terrified at his ferocious bark.

"What will we tell him?" whispered Basil, the second-ranking walrus. He well remembered how the Old Man had raved and ranted at him the last time the herd caught less than its quota of herring, and he had no desire to go through that experience again. Nevertheless, the walruses had noticed for several weeks that the water level in the nearby Arctic bay had been falling constantly, and it had become necessary to travel much farther to catch the dwindling supply of herring. Someone should tell the Old Man; he would probably know what to do. But who? And how?

Finally, Basil spoke up: "Things are going pretty well, Chief," he said. The thought of the receding waterline made his heart feel heavy, but he went on: "As a matter of fact, the beach seems to be getting larger."

The Old Man grunted. "Fine, fine," he said. "That will give us a bit more elbow room." He closed his eyes and continued basking in the sun.

The next day brought more trouble. A new herd of walruses moved in down the beach, and with the supply of herring dwindling, this invasion could be dangerous. No one wanted to tell the Old Man, though only he could take the steps necessary to meet this new competition.

Reluctantly, Basil approached the big walrus, who was still sunning himself on the large rock. After some small talk, he said, "Oh, by the way, Chief. A new herd of walruses seems to have moved into our territory." The Old Man's eyes snapped open, and he filled his great lungs in preparation for a mighty bellow. But Basil added quickly, "Of course, we don't anticipate any trouble. They don't look like herring-eaters to me—more likely interested in minnows. And as you know, we don't bother with the minnows ourselves."

The Old Man let out the air with a long sigh. "Good, good," he said. "No point in our getting excited over nothing, then, is there?"

Things didn't get any better in the weeks that followed. One day, peering down from the large rock, the Old Man noticed that part of his herd seemed to be missing. Summoning Basil, he grunted peevishly, "What's going on, Basil? Where is everybody?"

Poor Basil didn't have the courage to tell the Old Man that many of the younger walruses were leaving every day to join the new herd. Clearing his throat nervously, he said, "Well, Chief, we've been tightening things up a bit. You know, getting rid of some of the deadwood. After all, a herd is only as good as the walruses in it."

"Run a tight ship, I always say," the Old Man grunted. "Glad to hear that everything's going so well."

Before long, everybody but Basil had left to join the new herd, and Basil realized that the time had come to tell the Old Man the facts. Terrified but determined, he flopped up to the large rock. "Chief," he said, "I have bad news. The rest of the herd has left you."

The old walrus was so astonished that he couldn't even work up a good bellow. "Left me?" he cried. "All of them? But why? How could this happen?"

Basil didn't have the heart to tell him, so he merely shrugged helplessly.

"I can't understand it," the old walrus said. "And just when *everything* was going so well!"

Anonymous

The walrus story is amusing but in real life the effects are often tragic. The following is from *Harpers,* December, 1972. It is a book review of David Halberstam's *The Best and the Brightest.* The reviewer, retired General James Gavin, writes:

The war was under way whether we realized it or not. Optimistic reports came back from time to time interspersed with requests for reinforcements. Carefully organized briefings were prepared for visitors, and few were able to see beyond the roseate facade that confronted them. In an effort to get the facts, Secretary of Defense Robert McNamara made a trip to Saigon; he was elated at what he saw and heard.

McNamara's role was an exceedingly difficult one. In the State Department there was some skepticism about Vietnam from the very beginning, and George Ball was a consistent critic of the war. But Ball had no counterpart in the Department of Defense, and McNamara was forced to rely heavily on reports from Saigon. From time to time he returned to Vietnam, but on each occasion he again was given a very optimistic report. (Junior officers who did not render optimistic reports to Saigon were relieved of duty.)

In April of 1963 the chief of our Saigon Mission, General Harkins, met with McNamara and Roger Hilsman of the State Department, as well as others, in Honolulu. Halberstam reports the meeting: "Harkins was almost euphoric. He could not give any guarantees, but he thought it would all be over by Christmas. McNamara, listening to him, was elated."

(The optimism wasn't only from Saigon; people in the White House helped. General Taylor was President Kennedy's military advisor.)

As the war went on the President himself became deeply troubled by the reports he had been receiving. The reports emanating from Ambassador Lodge, who was then our emissary in Saigon, were generally rather pessimistic. On the other hand, the reports from the chief of our military Mission, reporting through the Department of Defense, were quite optimistic. In late 1963, the President sensed a serious rift developing in Washington between State and Defense. In order to get at the facts, the President asked Hilsman of State to draft a cable to Saigon reflecting considerable doubt about the progress of the war. When the answer came in, Ambassador Lodge's report was entirely pessimistic, while Harkins' report was markedly upbeat. It was puzzling until one of the White House aides found a reference in the Harkins cable to an outgoing cable of Taylor's. As Halberstam reports it "They checked out the number of the Taylor cable but could find no record of it in the White House. Sensing that something was wrong, one of the White House aides called over to the Pentagon for a copy of the Taylor cable." It was "a remarkably revealing cable from Taylor to Harkins explaining just how divided the bureaucracy was, what the struggle was about"—in effect, how to answer the White House cable.

Averell Harriman suspected something unusual at once and Kennedy was to remark later, "Harriman is really a shrewd old S.O.B." At the conclusion of the meeting at which this information was disclosed, Kennedy took Taylor into his office. There is no record of the conversation that took place.

The consequences of not telling the truth, of being more worried about careers than the truth, was a prolongation of a terrible war, with all the deaths and maimings and human tragedy! Gavin's review continues.

Halberstam is very severe with McNamara, finally concluding that he was, "there is no kinder word for it, a fool." I would be personally inclined also to blame those in uniform who misled him with their faulty intelligence estimates and optimistic reports. He needed a man with the honesty of Stilwell, who upon being driven out of Burma in an earlier war, said to the press, "I say we got the hell beaten out of us and we are going to do something about it." Halberstam points out that "the idea of a contemporary American general ever admitting that he had taken a hell of a beating is inconceivable."

If a man harbors any sort of fear, it percolates through
all his thinking, damages his personality, makes him
landlord to a ghost.
Lloyd C. Douglas

The following is an example from business in which lack of courage ended a promising career:

The division controller was explaining to the general manager (his peer, both worked for the president) that the manager for transportation systems, Jim Olsen, was really not credible on this Boston bid.

"First he said last week that it was a federal bid with federal contract terms and now he has changed his mind. I'm not sure I believe him when he tells me things."

The general manager met with Olsen privately and asked whether or not he had been mistaken when he told the controller that the bid would be a federal one.

"Yes, I was," he said. "He pressed me very hard for an answer so even though I wasn't sure, I gave him my best answer."

"Did you tell him you weren't sure?"

"Well no, I felt that it would look bad if I didn't know, so I told him as though I did know."

"Look, Jim," said the general manager, "you've really hurt your credibility and I don't think you should tell these people anything unless you are sure and if they then want your estimate, label it as an estimate, and tell them what you think but don't let them push you into giving a position that you are not ready to give."

"Well, he was pressing me pretty hard," he said. "I really felt that your organization and I would look bad if I couldn't give a good answer."

The general manager shook his head. "Jim, you're losing your credibility. I don't care who asks you for a position. If you are not sure, state that you are not sure. In trying to look good you're really hurting yourself because when it later turns out that you were shooting from the hip, so to speak, you lose your reputation."

"But he is the division controller," protested Olsen.

"Look, Jim," said the general manager, "we pay you a lot of money and you are a high-level guy. I don't care if he was the division controller. If he presses you for a position and you don't have one that you are really sure of, don't give him one. It's better to say, 'I don't know and I will get back to you' than to gamble that your answer is right. These people are tough-minded people and they will not let you get away with wrong answers too often."

Two weeks after this conversation, the division president, in a similar situation, asked Olsen for some facts. Not willing to admit that he didn't know the facts, Olsen again gambled and presented his 'facts' of things which were only half-known. The division president upon further questioning of other people found out that Olsen had been shooting from the hip. Angered, he mentioned this to the general manager.

The general manager decided that Olsen just was not courageous enough to withstand the possible disapproval of the high-level executives and would make up an answer if necessary in order to escape the situation of the moment. In short, he decided that Olsen could not be trusted to run important undertakings.

> Courage is fear that has said its prayers.
> *Karle Wilson Baker*

In short, indiscriminate submission to authority and indiscriminate resistance to it are both childish. The mature person is characterized by his ability to decide, according to morally significant criteria, when to cooperate with authority and when not to.
Thomas Szasz

It wasn't until quite late in life that I discovered how easy it is to say, "I don't know."
W. Somerset Maugham

We pay a heavy price for our fear of failure. It is a powerful obstacle to growth. It assures the progressive narrowing of the personality and prevents exploration and experimentation. There is no learning without some difficulty and fumbling. If you want to keep on learning, you must keep on risking failure—all your life.
John W. Gardner

It is better to go down on the great seas which human hearts were made to sail than to rot at the wharves in ignoble anchorage.
Hamilton Wright Mabie

Courage is the price that life
    exacts for granting peace,
The soul that knows it not,
    knows no release
From little things.
Amelia Earhart Putnam

It requires greater virtues to support good than bad fortune.
La Rochefoucauld

The absence of courage is a fault that few are willing to confess. We even invent names for it, which are only unconscious excuses. We call it prudence, or respectability, or conservatism, or economy, or worldly wisdom, or the instinct of self-preservation.
Henry Van Dyke

Success is never final and failure never fatal. It's courage that counts.
George F. Tilton

Fear is an acid which is pumped into one's atmosphere. It causes mental, moral and spiritual asphyxiation and sometimes death; death to energy and all growth.
Horace Fletcher

If my flesh knew how far my courage is soon going to carry it, it would be totally paralyzed.
Sancho, King of Navarre

The harder the conflict, the more glorious the triumph. What we obtain too cheap, we esteem too lightly; 'tis dearness only that gives everything its value. I love the man that can smile in trouble, that can gather strength from distress, and grow brave by reflection. 'Tis the business of little minds to shrink; but he whose heart is firm, and whose conscience approves his conduct, will pursue his principles until death.
Thomas Paine

Out of the night that covers me,
    Black as the pit from pole to pole,
I thank whatever gods may be
    For my unconquerable soul.

In the fell clutch of circumstance
    I have not winced nor cried aloud.
Under the bludgeonings of chance
    My head is bloody, but unbowed.

Beyond this place of wrath and tears
    Looms but the Horror of the shade,
And yet the menace of the years
    Finds and shall find me unafraid.

It matters not how strait the gate,
    How charged with punishments the scroll,
I am the master of my fate:
    I am the captain of my soul.

William Ernest Henley

Courage is not simply one of the virtues but a form of every virtue at the testing point, which means at the point of highest reality.

C. S. Lewis

You are never so near to victory as when defeated in a good cause.

Henry Ward Beecher

Far better it is to dare mighty things, to win glorious triumphs even though checkered by failure, than to take rank with those poor spirits who neither enjoy much nor suffer much, because they live in the great twilight that knows not victory nor defeat.

Theodore Roosevelt

One man with courage makes a majority.

Andrew Jackson

Physical courage, which despises all danger, will make a man brave in one way; and moral courage, which despises all opinion, will make a man brave in another. The former would seem most necessary for the camp; the latter for the council; but to constitute a great man both are necessary.

C. C. Colton

Boldness

> ... and not, when I came to die, discover that I had not lived.
>
> *Henry David Thoreau*

Boldness is close to, but separate from, courage. One can be courageous and not bold. The courage may be a quiet, steady, unseen courage.

Boldness is close to self-confidence, but it goes beyond self-confidence. It is the frequent outward expression of independence and courage. Boldness does not mean antagonism or rudeness. It means lack of fear and action-oriented. The bold question seeks to find information, not to disrupt. The management that resents a frank question is a weak one. The bold question will either get information or show management to be weak. Too often people are racked with fear and qualms that the question they have in their mind (that is keeping them from really understanding) is either (a) obvious or (b) imprudent. To ask an obvious question might show they are "dumb" or not knowledgeable. To ask an imprudent one says they are "difficult." So they don't ask, and management gets off the hook easily.

There have been many times a person has asked me a question I wish he hadn't. But I respect him for it, even if it causes me temporary embarrassment. He's a thinker and has courage.

I have watched the lowest level employee in the meeting challenge the highest, and almost always come out ahead for the challenge.

To be sure, there are those "executives" who will be so petty as to take offense at the questioner who may ask the top executive "why" (on a decision that may change the questioner's life). But even there the questioner is better off, because the company run by such an executive is in trouble, and it is better for the "bold one" to find out quickly the state the company is in.

Boldness gets results. It is an outward, pushing, risk-taking activity.

The "general manager's" attitude is drilled into the sales force of a large electronics firm. They are told that everything the company does is under their control, if necessary. They are told to make things come out right. And they often do. They demand to review the production schedule. When told that that is none of their business, they persist and appeal to higher authorities. And they usually get to see the schedule. They check everything and are rarely surprised.

Immense power is acquired by assuring yourself in your secret reveries that you were born to control affairs.
Andrew Carnegie

Treat everyone equally and as equals. This simple rule avoids so much pain and trouble, and commands respect from all. Your superiors think, "This individual is not awed by me or the Board of Directors. This employee has presence, control, and self-confidence and is worth listening to."

Your subordinates think, "This boss respects me. I can't let someone like that down."

Robert C. Townsend, author of *Up the Organization,* has made a videotape in which he discusses some of his ideas on management. In one delightful sequence, he pictures a retired president of a firm, who is kept on a retainer, to come back occasionally and run a special effort.

One of the benefits of having the ex-president around is that the special effort gets the necessary management attention.

He pictures the board of directors in a meeting when all of a sudden in wanders the ex-president, who says, "Hey, guys, stop. I need a nail or the special effort will fail."

All stop and turn their attention to getting him a nail. Then they return to what they were doing.

Perhaps I love this little vignette because of the relish and style with which Townsend relates it, perhaps because the idea of someone *wandering* in to a board of directors meeting and saying "Hey, guys," is delicious. It is the stuff dreams are made of. Townsend has touched the need for boldness in a direct way.

An agency head was telling me that the United Kingdom had paid the ten million dollars for a device that my company had sold to the agency. The agency in turn sold it to the U.K.

I wasn't impressed that the U.K. had paid. I never doubted they would.

"So what?" I said.

"You don't understand. They paid in three months."

"This was fast, but so what?"

"No, you still don't understand. We didn't have the authority to sell it to the U.K."

Now I understood—and was impressed.

The agency—and my friend—had taken a daring risk. They had spent ten million dollars without authority and shipped the goods to the U.K. I admired his boldness. It had worked!

> He that leaveth nothing to Chance will do few things ill, but he will do very few things.
> *Lord Halifax*

The Lack of Boldness

The lack of boldness is easily seen, fortunately.

A salesman was discussing a key account, and the general manager asked if the engineer assigned to the account was "up to the task."

"Yes, I think so," replied the salesman.

The conversation proceeded and again the question was asked and the same answer was given.

The third time, later in the conversation, the salesman replied, "No, he isn't."

Another business example:

A critical question on a $5-million contract was unanswered.
The general manager asked the middle-level, responsible manager
to get the question answered.

"I can't. You should call the contracts group and ask," he told
the general manager. "Why can't you?" asked the amazed general
manager, since the middle-level executive had spent two years
working with this customer.

"Only our contracts people can talk to their contracts people,"
he replied.

The general manager blew up. "It's *your* customer, *your* contract,
your responsibility. You talk to whomever you want."

The words didn't help. The middle-level manager was timid.

May you live all the days of your life.
Jonathan Swift

Some people believe that in any business transaction between two
organizations, vice-presidents should talk to vice-presidents, presidents
to presidents, directors to directors, etc. For a director to talk to a
president is too "daring"; it is somehow "impolite." Such people are
"status-awed."

Look at two companies working together on a large military proposal.

	Computer Co.	*Radar Co.*
Level 1	President	President
Level 2	Vice-president	Vice-president
Level 3	Director sales manager	Division manager
Level 4	Project manager	Sales manager
Level 5	Project coordinator	Project manager

Lack of boldness says a Level 3 can't call a Level 1.

"Status-awed" people believe that it is permissible and correct
that one level away from each other can call each other. Thus a Level
2 *can* call a Level 1, although it is better to keep the levels exactly
equal. It is always dangerous, they believe, to have more than one
level difference in any communication, especially an upward one. It is
"wrong" for a project manager to call a president. This foolish belief
has hampered the effectiveness of otherwise outstanding executives.
I've seen these people stare wildly when a Level 3 says, "Let's call a
Level 1." I've seen time and energy wasted as a Level 3 briefs a Level 1
in the Level 1's company so that the Level 1 can call the Level 1 in
the other company.

There are times, of course, when the message is delicate, when a
Level 1 should call a Level 1. But usually that call should be made
by the individual who knows the most and can be most effective.

> A man who has never been in danger cannot answer for
> his courage.
>
> *La Rochefoucauld*

Barbara Tuchman in *Stilwell and the American Experience in China* details a momentous failure of boldness.

Stilwell—the hero of the story—is beset by a backbiting ally, General Chenault of the Flying Tigers. Chenault, with an effective apologist in Joe Alsop, claims erroneously that with more supplies to them— and fewer to Stilwell—they can beat the Japanese with air power alone.

General George C. Marshall, Chief of the Army and guiding genius of America's war effort, sees the fallacy of this and wins dispute after dispute in Washington on the Stilwell point of view. But Alsop's persuasive language, coupled with the "China Lobby," continues to press.

George C. Marshall decides to have Stilwell meet President Roosevelt on one of Stilwell's few visits to Washington.

Marshall tells Stimson, Secretary of War, who is supporting Marshall's position, that Stilwell will win the day with FDR by giving firsthand, persuasive information. Stilwell can be devastating in his analysis, says Marshall.

The meeting is held. Marshall lays the background and turns the meeting over to Stilwell. FDR and Stimson wait expectantly. Stilwell hangs his head, says nothing.

Marshall prompts him, asks him questions. Stilwell mumbles. He can't be heard.

Marshall presents Stilwell's arguments, but they lack the force, conviction, and detail of Stilwell and his knowledge. The meeting is a disaster.

FDR later asks Marshall if Stilwell was ill. FDR decides for Chenault and for a brief time supplies are diverted to Chenault—until it becomes obvious that this is a waste.

Stilwell wasn't ill; he was awed! He lost his chance by not being bold.

> It is native personality, and that alone, that endows a
> man to stand before presidents or generals, or any
> distinguished collection, with aplomb—and not culture,
> or any knowledge or intellect whatever.
>
> *Walt Whitman*

Lawrence O'Brien, writing in *No Final Victories* about Joe Kennedy, the father of John, Robert, Teddy, and the others, states that the millionaire once told him that if he were ever dealing with someone important to him, he should picture that person sitting there in long red underwear. That's what Joe had always done in business, he said.

Boldness will be an asset in most companies and a defect in a few. The company is the loser when it is not an asset.

A chairman of the Board once told me: "Most people will not talk about the things that are most important to them. It's as if they are afraid that if they talk about them, they'll change them. And since they are *so* important they are afraid that the change may not be good. So they don't talk about them."

Boldness is the outward thrusting of courage. It complements courage and is essential to rising in large organizations. It must be managed by the riser so that it does not offend the beliefs of the organization.

... alas for those that never sing,
But die with all their music in them.
Oliver W. Holmes

The great tragedy of life isn't that men perish, but that they cease to live.
W. Somerset Maugham

In short, he who first seizes the word imposes reality on the other; he who defines thus dominates and lives; and he who is defined is subjugated and may be killed.
Thomas Szasz

To dare every day to be irreverent and bold. To dare to preserve the randomness of mind which in children produces strange and wonderful new thoughts and forces. To continually scramble the familiar and bring the old into new juxtaposition.
Gordon Webber

The great man is he who does not lose his child's heart.
Mencius

Common sense does not ask an impossible chessboard, but takes the one before it and plays the game.
Wendell Phillips

Men of genius are often dull and inert in society; as the blazing meteor, when it descends to earth, is only a stone.
Henry W. Longfellow

Ambition is the motor that drives the climber forward. Most executives are "driven" people in the sense that they have a strong drive to succeed that pushes them to expend energy. The ambitious individual finds a way, strives harder, works longer. The ambitious individual is always pushing!

This drive usually generates *high energy*. "Calm" and "slow" and "methodical" do not often characterize today's executive. The ambitious make things happen. You plan your next job and the job after that. You work to make openings for yourself; you force things to occur. The person who is not ambitious will often wait for things to happen.

Ambition differs from "willpower." It feeds willpower, to some extent, but it is a longer term, deeper characteristic. We all know people who have willpower but who are not ambitious; who are intense, or results-oriented, and not ambitious.

Sources of Ambition

There are two main reasons why people are ambitious, why they are pushers, drivers and the chiefs; a) because their "not OK" status is driving them to accomplish, b) because even in the "OK" status their basic beliefs tell them that they are here to achieve or to accomplish something for humanity. Basically this is the religious or messianic complex.

> ...his secret: timidity. To feel the equal of men, he must be their master.
>
> *André Maurois*

There are many ways to achieve—and thereby assuage inferiority feelings.

- Achieve power over people.
- Accumulate money.
- Gain reputation for mental accomplishments.
- Gain reputation for athletic skill.
- Be accepted socially by one's peers.

One of any of the above will help a person achieve self-esteem. Obviously one would like to accomplish all of them.

> I have offended God and man because my work has not reached the quality it should have.
>
> *Leonardo da Vinci*

Dreams have fired human efforts for years. The word dream is often used to describe very hard-to-achieve goals. Dreams spring from beliefs, and in turn fire the ambition. We are urged to have dreams, to seek to do the impossible, to explore and find new ways, to *do* the impossible.

A person's goals at the age of 25, 35, 45, and 55 are apt to be very different goals. This should be kept in mind by high-level managers as they attempt to motivate their subordinates. It is easy to assume that your subordinates will want the same goals as you do, but this assumption is often wrong. An organization must expect an individual's ambition to wane with time or as the individual attains some of the personal goals by middle age. The idea that one would deliberately slow down one's career growth is almost anti-American.

The concept of opportunity knocking only once, of grabbing your chance or else, of catching your tide, etc., is drilled into us. Don't let opportunity pass! Yet persons who have the correct qualities should be able to get a decent job and support their families—and they need not grab every opportunity that flies past.

Bill Moyers, President Lyndon B. Johnson's aide, showed great independence when he left the then Vice-President Johnson's staff to join the Peace Corps. Johnson didn't like people to leave him, especially when he was suffering through the limbo of the Vice-Presidency. But Moyers left. And it didn't seem to hurt him since Lyndon took him back in a key job after becoming President.

Not everyone is ambitious for the same things. Some want to be executives; some want to be scientists; others want to teach. Not all professors want to be deans.

I was going through the formal, yearly appraisal of a subordinate. I was telling him that he had to be more bold and more outgoing if he wanted to be a manager.

"I don't want to be a manager. I just want to be a superb technical analyst."

I was stunned! Didn't everyone want to be a manager?

I never discuss performance or future careers without first asking what are a man's ambitions.

Ambition will drive some people to do anything, even to risk their lives.

A Colonel: In combat, you are not accepted right away. You've got to prove yourself time and time again. . . . I wanted to prove myself so I had my life on the line a few times . . .

Ward Just

Ambition and realism usually come in the same person. An ambitious individual will be willing to compromise; in fact, perhaps too willing. Ambition and integrity are too often *not* found in the same person. Integrity can get in the way of the ambition.

> Ambition is like hunger; it obeys no law but its appetite.
> *H. W. Shaw*

Without ambition, you can still make it to the top. With superb qualities you can find yourself at higher and higher levels almost without effort. But your chances are fewer. Ambition keeps most people pushing and driving and in the race.

When a person . . . feels that he will aways fail, then battle he must—the competition must be recurrent and constant, for he cannot reassure himself for long, not unless one success follows another. Defeat is inevitable.

News Front

If you aspire to the highest place, it is no disgrace to stop at the second or third.

Cicero

One realizes that the beginning of every life is fraught with a more or less deep feeling of inferiority when one sees the weakness and helplessness of every child. Sooner or later every child becomes conscious of his inability to cope single-handed with the challenges of existence. This feeling of inferiority is the driving force, the starting point from which every childish striving originates.

Whenever we see persons constantly in motion, with strong tempers and passions, we can always conclude that they are persons with a great feeling of inferiority. A person who knows he can overcome his difficulties will not be impatient. Arrogant, impertinent, fighting children also indicate a great feeling of inferiority. They are compensating . . . overcompensating.

Alfred Adler

No one but the paranoiac is free from tremblings of insufficiency.

News Front

This world belongs to the energetic.

Ralph W. Emerson

Both the high- and low-level manager must have the insistence to demand performance from subordinates. And they must demand performance from superiors and peers as well.

An executive must reward subordinates. And, if they do not perform, the executive must admonish, guide, help and, when all else fails, remove them. The higher the executive goes the more important this becomes. Many managers are quick to reward but far too slow to punish.

We must have standards to which to repair.
George Washington

Punish is perhaps the wrong word. Managers should *remove* subordinates if, after guiding and pointing out mistakes to them, they still do not seem to understand. It is essential for the executives to be demanding in order for the organization to continue to function smoothly. An executive chooses subordinates and rises or falls to a large extent on their success or failure. An executive who chooses poor subordinates or mediocre subordinates will fail. An executive who chooses outstanding ones will succeed. No executive has a 100 percent batting average when it comes to choosing the right subordinate. When the executive has made a mistake, it is up to the executive to correct it.

Once it is clear that the wrong subordinate has been chosen and has not lived up to the executive's expectations, then it is necessary for the executive to remove that subordinate and put a new choice in the vacated position. This can be a very emotional experience for most people because it represents failure. The subordinate has failed. The executive chose the subordinate and, therefore, has failed also. In addition, there may be a friendship between the two individuals. There will always be reasons for not taking a poor choice out of the job, for making do, for muddling through. When, finally, to make the decision that the subordinate must go is a very difficult question. But clearly, an executive who never makes that decision is doomed to fail.

It is often easier to fight for a principle than to live up to it.
Adlai Stevenson

General George C. Marshall, the Chief of the U.S. Army during World War II, had a statement that he used to quell the objections of subordinates when he was promoting a man out of sequence. He would say, "We owe it to the men."

This philosophy should hold in all organizations. To keep an organization healthy, the executive must remove failing subordinates. "We owe it to the company, the men, the stockholder."

But what about the poor employee being removed? Sure it's tough on the employee, but the employee still has a job and a good salary. All people take risks as they climb the ladder; they may have to go back down. People tend to overreact to a demotion, as though those demoted are suddenly of no value whatever. Yet people still take it very hard, and it is a difficult and emotionally charged task to demote a subordinate. But everything is relative.

> They were having dinner out on a Friday night and the vice-president of production was bemoaning the fact that he'd had a tough day.
>
> "I had to take a man out of a high-level job today. His career is dead-ended and he was really upset."
>
> The dinner companions were a doctor and his wife. "I had a tough day too. I had to tell a patient he had cancer of the larynx."
>
> The vice-president decided that maybe his job was not that tough after all.

> Adversity has made many a man great who, had he remained prosperous, would only have been rich.
> *Maurice Switzer*

Each organization sets standards; each expects so much of its managers. The question arises: If my subordinate is performing in an "OK," average, not outstanding manner, and has not responded to counseling —the individual will never be outstanding—and there is another subordinate who is available and can do the job in an outstanding manner, should I remove the average performer? Or should I remove only people who are failing? The answer lies in the organization, in the views of the top executives. In some organizations, the average performer will remain; in others, be removed. The organization that removes the average performer will be a more vital, aggressive organization. But it will be one that is tough to work for because it *is* demanding.

Some executives I know have all the other qualities of the executive, but they are reluctant to exercise their authority to remove subordinates. When a subordinate is not performing well, they try to help the person. When the subordinate continues not to perform well, the executive works harder and harder and harder until finally the executive is overwhelmed by work and the organization begins to falter and fall behind.

These *executives* must be removed. If an executive does not police and cleanse the organization, then the executive's superior must do the job. At the high levels of larger organizations, the higher superior does not have the time and/or knowledge to run the subordinate's organization. Therefore, the subordinate executive must go.

Not to laugh, not to cry, but to understand.
Anton Chekhov

Should a superior report upwards the failings of subordinates? Will that harm their careers? Should the superior "manage the news"?

The question itself has a flaw in it. In addition to asking "Will that harm their careers?" you should also ask, "What are they doing to their *own* careers?" People forget that the boss, too, is constantly being appraised.

The failure of subordinates should be handled with complete candor with your own superior. "Jones 'blew' it. He didn't see that the zither wouldn't work," you say.

"What about Jones?" asks your boss. "Is he in the right job? Should we move him out of there?"

"Jones is good. He's smart and aggressive and knows the business. The customer likes him. He just tends to be unrealistic at times. I've talked to him about this and he recognizes his mistake. We should watch him in this area. Overall, he's got potential to go much higher." The boss may not agree with the evaluation. He may want to point out that you are being too easy on Jones and that he has been unrealistic too often. But the exchange is realistic, open, and nothing is hidden. Your superior and you are communicating and two minds are addressing problems and assessing. Jones's career should not be harmed by such an exchange.

Some people believe this is a cowardly approach and that you are blaming a subordinate for the problem. They argue that the report to your boss should be "My team and I really blew this one. Here's how I'm going to fix it." This, they argue, keeps the heat off Jones and makes you look courageous and "big." The reason this argument is so widely used is that it *does* have some merit; it *does* emphasize positive qualities of courage and maturity, But it also violates realism. If you *accurately* state what has happened to your superior and show the failure of your subordinate, your boss and you know that it is *still* your responsibility—the failure—and *your boss's!* It is your area, your responsibility, your subordinate, your problem. To take the blame is foolish bravado; the superior has a right to know who made the mistake. Your boss deserves to know in order to be careful of Jones in the future on this issue.

"But this *kills* Jones," people will say. It shouldn't. The top executive in this chain with emotional maturity knows that people make mistakes and will not count Jones out for one mistake.

66

> Few people have sufficient wisdom to prefer censure, which is useful, to praise, which deceives them.
>
> *La Rochefoucauld*

Making Demands of Superiors and Peers

It is not enough to make demands of your subordinates only. You must demand performance from yourself, your peers, and even your superiors. The superior may resent the demand when it occurs (the amount of tact and the manner of the demand are important) but in the long term will recognize that you are only doing your job.

No one likes to be on the receiving end of demands, so making demands should be done tactfully. Here is a tactful demand placed upon a higher level co-worker (but not upon a direct supervisor).

> A salesman had the customer ready to sign, but the service manager told the salesman that he wasn't going to maintain the machine if it was sold. This was clearly against the company policy; it was the service department's job to maintain anything that was in the sales book—and this item was!
>
> The salesman first tried cooperation. He said he'd get the customer to delay installation until the manager could train one of his men on the machine. Although this was generous on the part of the salesman, the service manager still said no.
>
> Now the salesman used force. He did it nicely, but it was force!
>
> "Look, the way I see the world, it's your responsibility to maintain this machine. You've shown me nothing that says you don't have to. Therefore, the way I see it, your position is wrong. Now, unless I get your agreement to maintain this machine, I've got no choice but to go to your manager and ask him to overrule you. Maybe you can show me why I'm wrong and, if I am, I'll have learned something. If I'm not, I'll have made the sale."
>
> The service manager agreed to maintain the machine.

Often the most competent managers will avoid being demanding of high-level managers.

> An outstanding technical manager is so nice a person that he hates to tell management bad news. He'll let sloppy information and even misinformation be presented without speaking up and clarifying things. To do so would point an accusing finger at the presenter.
>
> He'll go out after the meeting and try to fix things, and being as capable as he is, he usually succeeds.
>
> I have watched his boss orchestrate meetings with high-level management, constantly asking the competent technical manager,

"Do you agree?" The answer is frequently no, but the asking must be done to get the no out in the open.

On technical issues he is superb!

Being too solicitous can be disastrous!

A high-level manager who ran a million-dollar proposal was telling a friend about his experiences. "It was awful," he said. "There were times that the pressures got so bad, I just broke down and cried. There were times I didn't think I could make it through."

"Later, when the proposal was lost," he said, "they told me I wasn't tough enough, that I listened to the excuses of manufacturing and of engineering and I settled for less than they could have done had they been pressed to the wall." He paused, "Maybe they are right."

The upcoming manager must tell the boss what is needed.

A 'disaster' was underway. "Why didn't you tell me?" said the vice-president.

"I knew you had a run-in with the X division president over this bid and I didn't want to cause you more grief," said Brown. Brown had been trying to make life a little bit easier for the vice-president and it had now 'blown up!'

The vice-president paused: "You made a mistake. They pay me more than they pay you and one of the reasons is that I have to stand more 'pain' than you do. You should have told me!"

Trying to spare your bosses is a risky business; it often leads to surprises, and bosses do *not* like surprises—epecially bad news ones. The boss is paid more than you are; has more experience than you do; and can see things you can't. The boss wants to be forewarned! Keep your boss informed about the possible problems on the horizon.

I have seen executives who had *all* the qualities and abilities, except insistence. As their subordinates fail, they work harder and harder and harder. It is a sad situation, as the executives were superb—but they were incapable of making demands. The executives had to be removed.

> Do not pray for easy lives. Pray to be stronger men. Do not pray for tasks equal to your powers. Pray for powers equal to your tasks.
>
> *Phillips Brooks*

WILLPOWER

> I have brought myself by long meditation to the conviction that a human being with a settled purpose must accomplish it, and that nothing can resist a will which will stake even existence upon its fulfillment.
>
> *Benjamin Disraeli*

There are times when you must make up your mind that it is going to be your way and no other. Some of the most effective executives I have seen can almost dominate others by sheer willpower. They have committed their heart and soul and reputation to the achievement of an objective, and their willpower is almost a palpable thing that carries along subordinates and sweeps away opponents. It was said of Winston Churchill that grown men were afraid of him.

Without willpower, one lacks perseverance and intensity. Willpower needs no definition; it is the determination and commitment that lead to the goal. I include under willpower the idea of being a results-oriented individual. Great effort shows willpower, but results often show it more clearly.

Effective executives are ones who exhibit willpower because they want an objective met, and they inspire their subordinates to go forward to it. They are intense because they believe in the goal, and they are intense in order to lead. This positive intensity which grows from beliefs is very critical to the achievement of position and power. Many fine individuals possess all of the other traits but lack this one. It is something that cannot be taught.

> Thinking well is wise; planning well, wiser; doing well wisest and best of all.
>
> *Persian proverb*

Unfortunately in many companies the desire to "look good" takes precedence over the desire to achieve. This is especially true in companies that are very successful—they can afford these "look-good" executives. Executives of these companies learn to keep out of trouble, to look sage and wise, to never attempt anything hard, and to learn the "in" phrase and what the boss wants. It works, unfortunately.

I include under willpower the urge to achieve results, as contrasted to the desire to simply perform well. This could be called the results-oriented quality.

Results-oriented people like to win. They play to win. Watch them at their sports. They play tennis or squash with a vengeance. They often don't seem to be as good as their opponents, but they *win!* All major league coaches know that you cannot judge a player just by the statistics—batting average, fielding percentage, even runs batted-in.

There is an unmeasurable something coaches call "hustle" or "clutch playing." It doesn't show in any statistics, because there is no way to show it. But some ball players are always coming up with whatever is necessary, when necessary—a great catch, an extra base, an incredible throw. They get results; they win; their team wins.

It is not enough that we do our best; sometimes we have
to do what is required.
W. S. Churchill

Watch others who are not results-oriented. They play tennis, perhaps, beautifully. Their shots, form, style, and strategy are superb, but they don't win. Something always happens; they just don't seem to have the winning habit. They don't have the will to win.

Our power over the world is far greater than we dream.
We fashion everything we touch in our own image.
Eric Hoffer

Reputation should never substitute for results. Merit should be based on results.

A corporate vice-president once addressed a management class and stated that winners seemed to keep on winning. They seem to shape events so that the events come out in their favor. This is what we mean by results-oriented. They drive and drive until they get their way. The idea that "Well, I've done my best; let fate decide" is just not acceptable to them. They will do more and more and more until their desired result is in hand.

Willpower is persevering despite obstacles. F. D. Roosevelt, four times elected president of the United States, was disabled by polio for ten years before re-entering public life. Winston Churchill was out of power for ten years before he was accepted back into the English Cabinet as First Lord of the Admiralty—at age 60. Charles de Gaulle waited through his country's defeat and exile before coming back to take over France. Mao Tse Tung is the leader of 800,000,000 people.

He spent twelve years in a cave before he took power. Twelve years! In a cave! Lenin spent sixteen years in exile before overthrowing the czar in 1917.

Willpower is striking to see!

A high-level manager was seriously injured in an auto accident. He spent five hours in surgery. One of his subordinates, an old friend, helped push him on the table out of the recovery room. "Jim," said the friend, "this is the first time I've ever been able to push you around."

Through jaws wired shut because his jaws were broken, through the grogginess after a five-hour operation, he muttered: "It'll be the last."

Lack of Willpower

"Can John Jensen do this job?" The executive was talking about a high-level tough assignment.

"Well. . . ." the subordinate hesitated. "John is a nice guy."

This meant that John didn't get the job. Saying John was a "nice guy" was saying that he lacked willpower, that he would compromise and placate too much. In being recommended for a difficult job, a label of "tough and demanding" is far better than "nice guy."

> Words without actions are the assassins of idealism.
> *Herbert Hoover*

Ph.D.s are often more interested in the idea than the result.

A college assistant dean told me that many doctoral candidates had no idea how to write their theses. They knew a great deal about a very narrow subject, but could not relate why the subject they knew so much about was important. They did not know where the special subject fit into the order of things, what cause or result was. They wrote their theses on their particular subject because "someone suggested it years ago."

There is no question about the intellect or work habits of Ph.D.s. Their achievements show these. But too often they are not results-oriented. They need someone to suggest an area of work. Their willpower is not focused.

It's not simply that Ph.D.s don't make it to the top in large organizations; they often *fail* to perform, even at the lower echelons. Technical Ph.D.s often argue that no one can evaluate their work. They fail because their willpower lacks focus. They are more interested in process than results.

Some people seem to know what has to be done to achieve a result. They "see" who the blockers are; they recognize vital, needed steps. And they do the necessary things. Sometimes they do them without flourish, without great effort, and sometimes almost effortlessly. Some of their peers work frantically and feverishly to achieve results, yet seem not to achieve them. They don't see the needed steps.

Why some "see" and others don't is perhaps intellectual or perhaps emotional—a lack of will—or both. But these people *should* do better; they try so hard!

Some lack the tough-minded *commitment* to the objective that is so often needed. Often it takes unpleasant confrontations to get results. It often means being demanding to the point of straining friendships and even good manners.

> A large corporation was putting out a $10-million bid. Three or four new and risky developments were included, and higher level sign-off was required.
>
> The proposal manager, who would also do the job if it was won, was presenting to the general manager of the radar department, preparatory to briefing the president.
>
> He explained that he felt that an increase of 2.5 in power/return could be achieved, but that the legal department had stated that that would require the division president to go even higher for approval—to the corporation vice-president for aerospace.
>
> "Any gain more than 2 has to be signed off at higher than division because of the risk. We lost our shirt a few years ago on one," the lawyer had said.
>
> "So I backed the gain down to 2," said the project manager.
>
> "Will it be harder to win with only 2?" asked the general manager.
>
> "Yes."
>
> "Can you make 2.5 on schedule and within cost?"
>
> "Yes; sure can!"
>
> "Then let's go to the boss's boss. We can do it. We need the sale."
>
> "But the lawyers and policy people think we'll have a hard time getting it through!"
>
> The general manager was perplexed.
>
> "Wouldn't you rather fight for what you think is right, have the tough time inside the company and more chance to win? If the top guy won't let us take the risk, then he at least understands that we thought we should and that we are less likely to win if we don't. It was two years ago we lost the dough."
>
> They brought it "upstairs" and got approval.

This process is a very common one. The staff—finance, legal, personnel departments—want to be safe and if they "force" the proposal manager into too many compromises, the proposal will not sell.

"Force" is the wrong word. "Wear down" is a more accurate description of the process. Proposal managers *must* be intense about what *they* want, and they must actively fight this wear-down procedure. They must be bold, demanding of their superiors, insisting that the superiors get involved to stop the process.

"Listen, boss," they should say to the general manager, "I think the legal guys are wrong and I've had two meetings with them on this. I need to get past their delaying tactics. You've got to help me. Let me set up a meeting and you can judge and then overrule them or take it higher."

General managers expect these kinds of tangles and they know it is part of their jobs to step in and fix the thing.

The *last* thing they want is to have proposal managers worn down. Yet they can't tell the lawyers not to warn of dangers! The process works only if the proposal managers are results-oriented. If they're not, the chances of winning are cut drastically.

General manager's *must* be results-oriented, and intense, and in possession of great willpower.

The truest wisdom, in general, is a resolute determination.
Napoleon

I run until I hurt and then I run until I'm in pain and I keep running until I'm in agony. And when I'm in agony, that's when I break records.
A student of Jess Lair

Unapplied knowledge is knowledge shorn of its meaning.
A. N. Whitehead

Activity back of a very small idea will produce more than inactivity and the planning of genius.
James A. Worsham

Trouble. The best way out is always through . . . once you are in.
Joseph M. Fox

The real difference between men is energy. A strong will, determination can accomplish anything and in this lies the distinction between great and little men.
Thomas Fuller

For while the tired waves, vainly breaking,
Seem here no painful inch to gain,
Far back, through creeks and inlets marching,
Comes silent, flooding in, the main.

And not by eastern windows only,
When daylight comes, comes in the light.
In front the sun, climbs slow, how slowly,
But westward look,
    the land is bright.

Arthur Hugh Clough

Life yields only to the conqueror. Never accept what can be gained
by giving in. You will be living off stolen goods, and your muscles
will atrophy.

Dag Hammarskjöld

The woods are lovely, dark and deep,
But I have promises to keep,
And miles to go before I sleep,
And miles to go before I sleep.

Robert Frost

If you want to hit a bird on the wing, you must have all your will in
a focus. You must not be thinking about yourself, and, equally,
you must not be thinking about your neighbor; you must be living
with your eye on that bird. Every achievement is a bird on the wing.

Oliver W. Holmes, Jr.

We mount to heaven mostly on the ruins of our cherished schemes,
finding our failures were successes.

Amos Bronson Alcott

The lure of the distant and the difficult is deceptive. The great
opportunity is where you are.

John Burroughs

The only things in which we can be said to have any property are
our actions. Our thoughts may be bad, yet produce no poison; they
may be good, yet produce no fruit. Our riches may be taken away
by misfortune, our reputation by malice, our spirits by calamity, our
health by disease, our friends by death. But our actions must follow
us beyond the grave; with respect to them alone, we cannot say that
we shall carry nothing with us when we die, neither that we shall go
naked out of the world.

C. C. Colton

74

> There have been a few moments when I have known complete satisfaction, but only a few. I have rarely been free from the disturbing realization that my playing might have been better.
>
> *Ignace Jan Paderewski*

EMPATHY

Empathy is vital to sales ability, to leadership, to managing. Empathy means seeing the world through the other individual's eyes. Some people can "put themselves in the other's shoes." This quality is essential for effective people-interaction.

> When I'm getting ready to reason with a man, I spend one-third of my time thinking about myself and what I am going to say—and two-thirds thinking about him and what he is going to say.
>
> *Abraham Lincoln*

Empathy makes executives human to their subordinates. It precedes sympathy, but is different from sympathy. Executives can have empathy and still fire the poor performer. Without the balance of empathy, a self-centered person will lose the people-interaction skills that are so necessary to successful operations.

The ability to view events and circumstances from the other person's point-of-view does not mean you must share or agree with that point-of-view, but only that you can appreciate it and understand it. Empathy is vital to communications skills.

A very fine salesman told his secret one day—even if he didn't understand a technical discussion, he could, by watching and listening very carefully, assure that the parties communicating were really communicating.

By watching the physical reactions more than the verbal, he could tell if a sensitive point was accepted or not. And if it was not, he would steer the discussion back to the point sooner or later to get it resolved. "It always amazed me," he said, "that I could be a factor in negotiations on issues in which I had no capabilities. Yet, by being sensitive and alert, I could make sure that disagreements weren't overlooked. I could assure that key points— even though I didn't understand them—were understood. I could communicate, even when I didn't understand. If I understood, well, so much the better."

> He has the right to criticize who has the heart to help.
>
> *Abraham Lincoln*

75

Perhaps the greatest way to exhibit empathy is to somehow let people know that you will not judge *them*. You may judge their acts, but not them. This is a fine, but critical, distinction. People are often willing to admit that their acts are wrong ("I shouldn't have yelled at the customer...."), but are almost never willing to accept *personal rejection*.

If persons feel that you will not reject them personally, they will be more at ease with you, more open, more agreeable. But judge them personally and you'll never get them to open up again. There is a fantastic amount of information to be gained (or lost) depending on the attitude one displays toward peers, customers, boss, and subordinates.

Great Spirit, help me never to judge another until I have walked in his moccasins for two weeks.
Sioux Indian prayer

People who are very empathetic have a habit of being talked to. People tell them things, important things. They tell them about troubles and pressures, opportunities and dreams.

> An assistant general manager had a great means of gathering information—he listened. And all sorts of people in the organization talked to him, whether he was their boss or not. They would ask for advice, sometimes; help, sometimes; and sometimes just for a listener, someone to talk to. He was always willing to listen; he made time.
>
> "I'm really upset, Joe; I don't know what to do. Jack (his boss) doesn't listen to me. I've told Vin (the vice-president) I want a new job and he says, 'Hold on.' "
>
> This little monologue is common to most large corporations. Change the names and titles and you have every corporation, every division.
>
> The point here is that "Joe" has nothing at all to do organizationally with the speaker or his boss, Jack. He is almost a total outsider.
>
> The speaker comes to him because he needs someone to talk to, someone who will not "turn him in," who will help, even if it is only giving advice.
>
> What Joe gets is the satisfaction of helping, of course, and friendship. And *he gets information*. He hears firsthand the flaming problems—information that is very helpful to him.

See everything, overlook a great deal, correct a little.
Pope John XXIII

Tact

I think tact is 90 percent how to state sensitive things without hurting feeings. It is much more than just *not* stating the sensitive things. It is the decision of what words you use to convey the idea, and the way in which you state the words—softly, humorously, offhandedly, etc.

> Your superior has been defensive in answering questions from his boss. You want to tell him to help him. How do you tell him? It depends.
>
> It depends first on your relationship with him. If you know him very well, you may just tell him.
>
> Or, you might say, "The big boss seemed edgy and easy-to-anger today, didn't he?" Hopefully this will start a conversation in which you can tell the boss that he was defensive.
>
> Or you can kind of take the blame yourself. "I should have been more aggressive, don't you think? I kind of got defensive too fast."

Tact is diplomacy. It is saying things in a manner that can be accepted by the listener. Some people are masters at giving bad news tactfully and gently, so that the listener gets the message and doesn't get angry and hurt. ("There are one or two things you could do that would help me tremendously.")

> **Men must be taught as if you taught them not,**
> **And things unknown proposed as things forgot.**
> *Alexander Pope*

A superior communicator is able to convey difficult messages with grace and nonabrasive words and manner. The person who can do this makes for fewer enemies than the person who does not.

People do not like bad news, and yet managers *must* give bad news —to peers, subordinates, and superiors. If it is done in the right way— apologetically, with sympathy, with care toward feelings, the news is more easily accepted.

> A high-level manager cut a man's pay as punishment for particu- larly bad behavior. He spent about nine hours, over a week or so, explaining to the man whose pay was cut, why it was cut, why it was necessary.
>
> The man never liked it, but he finally understood that the boss was not happy about it either, but felt that discipline demanded it.
>
> The nine hours were worth it. They've since promoted the man.

> **Every great man is always being helped by everybody;**
> **for his gift is to get good out of all things and all**
> **persons.**
> *John Ruskin*

Too Much Tact

Tact can be taken too far, however. Sometimes the tactful speaker can so soften the message (in order to avoid hurting or disappointing) that the message never arrives.

I had been given the assignment of finishing the contract signing for $40 million worth of computing equipment. The customer had signed a letter of intent. The sales executive, Bill Adams, who had gotten the order this far had been promoted—to a large extent as a reward for the $40-million order.

As I dug into the job, I found that the customer didn't know what he was going to do with the computers. He had some vague plans and was thrashing about trying to shape them up.

After months of wheel spinning, the vice-president of the customer's firm asked for a restatement that my company would assist them in a certain way. In essence, we were becoming a junior partner in the planned endeavor. Our firm said no, we weren't interested.

Then it came out that the customer felt that Adams had stated our firm would assist in the manner they desired. Inquiries revealed that Adams had checked the idea with the division president, and had been speedily told no. Adams stated he had told the customer no.

We told the customer this. He thought for a while and said, "You know, he never did say yes, but he was always so positive and pleasant we always felt we would work it out."

The $40-million order was canceled.

But that is not the end of the story. Just before it was canceled, Adams called me.

A: Joe, you've done a good job, but you have to close this order. You can do it.

F: Well, we're trying, but it looks grim. They want commitments from us that we aren't going to give.

A: You can do it.

F: We'll sure try.

A: (With a chuckle) If you don't, Joe, it's your fault. You've had the time and people to do it.

F: (Sharply) No, Bill, it'll be your fault. Just because you chuckle when you try to lay the blame on me doesn't mean it's not a nasty thing to do. You led these people to believe things that weren't true. It'll be your fault if I can't pull it through.

A: (Still pleasant) Well, Joe, you can think that if you like. . . .

F: I'll not only think it, I'll state it to anyone who asks. Look, I've got to go. Is there anything else?

A: No, good-bye.

F: Good-bye.

> Scoundrels are always sociable.
>
> *Arthur Schopenhauer*

The crux here is that Adams had said things far too nicely to the customer, and now he was trying to do the same thing to me. With a friendly approach and a chuckle, he wanted me to admit that if the thing fell apart, it was my fault. He was so nice about it. How could I say no? Had I said yes, he would have quoted me to my bosses ever after, stating I agreed it was "up to me; all up to me!"

> One can smile and smile and be a villain.
>
> *William Shakespeare*

People who have fine empathy are careful of how they start a sentence.

One of our middle-level managers suffered severe chest pains while he was spraying his lawn one spring Saturday. He was put in the Cardiac Care Unit of the hospital.

On Monday morning I got two reports. (1) "Did you hear that Al is in the Cardiac Care Unit. But they think it was the weed killer, etc." (2) "Did you hear about the false alarm on Al. He is in the Cardiac Care Unit, etc."

The first opening causes a spike of anxiety, the second does not. Clearly the second is more empathetic. My nerves survive better with the second.

The point of this is that words can stir many emotions and the sequence in which ideas or facts are presented is crucial. While this is not tact per se, it is a good example of the kind of thought that should go before speaking, if time permits. When people are conscious of the effect of their words and make an effort to select words and to order the facts so as to have right impact, they soon find that they are getting adept at it, that it becomes an automatic thing. That is very different than just stating what is on your mind.

> The man who can put himself in the place of other men, who can understand the working of their minds, need never worry about what the future has in store for him.
>
> *Owen D. Young*

Lack of Empathy

Perhaps an example of lack of empathy will clarify the idea.

A vice-president was brilliant but unfeeling. The executive conference recessed briefly as the president was called to the phone.

The other vice-presidents and executives spoke in small groups about various things. Joe Smith, assistant to the president, was talking to the personnel director about a problem. Suddenly, the low murmur of voices was rent.

"Joe, Joe," yelled the unfeeling vice-president urgently.

"Yes, what's wrong?" answered Smith. Everyone fell silent to hear what was so urgent.

"Get us some coffee."

Smith felt like a waiter, not the assistant to the president.

Treating subordinates—your own or others—as lackeys does not endear you to them. Smith became a vice-president himself and did not have much use for the "get us some coffee" man.

The subject of management is man; the objective of management is the moving of man's mind and will and imagination.
David E. Lilienthal

Empathy takes the pain out of the perfectionist. How often people with outstanding qualities are perfectionists, who want perfection from subordinates—or else. They don't get it, of course, and they do not get the top jobs, either.

A sad phenomenon of human enterprise is that often persons' empathy suffers as their brilliance grows and as their knowledge deepens. Brilliant individuals keep repeating "You see, if A equals R, then S must be. . . ." and most listeners don't have a comparable intellect that would allow them to make that conclusion. The brilliant ones, instead of having empathy and going slowly, too often just quit trying or just keep repeating themselves.

There are two worlds: the world that we can measure with line and rule, and the world that we feel with our hearts and imagination.
Leigh Hunt

There are indeed two worlds, and high-level managers must deal in both. They must have the knowledge and mental power to get things made, or shipped, or sold. And they must deal with people, constantly with people. For getting along with people they must share (or seem to share) their beliefs and they must have certain personality qualities.

Engineers are often not "good with people." *The Levinson Letter* by Harry Levinson makes the following observations:

> Speaking of engineers, Drs. Alvin Rudoff and Dorothy Lucken of San Jose State College (*Science* 11 (June), 1971) say that, though engineers are heavily family-oriented, relationships within the family, though intact, may be strained. . . . The engineer's training as well as his entire occupational emphasis is directed toward the manipulation of objects. This focus is then said to carry over into his relationships with other human beings. . . . In engineering settings there are few smiles, little joking, hardly any small talk, and no nonsense. Apparently physically relaxed, there is a sense of intellectual tension. One gets the feeling that mathematical formulas and the drawing boards are too often used as mechanisms for a retreat from the realities of problems and not merely as tools for their solution. Although too harsh a characterization, the environment in which the engineer works is somewhat akin to an intellectual concentration camp. This intellectual captivity seems to be as much a product of the profession as of a given organization. There appears to be no room for the passions of man. . . . When engineers move into management positions, this orientation, to whatever extent it is valid for any individual, makes the managerial task of dealing with people more difficult.

> Robert C. Heeney, a Montgomery County defense attorney for 25 years . . . flat out refused to put one particular group—engineers—on any jury hearing a criminal case. "They're hard-nosed," he says. "These people only know 2 and 2 is 4 and sometimes I need it to be 4½ or 5 and they won't budge."
>
> *Mary Ann Kuhn*, Washington Star

Now this is not to say that all engineers are insensitive to people. There are many engineers who are outstanding executives and are superb at people interaction. But they are in the minority.

> A high-level government official, talking to me about a sensitive, high-level personnel action: "This man is an outstanding engineer and that is one of the problems. He is not experienced in dealing with the Hill (Congress) and the politics of center versus center.
>
> "You know, when we went to engineering school, we were taught that every problem has a solution and there is an optimum solution. There are political problems that just don't have any solution!"

Perhaps it is the training engineers receive that shapes them. In any event, engineers should be alert to a lack of empathy on their part.

Empathy is the key to working with and through people. It is a quality critical to gaining and exercising power.

I will pay more for the ability to deal with people than
any other ability under the sun.
John D. Rockefeller

I do not understand how people can respond to a painting, to music,
to an idea, and yet go into the street and ignore the first beggar
who comes up to them.
Isabel Luisa Alvarez de Toledo y Maura,
Duchess of Medina-Sidonia

Tact is after all a kind of mindreading.
Sarah Orne Jewett

Talent is something, but tact is everything. Talent is serious, sober,
grave, and respectable; tact is all that, and more too. It is not a
seventh sense, but is the life of all the five. It is the open eye,
the quick ear, the judging taste, the keen smell, and the lively touch;
it is the interpreter of all riddles, the surmounter of all difficulties,
the remover of all obstacles.
W. P. Scargill

Anyone can wear the mask, few don't.
A student of Jess Lair

I'll always have to get the last word in—
maybe that's why I'm always the loser.
A student of Jess Lair

Empathy: your pain in my heart.
A student of Jess Lair

There is much good in the worst of us, and so much bad in the best
of us, that it hardly behooves any of us to talk about the rest of us.
Edward W. Hoch

He is greatest whose strength carries up the most hearts
by the attraction of his own.
Henry Ward Beecher

No man is good enough to govern another
without the other's consent.
Abraham Lincoln

82

If you would win a man to your cause, first convince him that you are his true friend. Therein is a drop of honey that catches his heart, which say what he will, is the greatest highroad to his reason, and which when once gained, you will find but little trouble in convincing his judgment of the justice of your cause, if, indeed, that cause be really a just one. On the contrary, assume to dictate to his judgment, or to command his action, or to make him as one to be shunned or despised, and he will retreat within himself, close the avenues to his head and heart; and though your cause be naked truth itself, transformed to the heaviest lance, harder than steel and sharper than steel can be made, and though you throw it with more than Herculean force and precision, you shall be no more able to pierce him than to penetrate the hard shell of a tortoise with a rye straw.

Abraham Lincoln

I do not need a critic; I am enough my own.
And there are many who leap to the task.
I need a friend, to help; and to be with me.

Joseph M. Fox

The concern for man and his destiny must always be the chief interest of all technical effort. Never forget it among your diagrams
and equations.

Albert Einstein

Think all you speak, but speak not all you think.
Thoughts are your own; your words are so no more.

Patrick Delany

There is more challenge in each square block of city slum than all the galaxy.
Between Brother and Brother, more awful distance,
Than the long boulevard of lonely space.
    It will be written that in 1969, primitive man canned himself . . .
    and catapulted through the void,
    While hunger, hate and sickness stalked his earth,
    Choosing not to try for Heaven, just the moon.
    The old gnarled black man, sitting in the seamy summer of
Seventh Street amidst the broken glass,
    Is wiser then the scientists at Houston
    He knows what vistas cry to be explored.

Representative Charles Joelson

*In the midst of winter I finally learned that there was in
me an invincible summer.*
Albert Camus

It is unusual to list cheerfulness in the catalog of executive qualities. Cheerfulness may not be quite the right word to describe this quality. "Pleasantness" may be closer. It is the quality that makes you be accepted by other people. It is very important to sales ability.

What I mean is an outward, radiating sense of goodwill, optimism, and unaggressiveness that sets at ease the people you come in contact with. They enjoy being with you; they are happy to see you; you are welcome.

You can be welcome personally *even if* you are unwelcome for business purposes. I have seen many instances of meetings when some of the participants are known in advance to be antagonists, yet the very people they are attacking are genuinely happy to see them—they like them—and after the meeting, even though they have successfully attacked and set back their causes (if not their careers) they still like them.

Such a quality is worth cultivating. For lack of better word, let's call it cheerfulness.

*Be sincere. Be simple in words, manners, and gestures.
Assume as well as instruct. If you can make a man laugh,
you can make him think and make him like and believe you.*
Alfred E. Smith

Most people are anxious to avoid difficult and nasty situations. When individuals come into a room looking glum or unhappy, an air of uncertainty is created. People are uncomfortable and wary.

The opposite is true if the persons are cheerful and relaxed. People are happy to see them, welcome them into their offices, and are anxious to exchange views. The more relaxed and cheerful, the franker the views that are discussed and the more complete and honest the information transmitted.

I have know high-level managers who possess the other qualities of an executive to an outstanding extent, yet who fail to continue to rise in the organization because they always look as though the sky is about to fall. They make their subordinates uneasy, and they make their superiors uneasy. Perhaps most important they make their customers uneasy.

Cheerfulness is more critical to gaining the executive job than in exercising it, but it is still important at the executive level in dealing with outside contacts such as customers, leaders, the government, the unions, etc.

> **A laugh is worth a hundred groans in any market.**
> *Charles Lamb*

The opposite of cheerfulness, graveness, is also a useful quality. When grave matters are being discussed, cheerfulness should be held in rein.

Unfortunately our culture judges somberness as being synonymous with wisdom. They are not synonymous and one should be on guard against those who wear masks of concern constantly. They should be suspected of lacking emotional maturity. They certainly lack cheerfulness.

> **With the fearful strain that is on me day and night, if I did not laugh, I would die.**
> *Abraham Lincoln*

There is no doubt that if people like you, they will try to find a way to help you. Sometimes it's a conscious effort to find a way; sometimes unconscious. But it's there. Empathy and cheerfulness in persons will usually result in their being liked.

> In the Watergate mess, a government lawyer mentioned to me that a certain high-level Department of Justice official "would escape clean." He said, "Everyone likes him. He is such a nice guy that people are going out of their way to *not* find things."

This probably seems hard to believe, but it fits what I have found in many serious situations.

> Then there was the case of the stolen cow. It was stolen from very unpopular miser, Jones, by the town clown, Smith, who was loved by all.
>
> After a short trial which showed conclusively that Smith took the cow, the jury returned and the foreman announced: "We find the defendant not guilty, but he has to return the cow."
>
> The judge exploded. "A perversion of justice! I'll fine you all for contempt." He sent them back.
>
> When they returned, the foreman announced: "We find the defendant not guilty, and he can keep the cow."

If they like you, they will find a way to help you.

How you say no is very important. If persons you are saying no to think that you are unhappy about being unable to help, you will not have earned an enemy. If they think you are trying to stop them, they look upon you as "the enemy!" You! *You* are the problem!

I was in a headquarters staff job and I fielded requests for the branch offices for help or for new products. I had a rule that I always made it clear that I was not the individual saying no, that I was the pleader of the case to a higher authority. That was my job.

Even when the request was for an item that had only hours before been turned down by the review board, I'd tell the branch that it was unlikely but I would check it once again. And I would! I'd talk to the head of the review board (or our vice-president) and mention that indeed another request had come in. Ninety-nine times out of a hundred it would not tip the balance of the decision. One time in a hundred it would.

In the ninety-nine cases I'd call the branch back and tell them I'd checked and was sorry, but no. They always appreciated that I'd tried.

A peer would tell them flatly no. He was disliked because he didn't empathize with the need of the branch.

Cheerfulness Is Not Always Appropriate

Being cheerful at the wrong time can be very bad.

A brilliant financial advisor seemed to take delight in finding reasons why something couldn't be done. Even when he'd say, "I'm sorry, you can't do this because . . . ," he seemed to be more pleased at his brilliance in finding a problem than upset at stopping an effort.

It was not long before every line manager was finding ways to use a different advisor. They did not want to work with the brilliant one. He felt he was just doing his job. He was, but he was alienating his clients, not by his opinions, but by his attitude.

Another example:

A rising manager was one of several that was being considered for a high-level job. He was rejected because "he never smiled." This reason may not seem to be sufficient to deny him the job, but the vice-president explained: "I want him to see my boss and my boss's boss without me. He must interface with the headquarters staff. He just doesn't set the right tone. His first impression is 'grim.' I don't want to be represented that way."

This story persuaded me to keep cheerfulness as a separate quality, and not subsume it under empathy or salesmanship. The lack of a pleasant demeanor, the lack of cheerfulness, had caused a middle-level manager to be passed over for promotion.

I don't like a man to be too efficient.
He's likely to be not human enough.

Felix Frankfurter

Too much gravity argues a shallow mind.

Johann Kaspar Lavater

An inexhaustible good nature is one of the most precious gifts
of heaven, spreading itself like oil over the troubled sea of thought,
and keeping the mind smooth and equable in the roughest weather.

Washington Irving

One of the great secrets of contentment is the refusal to take ourselves
seriously. To laugh at ourselves, to stand aside, and in imagination,
watch ourselves go by.

Gilbert Hay

The aura of victory that surrounds a man of goodwill, the sweetness
of soul which emanates from him—a flavor of cranberries and
cloudberries, a touch of frost and fiery skies.

Dag Hammarskjöld

There are those much more rare people who never lose their curiosity,
their almost childlike wonder at the world; those people who continue
to learn and to grow intellectually until the day they die. And these
usually are the people who make contributions, who leave some
part of the world a little better off than it was before they entered it.

William Sheldon

Many who think that they are taking life seriously are actually only
taking themselves seriously. Who takes himself seriously is overcon-
scious of his rights; who takes life seriously is fully conscious
of his obligations.

Joseph T. O'Callahan

Mediocrity requires aloofness
to preserve its dignity.

Charles G. Dawes

The worst cliques are those
which consist of one man.

George Bernard Shaw

The compulsion to take ourselves seriously is in inverse proportion
to our creative capacity. When the creative flow dries up,
all we have left is our importance.

Eric Hoffer

We cannot always oblige, but we can
always speak obligingly.
Voltaire

I shall not pass this way again.
Any good thing that I can do,
or any kindness that I can show,
let me do it now!
Let me not defer it or neglect it.
For I shall not pass this way again.
Etienne de Grollet

They might not need me; but they might.
I'll let my head be just in sight;
A smile as small as mine might be,
Precisely their necessity.
Emily Dickinson

Wondrous is the strength of cheerfulness, and its power of endurance
—the cheerful man will do more in the same time, will do it better,
will persevere in it longer, than the sad or sullen.
Thomas Carlyle

Unmitigated seriousness is always out of place in human affairs.
Let not the unwary reader think me flippant for saying so;
it was Plato, in his solemn old age, who said it.
George Santayana

The secret of happiness is this: Let your interests be as wide as
possible, and let your reactions to the things and persons that interest
you be, as far as possible, friendly rather than hostile.
Bertrand Russell

RESILIENCE AND DURABILITY

I am wounded
but I am not slain,
I'll lay me down
and bleed awhile
and rise and fight again.
Old Scottish ballad

Resilience is the ability to continue performing despite delays, disap-
pointments, risks, distractions, and other burdens. It may be likened to
tolerance of frustration. Most powerful executives have gone through
many frustrating experiences in their lives and they can take these in

stride and handle them. The higher one goes, the more frustrating the job can be; the more difficult to delegate, the more difficult to accept less than what you yourself could do. The higher level executive exhibits great perseverance and tenacity and "staying power." Resilience is a result of emotional maturity.

Sooner or later you discover that power doesn't grow as fast as you might think and hope. In large organizations you always have a boss. We have seen in the section on Realism that even the President of the United States has limits on his power. The same kind of frustration is evident in all large organizations. The executive is often pressed, and frustrated.

Many vice-presidents, despite their titles, often are as tightly managed as first-line managers. The frustration of such management is *doubled* since it is so unexpected at these levels of management. During the climb to the top levels, rising executives suffer innumerable blows to their egos and equilibriums.

> One rising executive had a very challenging contract to perform.
> He took a two-week vacation, only to find upon his return that
> his boss had reassigned his project manager. He had not been
> called, consulted, or warned in any way. The man was just gone.
> (The project suffered a major delay.)

There is a top in an organization and it is singular in almost all cases. The boss is the one boss. Unfortunately too many of the singular tops get very arbitrary in the manner in which they run the company. It is "their" company in the same way it was "my" baseball bat when I was ten years old. And they "can do anything" they want with it—including firing group vice-presidents because they "just don't seem to get on with them anymore."

Group vice-presidents are not a unique top; they report to someone; they are *dependent,* even if they earn $300,000 per year. Whenever you are feeling frustrated because your boss will not give you a "free hand," i.e., the boss makes you feel like a low-level manager instead of the executive you are, consider the following:

> The new president of a $ billion-per-year corporation once showed
> his frustration to a group of middle-level managers. An old ac-
> quaintance had said, "Congratulations on the Presidency." "Ha!"
> he said. "Let me tell you. I run the company when Al (the
> chairman of the board) doesn't feel like it."

What frustration! To have a big title, salary, and everything else, yet to have little freedom of action. Look at resilience in action:

> T. J. Watson, Sr., the founder of IBM, was a high-level executive
> of the National Cash Register Company. Mr. John Patterson, chief
> executive officer of NCR in those days—circa 1910—was a despot.

One way Patterson let executives know they were fired was to simply remove their office furniture over a weekend. When the executive showed up on Monday, he found another executive with different furniture and secretary in his location. It was a bit of a shock.

This happened to Tom Watson, but he just kept showing up morning after morning. Finding "his spot" occupied, he went home. He went on some trips.

After a few weeks of this, he arrived one morning to find his furniture and secretary back where they had been. He went back to work. Neither he nor his boss Patterson ever said a word about the incident to each other.

Watson's case was a bit bizarre, but such tensions, pressures, and impositions exist today.

The prevailing mode of operation of some executives seems to state: "See if you can catch your subordinate not aware of something that has happened in his area. Make him feel small and incompetent. This will keep him running real fast and the whole operation will be speedier." This approach works. It does keep the operation speedier.

A $60,000-a-year executive told me. "When I get called in to see the boss, the vice-president, I never know whether he is going to fire me, demote me, or promote me. I've worked for him for two years and that is the way he plays the game.

"I'm sure if I work for him for five years it will be the same. It's really frustrating."

This was no newcomer to executive ranks. He had worked in high-level jobs for years. It was simply that many executives "keep their options open" by never letting their subordinates know where they stand. They keep their subordinates on their toes by keeping them from ever feeling secure in their jobs.

There are many degrees to which this practice can be pushed. To keep all on their toes, the boss asks a lot of questions. Knowing this, everyone tries to be ready. The boss's reactions when they are not ready tells the story. One reaction is to quietly ask them to call when they get the answer. Or the boss can stomp and glower and rant and rave. And subordinates will be motivated to keep one step ahead of the boss.

We die daily—happy those who daily come to life as well.

George Macdonald

It is fascinating to watch a high-level executive go from a disaster to being a self-assured leader without breaking stride.

Vice-presidents can take an amount of abuse from their bosses that would leave any lesser man in prostration; they then turn immediately to another task without any outward evidence that they have just been clobbered by their boss. When he walks through the door, his team is waiting for him.

Their careers and futures ride to a large extent on him. They want him to be strong and successful. It helps them. When he's hurt, they worry. If their boss is always on the defensive, they start looking elsewhere for upper management support.

Some organizations operate on a cooperative, team-spirit, "we're-a-team" approach. But many operate on a do-your-job-well-or-else approach. There is a game children play called "King of the Hill." One child gets on top of a hill and all the others try to push or pull the winner off. Once off, another child takes top place and then is attacked by all the others. Something similar happens in organizations. Many, not all, want the boss's job. And some are very open and aggressive about trying to pull the boss down.

Bosses are usually never there for life. They can always make a mistake big enough to be removed from the hill. The child's game of "King of the Hill" usually doesn't last too long. The children get tired of it, or just tired. Unfortunately in today's organizational world, the game never ends. In the real world the game goes on and on and on and . . . on. Executives must perpetually put up with and thwart all the continual threats and moves against them. They can't get bitter, or too tired. They must be forever vigilant to the next attack. All this takes great emotional stability, and durability, and resilience.

Anthony Jay in *Management and Machiavelli,* published by Holt, Rinehart and Winston, states:

Worry and responsibility are part of the price of power. Real power does not lie in documents and memos outlining your terms of reference and area of jurisdiction: it lies in what you can achieve in practice. The boss's secretary can wield great power, like the king's mistress, without any authority at all—or at least not the sort you can show anybody. Equally, the head of a big division or company can be powerless, just as Lear was powerless, despite any number of theoretical powers. Power lies in the acceptance of your authority by others, their knowledge that if they try to resist you they will fail and you will succeed. And so the boss who does a Lear is liable to discover that Goneril and Regan, the production director and the marketing director, ignore his directives: and he realizes that the only statutory power he has left is to fire them. But it is made clear to him that if he does fire them, each has a better job waiting with an expanding competitor, and has arranged to take the twelve key men of his division with him. If the Lear has to report to a board, that is that: His power has vanished. But even if he owns privately 100 percent of this equity, he is still ditched. All he can do is accept defeat or do a Samson and destroy the firm; and while Samson makes a great tragic hero, he would have been an appalling managing director.

Comfortable leadership is a contradiction in terms. The leader must make sure everyone knows that the toughest decisions are his responsibility, that however great their worries they can in the last resort pass them to him, whereas he cannot pass them to anyone. They pay him for that with a part of their freedom, their independence, their autonomy—a sort of authority tax which he exacts and they pay with a willingness which is in proportion to their satisfaction with the use he puts it to. As long as they see he is using that authority of theirs to fight an important battle or carry out useful reforms, they go on paying, but when they see it wasted or frittered away, and also find they can get away without paying it, then they stop. If they realize that they are now taking the toughest decisions on their own they realize, as Goneril and Regan realized, that they are of greater value to the enterprise than he is.

My God! What is there in this place [the Presidency]
that a man should ever want to get into it.
James A. Garfield

Most executives have great physical stamina. Some fly from New York to Hawaii, spend one hour, fly back to New York, and continue working as though there had been no trip.

A general manager: "Ten years ago I ran a proposal that was a killer. We worked for four weeks, right through weekends. In the last week, we were working from 7:00 A.M. until midnight with no lunch.

"It was a madhouse. The people were at the edge of exhaustion. Some were just sitting in a stupor; others were ill.

"I was fighting everyone: Legal, production, engineering, finance—everyone. I had no patience left at all.

"Finally about 7:00 P.M. the Friday before Christmas, with my wife and small children 500 miles away, I just cracked and cried like a baby! It was awful. But we got the proposal out."

Most executives have stamina and energy to spare. They work prodigiously, yet never seem to get sick. Is this a cause of success, or the result of success? Psychologists argue that some people are healthier because they succeed, not that they succeed because they are healthier.

> What counts most in the long haul of adult life is not brilliance, or charisma, or derring-do, but rather the quality that the Romans called "gravitas"—patience, stamina, and weight of judgment—the prime virtue is courage, because it makes all other virtues possible.
>
> *Eric Sevareid*

Organization climbers can never stop producing. They must *always* meet their goals, look good, etc. Relaxation or an easy steady pace is out of the question if they expect to keep going up, up, up. Eternal vigilance can be very tiring. And it would be so nice to end the vigilance, to achieve the goal, once and for all! But it doesn't happen that way!

Anthony Jay in *Management and Machiavelli* says it well when he states the leader must constantly sift through the good news looking for evidence of future problems. He must be "eternally vigilant." He cannot afford to relax.

> Our greatest weariness comes from work not done.
>
> *Eric Hoffer*

Attend a "kick-off" meeting of a sales team just after the New Year. Two things occur: the team is congratulated for making their plan last year—and they are exhorted to make this year good, too—year in and year out, year in and year out.

Executives must always deal with problems. Ninety percent of their time is spent on problems; ten percent on victory dinners, celebrations, etc. And very often the celebration for a wonderful victory coincides with the discovery of a terrible new problem. Rarely is victory unstained by a concurrent encroaching defeat.

> An executive had a luncheon planned to celebrate the installation of the Picket Radar system. It had been a five-year, $100-million effort. It had been marked by tremendous efforts, congressional abuse (undeserved), management failures, and demotions. But at last it was ready.
>
> And at the lunch he was going to give out four $5000 awards— to people who had gotten it started, to those who had worked on it for years. It was an occasion in which to bask. They had made it!
>
> From 11:00 to 12:00 he had a review with a vice-president from a different division over some schedule problems on a system

to control a cement plant. There were schedule problems, but they didn't seem too serious.

At 11:50, while he was still feeling pretty good, disaster struck! The other division stated that there was no provision for recovery if one of the two automated lines failed. (The second one was there to take over if the first failed.) They said the operator would have to type in data for days before the backup machine could take over.

The vice-president relaxed. That was such a flagrant oversight that he knew his team couldn't be *that* dumb.

His team sat silently. They said nothing. They *were* that dumb.

At 11:55 he went to the luncheon, deeply troubled about the stupidity or incompetency of his management team.

The victory lunch was not as sweet as it was planned to be. It was still sweet, but his restless mind went back time and time again to this new disaster.

Sorrow and the scarlet leaf,
Sad thoughts and sunny weather,
Ah, me, this glory and the grief,
Agree not well together.

Thomas Parson

Even where you might expect tranquility and a slow pace, you will be surprised.

A college president told me recently, "I'm having a difficult time keeping this college afloat, much less thinking about what new projects we can undertake."

My grandfather always said that living is like licking honey off a thorn.

Louis Adamic

A vice-president who seemed to have the whole thing under control confided in me one day that he felt like he was in a small sailboat going through storms at sea. He would work furiously to get the boat out of one storm, only to have one or even two more descend on it at once. There was no breather; it was constant crisis.

He told me at times he felt like "breaking." That was the word he used. He felt like just sitting back and crying, or leaving the office and going home to bed.

He said he often would want to drive past the office, so he wouldn't have to go in and face the storms. He even liked going to the dentist because it was a half hour of "peace and quiet!"

94

His pride was caught: he couldn't let that boat sink. He'd just get it out of the storms, head for land and never go to sea again. But he never got out of the storms.

There were times when there were storms within storms, whirlpools, and sea monsters all at once. "The phone will ring and I'll think, 'Please don't let it be another problem. Please let it be a solution to one that is here now.'"

We endure in the absence of triumph.
John F. Kennedy

There is a distinct emotional difference between the job of judges and the job of lawyers. Lawyers plead cases. They are fortunate in that they can concentrate specifically on their arguments. They do not ignore the arguments of the other side but they have the luxury of not worrying about their own emotional and intellectual belief in those arguments. All they desire is to negate the other's arguments.

Judges on the other hand must decide, they must listen to cogent and powerful arguments on both sides and then make the final decision. They must often make a decision between two unpopular choices, where either choice is not very pleasant, and yet it must be made. When the choice is made, it will be described as the judge's decision. Lawyers can go home, forget about their involvement, and rest easy in the belief that they have done their job well. Even losing lawyers may have done their jobs well. They have been perhaps eloquent and brilliant and while the fact that they lost does not fill them with joy, it also does not fill them with shame. Judges, on the other hand, go home and worry about whether or not their decisions were right and the consequences of their decisions. In the final analysis, it is *their* decision.

Many executives are in jobs much like those of a judge. They must make the decision and on their shoulders rest the consequences of that decision. The emotional burden that executives must carry is substantial. They must "end" the careers of other executives. They must remove from executive position those of their friends who have lost their drive and imagination. They must stop the cherished plans of some of the best technical people in the organization, risking their ire (and perhaps their departure from the company). They are the judge; they must make the final decision.

There is a saying: "Delegation, not Abdication. Check on it." And rightly so. But in the real world you can't check everything—or you would be managing it yourself. So you rely on spot checks and very often these will flush out the critical problems. Occasionally, though, a disaster will occur that is not spotted by the checks until it is too late. The first reaction of most managers to disaster is guilt. "I let this happen!" Defensive thinking starts. "How am I going to explain this to the higher ups?" These thoughts are natural and healthy. But mature, tough executives take these "disasters" in stride. They *know* things are not always going to be right and that delegation means loss of control (and loss of some of the fun of doing things). They must live with that knowledge comfortably.

Vance Packard, in *The Pyramid Climbers* published by McGraw-Hill, writes:

> This need to be able to proceed with assurance in situations where, often, there are few hard facts raises a provocative question. Is the ability to proceed on a campaign in some ignorance an overlooked but very real asset in executives? John Hite, director of the Institute of Management, Johnson & Johnson, believes it is. He advises: "No matter how intelligent or able a manager is, one day his responsibility will exceed his knowledge. In fact this is *the* problem of modern management, and it is an emotional one. Most men cannot bear to be responsible for that which they do not know. Yet they cannot take high positions in management unless they can accept such responsibility without paying for it in ulcers or nervous breakdowns."

Man can climb to the highest summits, but only God can dwell there.
George Bernard Shaw

The job of high-level managers can be very lonely. Not always, but it often is. Their superiors are very busy, and often seem to be (even when they aren't) uncaring about them as persons.

> A high-level executive was getting little or no support from the president. At work he appeared durable and in control. One evening, however, he called a close friend at home, the assistant to the president. "You bastards down there are killing me. You will not listen to my. . . ." He went on and on. The assistant realized after a point that his friend was not only distressed but drunk. Being a wise assistant and good friend, he sympathized, and agreed. The next day he stopped by to see the executive, told him he'd help, was friendly.
>
> That was all that was needed. Some support.

"Sprinters" versus "Long-Distance Runners"

Almost all organizations have goals. And it's up to the executives to get the company to meet its goals. At the lower levels, managers can do the total job to be done. And faced with a severe challenge, they can *sprint;* they can put forth a burst of energy and activity and accomplish "miracles." For such a sprint and its results, they'll be recognized and marked as "comers," high-potential managers.

But the young comer can get confused. As we have seen, some executives will deliberately keep their subordinates worrying about their status. The managers have been rewarded for "sprinting" in the past and are tempted when they are moved to higher management to "sprint" themselves when one of their subordinate managers is presented with a crisis. At Level 2, this is probably acceptable, as they do not have that many crises and are "sprinting" only occasionally.

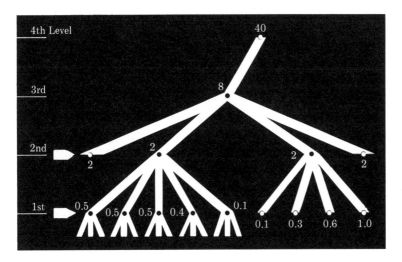

Figure 2.1   Crises per month. Crises means some problems that the lower-level manager and/or the staff cannot solve. Most problems they can and do solve, but some they cannot. These get pushed up to higher management.

Clearly, however, at high levels, they can no longer personally "sprint" for every crisis of one of the first-line managers. They will never stop "sprinting," and will exhaust themselves very quickly, and will never do their own job.

Rising managers must recognize that just as in track there are different skills and strengths for sprinting and for long-distance running, there are different skills and strengths for high-level management and for low-level management. This apparently obvious fact is often missed because:

- Rising executives have had "sprinting" behavior rewarded and *they know how* to sprint.

- The organization wants results, rewards results, and too often doesn't care who is sprinting as long as the "sprinting" gets results.

> Nothing is so fatiguing as the eternal hanging on of an uncompleted task.
>
> *William James*

Such organizations have a high dropout rate as the middle-level executives wear themselves out fast and fall by the wayside.

> A corporate planner once told a chairman of the board of a subsidiary, "You think that the top guys are really interested in you personally. Let me tell you; all they want is results. They send you out like a night fighter. They want you to come back; they want to win. But if you don't, they'll go hire another night fighter."

Now, don't jump to a conclusion that this is wrong, or inhuman. Sprinting works! It gets results. The corporation is not a family where you are assured of being loved. You must produce, and produce, and produce. You must develop the skills of the long-distance runner, *you* must hire and fire "sprinters"—or *you* will be replaced.

Perhaps all it takes is the independence to refuse to be a constant sprinter, to say (through your actions if not in words), "I know how to be a sprinter, but I choose not to spend my life sprinting. Either accept me as one of the top people, or tell me you do not, and I will decide what to do." What to do may be to leave, or to move backward in the organization—or keep sprinting.

Some people love to sprint. If there is no crisis for more than three days in a row, they'll create one. They throw themselves into the fray, performing miracles, working day and night. Such people are very valuable—as sprinters! But don't put them in charge of long-range planning!!

Why do they like to sprint? Probably because it is exciting, or because it enables them to prove to themselves once again that *they* can do it. All long-distance runners should have some sprinters as assistants so that they don't have to sprint when the next crisis arrives.

Career versus Family

Freud stated that in the end our lives came down to two things: Love and Work.

Work dominates the lives of most top executives. They spend their effort, time, and attention on work—and not on family, hobbies, or community. This is in itself neither good nor bad, but it must be examined in its results.

A top corporation executive once confided to me that he had reviewed the ten top people in his company and that nine of the ten had "severe" personal problems: divorce, alcoholism in wives or children, suicides in the family. He told me that years ago, and my own experience bears it out. Rising executives are often too willing to devote their entire energies to getting ahead. Ambition keeps them working, working, working. One should manage *life* the way one manages everything else—sensibly and in a balanced manner.

Psychologists point out that every choice one makes is a sacrifice. When one chooses fish in a restaurant for dinner, one gives up steak. The choice of being a top executive versus having a lot of time for other things is a very real choice and sacrifice. Maybe it can be alleviated by timing your arrival at the top to fit with the rest of your life. It takes great discipline to pass up opportunities that come in the early years. Choice is sacrifice. The choice is the individual's. If individual climbers don't manage their own lives, no one will. The organization is geared for results—not for social niceties

Look at the two time pie charts in Fig. 2.2 on page 100. Many people will choose number 1 because they love their families and want time with them. But they are also ambitious. And competitors in the race are often choosing number 2. The climber is torn. Number 1 may be more fun, but it pays less money.

Ambition usually costs at home. The individual must make the choice. The children are at home for one-fourth to one-half of the parent's life. If that time is spent climbing the ladder and *not* with the children, that should be the *decision* of the individual. Too often no decision is made; life is just lived!

One senior vice-president told a management class, "If you are not a vice-president by the time you are 40, forget it. You'll never make it."

The human cost of this is that the husband and father or the wife and mother is at the peak of his or her effort for the organization when the children are young and he or she is needed at home.

Why point all this out? Isn't it self-evident? No. It should be, but many executives never focus on the fact that they are not spending time at home. Few ever put it into words. I have talked to dozens of 40-year-old executives who have told me that they didn't realize what they were doing when they spent 90 percent of their energies at work. When they moved eight times in nine years!

Too often it has been assumed by too many people that to be an executive one must, or will be forced to, ignore the family or spend very little time with them. Although this is often true, I believe it is a situation that can be avoided.

Executives should manage their *whole* lives, not just their business lives. If business is taking too much of their time at an age when their children are still young, and at home, they should consider deliberately delaying their ascent. If they're really good, they'll make it later. And if they don't make it to the top, at least they won't be at the top with one unhappy family life behind them!

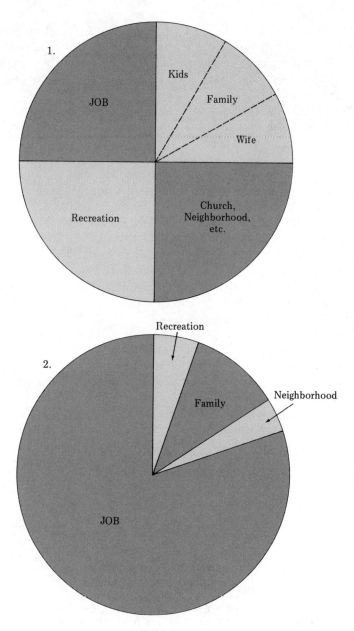

Figure 2.2 Two ways to spend your day (or your life).

It is very sad for a man to make himself servant to a
single thing; his manhood all taken out of him by the
hydraulic pressure of excessive business.

Theodore Parker

100

Psychologists tell us that in order to stay emotionally stable we should not put all our interests into one area. They point out that we would be severely impacted if all our hopes, all in one area, were dashed by luck, by choice, by a competitor, by our actions. Variety! Many interests, with no single one of them paramount will help ensure durability. Yet we see so often this warning ignored and people devoting their whole lives to their "career," their job—at the expense of their family, their friends (if any)—and ultimately at the expense of themselves.

To remain stable, persons should have many interests. Should they become totally absorbed in one activity, e.g., work, and ignore other activities, e.g., family, friends, hobbies, then they can be badly shaken —if not destroyed—emotionally if they meet with failure in their single chosen interest.

Not getting the next promotion, being moved sideways, or down, in the organization can unbalance a person who is totally immersed in work to the exclusion of other interests.

Objective; Subjective*

People split into two different groups—objective or subjective—based on inborn traits. The objective person is more outgoing, less sensitive, and enjoys working with people. The subjective person is more sensitive, and would prefer to work alone. Most people are clearly either objective or subjective, but some test ambiguously. Three-fourths of the people tested are objective. A subjective person with a high vocabulary has an outward appearance very close to objective.

Subjective persons may do well in sales for a time, but because they don't like it—it goes against their subjectivity—they will eventually leave or fail. Subjective people should work in the professions— teaching, writing, law, medicine—and will not *wear well* as executives. They can be outstanding executives, but they don't really want to be. Their durability and resiliency will wear out more quickly than that of an objective person.

> "Some people are just different," said my friend. "My boss at the radio station in Florida was the owner and general manager. I was working one Sunday and saw him come to the office. He was being sued by the FTC, in the process of getting a divorce, and was trying to run the radio station. He came in that Sunday, whistling, holding his secretary's hand, without a care in the world. Nothing fazed him."

---

* I am basically drawing upon the ideas of the Johnson O'Connor Research Foundation, Inc., for the ideas in this section. The Johnson O'Connor Research Foundation is an independent, nonprofit psychological testing and research activity that has been operating for over 50 years across the United States. I have found the Foundation's material of great value.

The radio station owner sounds objective.

Another example:
The task force was established very suddenly. The group vice-president simply said, "Start Monday." He tapped a division vice-president to head the task force on oil processing—even though that individual knew nothing about oil processing. No amount of protest could change the assignment.

Many people were gathered together from all parts of the company. And the European oil processing sales coordinator was told to be in New York on Monday. This word got to him in Paris on Friday. He was there on a trip; his home was in Stockholm. He dropped all his plans and caught a plane to New York on Saturday.

On Monday he kept asking the task-force leader what he was to do. Since that division vice-president didn't have the foggiest idea what *anybody* should do, he couldn't tell him.

The European man sat around in New York all week watching the division vice-president task-force leader getting educated.

The division vice-president in this case was subjective, and he was very unhappy and uneasy because this man had been yanked over to New York and he couldn't give him anything to do. He worried and fretted, thinking of how inconvenienced the European man was. The group vice-president, had he known, wouldn't have batted an eye. He was objective.

Objective managers are not inconsiderate. They are more demanding and expect people to work hard. But they are courteous, and pleasant. They are just not bothered by being demanding. Subjective executives are troubled because they must be demanding.

To know the pains of power, we must go to those who
have it; to know its pleasures, we must go to those who
are seeking it; the pains of power are real, its pleasure
imaginary.

C. C. Colton

The preceding quote seems to be correct for a subjective person. But not for an objective person. Objective persons do not take on the burdens of power. They shed a great amount of the personal pain that subjective persons carry.

The subjective individual takes it all *personally,* and most of the slings and arrows are not meant personally. But the subjective individual views the blows as personal attacks! And wears down!

102

Of wounds and sore defeat, I made my battle stay;
Winged sandals for my feet, I wove of my delay;
Of weariness and fear, I made my shouting spear;
Of loss and doubt and dread and swift oncoming doom,
I made a helmet for my head and a floating plume.

From the shutting mist of death,
from the failure of the breath,
I made a battle horn to blow,
across the vale of overthrow!

William Vaughn Moody

There is a kind of release that comes directly to those who have
undergone an ordeal and who know, having survived it,
that they are equal to all of life's occasions.

Lewis Mumford

Life is given for wisdom, and yet we are not wise; for goodness,
and we are not good; for overcoming evil, and evil remains;
for patience and sympathy and love, and yet we are fretful and hard
and weak and selfish. We are keyed not to attainment,
but to the struggle toward it.

T. T. Munger

Steel can be tempered and hardened, and so can men. In this world
of struggle, which was not designed for softies, a man must be harder
than what hits him. Yes, he must be diamond-hard. Then he'll not be
"fed up" with his little personal troubles.

Herbert N. Casson

The fountain of content must spring up in the mind; and he who has
so little knowledge of human nature as to seek happiness by changing
anything but his own disposition will waste his life in fruitless efforts
and multiply the griefs which he proposes to remove.

Samuel Johnson

I returned and saw under the sun that the race is not to the swift,
nor the battle to the strong, neither yet bread to the wise, nor yet
riches to men of understanding, nor yet favor to men of skill, but
time and chance happeneth to all of them.

Ecclesiastes 9:11

Man is born broken. He lives by mending.
The grace of God is glue.

Eugene O'Neil

If people bring so much courage to this world, the world has to kill
them to break them, so of course, it kills them. The world breaks
everyone and afterwards many are strong at the broken places.
But those it cannot break, it kills. It kills the very good and the very
gentle and the very brave impartially.

Ernest Hemingway

It is not the critic who counts, not the man who points out how the
strong man stumbled, or where the doer of deeds could have done
them better. The credit belongs to the man who is actually in the
arena; whose face is marred by dust and sweat and blood; who strives
violently; who errs and comes short again and again; who knows the
great enthusiasms; the great devotions; who spends himself in a
worthy cause; who, at the best, knows in the end the triumphs of high
achievements; and who, at the worst, if he fails, at least fails
while daring greatly.

Theodore Roosevelt

Suffering becomes beautiful when anyone bears great calamities with
cheerfulness, not through insensibility but through greatness of mind.

Aristotle

The responsibilities . . . are greater than I imagined them to be, and
there are greater limitations upon our ability to bring about a favorable
result . . . it is much easier to make the speeches than it is to finally
make the judgments, because unfortunately your advisers are frequently
divided. If you take the wrong course, and on occasion I have,
the President bears the burden of the responsibility. . . . The advisers
may move on to new advice.

John F. Kennedy

One of the paradoxes of the leader is that
he cannot succeed without confidence or without doubt.

Anthony Jay

My time is not yet come either; some are born posthumously.

Friedrich Nietzsche

3
The Beliefs and
Mental Qualities

The belief qualities and the mental qualities are:

Belief { Beliefs
          Integrity

Mental { Intellect
          Logic
          Nimble-mindedness
          Knowledge

The belief qualities are critical to rising executives. If their beliefs mesh with those of their superiors, they are in the race. If their beliefs don't, and they do not disguise the fact, then they may be out before the race even starts.

Integrity, we shall see, is absolutely necessary at all levels.

The mental qualities are interesting in that those you might suspect of being most important usually are not. The most important mental ability for the executive is nimble-mindedness.

By the time people get to be lower-level managers, they have probably shown that they have enough brainpower to function at any management level.

A first-rate mind is a fine asset for an executive but it is clearly not a necessity. Many outstanding executives have second-rate minds only. It is not just the mind; it is how one applies it. Allan Nevins once wrote that Franklin Delano Roosevelt had a second-rate mind in first-rate application, and that that combination was clearly superior to a first-rate mind in second-rate application.

Beware when the great God lets loose a thinker on this planet.

Ralph W. Emerson

BELIEFS

If we work marble, it will perish; if we work upon brass, time will efface it; if we rear temples, they will crumble into dust; but if we work upon immortal minds and instill into them just principles, we are then engraving upon tablets which no time will efface, but will brighten and brighten to all eternity.

Daniel Webster

Personal beliefs shape your every judgment and every decision. To illustrate how critical beliefs are, contrast for a moment two kinds of people—those that believe they have a duty to society—and those that believe society owes everything to them.

Now vest in these individuals all the other qualities that we have listed, and put these individuals in precisely the same executive position in a large company. Clearly, the decisions made by individual 1 and individual 2 will be significantly different, because they are made against the backdrop of a different set of beliefs.

Beliefs are very vital to shaping the personality, and since personality is in a never-ending evolution, beliefs are constantly at play. Beliefs come first. Persons do not act in conflict with what they believe, regardless of their abilities, whether they be superb or deficient. The thing that first shapes humans is what they believe in.

What one's beliefs may be is of little importance in being a leader, for even people with idiotic beliefs attract a following. Any strong belief makes a leader; witness some of our lunatic fringe movements, like the American Nazi Party.

> **A man becomes the creature of his uniform.**
> *Napoleon*

A few people have no beliefs. Complete pragmatists can be effective executives, but they can also be dangerous ones. The person who has no beliefs, and is simply an opportunist, may well be effective in the sense of getting things done. However, such a person will not be a "good executive" if by "good" we mean complete and supportive to the entire society. Opportunists may be good for their corporations' balance sheets, but in the long run, if they violate the modes and customs of their society, if they do not share the same beliefs that their society shares—in the long run their corporations will suffer.

Different Societies—Different Beliefs

Beliefs differ from nation to nation!

> Look at the kamikaze pilots of Japan during World War II. These people were completely willing to die for their country and indeed believed it a great honor to fly to their death at the end of World War II.

> The German Army was able to maintain an incredible discipline in the final disastrous months of the war because the German people were imbued with a belief and respect for authority. It is not an accident that the Japanese and Germans were able to mount a war machine with an effectiveness far beyond what their numerical population would lead one to believe. The basic beliefs of the countries enabled them to get far more from their people.

And in today's world:

> In some countries it is perfectly ethical (conforming to the country's ethic) to agree on one set of things, type a different set in the contract, and try to trick the other fellow into signing without looking.

Examples of how cultural beliefs can affect one's performance are obvious once recognized.

> In the United States, if a man doesn't "look you in the eyes," he is dishonest or totally subservient. In the United States, it is acceptable for a leader to sit down with his employees and discuss where the organization is going.

> In a South American country, both of the activities above are interpreted very differently. To look a man in the eye is to show disrespect. For a boss to discuss where the organization is going is to show total lack of control.

These "beliefs" are usually not even recognized by people until they are pointed out to them. Just as people cannot sense the air around them, people absorb their culture and beliefs unknowingly.

Every man carries with him the world in which he must live.

F. Marion Crawford

The following incident which occurred on a visit to Japan shows how beliefs can shape the whole climate of the business enterprise.

> We were six, sitting in the lounge, waiting for a seventh to come down for dinner. The TV was showing a Japanese situation comedy, and the one Japanese with us was explaining what was happening. A commercial came on, showing a young Japanese banging away at an adding machine. Numbers flew through the air at an increasing rate. The machine operator was perspiring.

> He took out a small bottle of pills, shook two pills into his hand, and gulped them down.

> "Excedrin," one of the Americans cried. "They have Excedrin headaches and commercials here, too," he said, referring to the popular headache tablet commercial.

> "Oh, no," said our Japanese friend, "that is vitamins."

> The Washington Post recently reported on a factory in Macon, Georgia, that is owned by a Japanese company, has a Japanese president, and American workers. They quote the Japanese plant manager/president "I am working for employees—not myself. I forget my wife, my children. I love 110 people. Even sleeping, I worry about them."

The Japanese have a very strong "work ethic." To be asked to work on a weekend is an honor, not an imposition.

The French writer and social observer, Jean-Jacques Servan-Schreiber, has written that the reason for American Industrial predominance abroad, and for its successful management at home, is rooted in the fairly radical concept of a free public education to every boy and girl born in this country.

> The function of values is to give us the illusion of purpose in life.
>
> *John P. Grier*

Different Organizations—Different Beliefs

> With most people unbelief in one thing is founded upon blind belief in another.
>
> *Georg Lichtenberg*

For persons who spend their entire working careers with one company, it is difficult to point out the "culture" of that company. It is often up to outsiders or to a new employee from a different company to point out the features of the culture. Fast-rising executives either consciously or instinctively identify these cultural features and use them in their power struggle.

A marketing manager was battling the engineering division. The meeting was made up of the vice-president, various managers of engineering, and the young manager, his boss, and the vice-president of sales. The group vice-president over both sales and engineering was chairing the meeting, which was heated.

The young manager knew the "culture" of the company. To be bold was to be good. He attacked head on. He told the group vice-president that the engineering division had not been working on the problem until just a week ago.

The vice-president of engineering was enraged. "That's not true," he stormed. "I resent your saying it; it's not pertinent."

"It certainly is pertinent," said the young manager. "It means we're starting late and we all should start with that clearly in mind. And I am right. Tell me who has been working on it?"

"Umm—Brooks!"

"No, Brooks started on this just this week. If you think I'm wrong," the younger manager pointed to the phone, "call him. His number is 6401."

A long silence ensued. The engineering people looked at each other. No one moved.

"Well," said the group vice-president, "does anyone want to call Brooks?"

Silence.

The meeting continued with the young manager in a much more respected, believed position.

In some companies the young manager would be guilty of impudence to confront a vice-president in so direct a manner. But in this particular company such candor and aggressiveness were encouraged. The young manager had observed that. A less perceptive or newly arrived (from some other company) manager may not have known that the "culture" would respect such boldness, even if the young manager had been wrong. In this particular case, he had been right.

Large organizations are like societies and many have very specific beliefs that permeate the entire structure and determine business goals and, therefore, all key decisions.

A large, billion-dollar company has a practice that everyone— even the chairman of the board—is called by his or her first name. The practice eliminates unnecessary formality, and eases communication. When a person calls someone else "Mister," it is a sure tip off of a new employee who doesn't know the company.

Bring ideas in and entertain them royally, for one of them may be the king.
Mark Van Doren

Beliefs Change with Time

Beliefs change with time. What was acceptable to our forebears two hundred years ago is considered an atrocity today. A recent book on some British history talks about some of the slave ships that plied their trade in the eighteenth century. A court case in Britain examined whether the 130 human beings thrown overboard to lighten the ship in stormy weather constituted an act of jettison or an act of fraud. The insurance company had to pay for the financial loss if it was judged to be an act of jettison. The idea of barbarism had not yet emerged, it seems.

Man is so inconsistent a creature that it is impossible to reason from his beliefs to his conduct, or from one part of his belief to another.
Thomas B. Macaulay

The history of the Intelligence Agencies in the United States shows twists and turns of society's beliefs.

In 1929 the then Secretary of State, Henry Stimson, directed that the "Black Room" that was operating in the War Department decoding the messages be shut down.

"Gentlemen," he said, "do not read each other's mail." This closing set back for several years the intelligence efforts of the United States. Fortunately these efforts were revived in sufficient time for them to play a very key, if not absolutely vital, role in World War II. Decodings of intercepted messages of both Japanese and Germans were vital to several major victories and to the entire conflict.

If persons spend more time with their families than the "company belief" allocates, then they are judged unambitious, or even lazy. This company belief is very crucial. *It* sets the tone, the expectation.

Beliefs Set Goals and Style

Beliefs beget goals and goals can be visions. Visions can fire the workers and managers of a firm; they are *committed* to the *cause*, they will conquer. Nothing is so powerful as this kind of spirit and commitment and, if morale is low, it is often because the vision is weak or confused. "Yes, but where are we going?" will be the answer to an exhortation to do better, to work harder.

> To live in the presence of great truths and eternal laws, to be led by permanent ideals—that is what keeps a man patient when the world ignores him, and calm and unspoiled when the world praises him.
>
> **Dr. A. Peabody**

Nothing is so obvious to subordinates as a clash of visions on the part of two supervisors. And if one works for the other, is the other's subordinate, watch out. There's trouble afoot! If the president wants a manufacturing business and the vice-president wants a consulting business, the future is troubled indeed. The clash/crash of ideologies is coming, so better pick sides based on (1) who you want to win or (2) who you *think* will win, often different from (1).

Such differences in goals can be catastrophic to an organization. The president must have it out with the vice-president. The president must clarify the goals—and get agreement—or the lower ranks will be in confusion.

Speech writers are very important people within the White House with a lot of power and prestige. This surprised me when I first heard it. Why? All they do is 'wordsmith.'

111

No, they get to articulate beliefs and goals, and if the leader accepts the formulation and gives the speech, they are setting policy, setting objectives, and calling out a direction!

The followers will hear the call and respond. The organization has changed—because a speech writer put *his own* ideas forth, and the leader said yes to them.

The aim, if reached or not, makes the life great:
Try to be Shakespeare, leave the rest to fate.
Robert Browning

Beliefs are used to keep morale high. A goal is defined and then the effort to reach it is made a crusade. In San Francisco in the early 1900s, A. P. Giannini founded the Bank of Italy on personal beliefs that violated all the established wisdom. It was a bank to help the "little" people. It *solicited* accounts—a new idea in banking. It loaned money to working men. Giannini was sneered at by the big bankers of the city. Today, his bank, the Bank of America, is the largest in the country.

When a small company starts out, its goals have a lot to do with what is important and how the company operates. If revenue growth is sought—even at the expense of profit—in order to make the stock price rise, the company will act very differently than if the goal is to remain a small, quality-first firm. "I just couldn't keep making questionable decisions to keep the stock inflated," a Nobel Prize winner in physics once told me. "I had to leave."

The true joy in life is being used for a purpose
recognized by yourself as a mighty one.
George Bernard Shaw

Style

Beliefs have a great effect on style, because they determine what means are allowed. And what means are used add up in total to an individual's style. How hard can you press to get your objective? Can you fire people? Indiscriminately? Are knockdown, drag-out fights acceptable? Or are aggressions to be masked, to be kept hidden? Is profit all important, very important, unimportant, or secondary? These questions and others when answered add up to style, and they follow almost directly from beliefs.

A man must not swallow more beliefs than he can digest.
Henry Brooks Adams

Being out of style can be disastrous.

112

The marketing arm can be very style conscious. If you are a "scientific" type, you are an "egghead," an oddball. You don't fit.

Once a manager was heard to say, "Heck, he even gets his hair cut like an engineer."

Style has a way of becoming practice, and practice has a way of becoming policy.

The chief executive officer of Pepsi-Co. is a health enthusiast, according to Robert Scheer in *Esquire,* April 1975. Scheer, after commenting that the chief executive officer is a jogger, etc., comments that any rising executive had better be seen jogging at lunchtime and be seen in the gym.

Beliefs to a large extent set goals, set style or philosophy, determine which means are acceptable, which are not. Beliefs can be like the air around us, invisible but critical. Effective managers study the beliefs of their organizations, listen carefully to the speeches of the chief executive, read carefully the in-house newspaper. And they deviate only with great care.

Oh, wise men, riddle me this?
What if the dream come true?
What if the dream come true
And if millions unborn
Shall dwell in the house that I shaped in my heart,
The noble house of my thought?

Lord, I have staked my soul.
I have staked the lives of my kin
On the truth of thy dreadful word.
Do not remember my failure.
But remember this, my faith.
Paedric Pearse

No man has earned the right to intellectual ambition until he has learned to lay his course by a star which he has never seen. . . .
For I say to you in all sadness of conviction that to think great thoughts you must be heroes as well as idealists.
Oliver Wendell Holmes, Jr.

It is the sad destiny of a prophet that when, after working twenty years, he convinces his contemporaries, his adversaries also succeed, and he is no longer convinced himself.
Friedrich Nietzsche

How common it is to hear people say a man ought to have the courage of his convictions; how rare it is to find a man who will say that one ought to have the courage to change one's opinions.

Arthur Christopher Benson

Important principles may and must be inflexible.

Abraham Lincoln

It must be considered that there is nothing more difficult to carry out nor more doubtful of success, nothing more dangerous to handle, than to initiate a new order of things. For the reformer has enemies in all those who profit by the old order and only lukewarm defenders in all those who would profit by the new order.

Niccolò Machiavelli

Men do not succeed in business or in life, no matter how intelligent they may be, no matter how sharply their aptitudes are defined, no matter how brilliantly they may be educated unless they are oriented toward the proper goals and have the drive or motivating force to succeed. One has to want something mighty hard and keep on wanting things all his life. . . .

Wallace H. Wulfeck

If a man does not keep pace with his companions, perhaps it is because he hears a different drummer. Let him step to the music which he hears, however measured or far away.

Henry David Thoreau

The most patriotic thing I can do for my country is to remain solvent.

James E. Sinclair

I have in mind a plan of development which would make radio a "household utility" in the same sense as the piano or phonograph. The idea is to bring music into the house by wireless. While this has been tried in the past by wires, it has been a failure because wires do not lend themselves to this scheme. With radio, however, it would seem to be entirely feasible. The receiver can be designed in the form of a simple 'Radio Music Box' and arranged for several different wavelengths, which should be changeable with the throwing of a single switch or pressing a single button. . . .

David Sarnoff

The mind of Eddie Carbone is not comprehensible apart from its relationship to his neighborhood, his fellow workers, his social situation. His self-esteem depends upon their estimate of him, and his value is created largely by his fidelity to the code of his culture.

Arthur Miller

114

Expedients are for an hour, but principles are for the ages. Just
because the rains descend, and the winds blow, we cannot afford
to build on the shifting sands.

Henry Ward Beecher

All truths begin as blasphemies.

George Bernard Shaw

Our emotions are the driving powers of our lives. When we are aroused
emotionally, unless we do something great and good, we are in danger
of letting our emotions become perverted. William James used to tell
the story of a Russian woman who sat weeping at the tragic fate
of the hero in the opera while her coachman froze to death outside.

Earl Riney

INTEGRITY

Is there not a sort of blood shed when the conscience is
wounded? Through this wound a man's real manhood
and immortality flow out, and he bleeds to an everlasting
death.

Henry David Thoreau

Almost every list of executive traits will show the quality of integrity.
However, it is an oversimplification to just list integrity, state that it
is an absolute requirement, and go on from there. Why is integrity
important to being a good and effective executive? Why do so many
lists of executive qualities include it?

To a certain extent there is wishful thinking in the inclusion of
integrity in the lists. It is a reflection, and a happy reflection, of the
American idea of righteousness. All of us want the boss or person we
are dealing with to be true to the same set of ideas that we believe in.
We want to deal with a boss who will be trustworthy, that is, one
who has integrity, and who will be somewhat predictable.

Integrity: soundness of an adherence to moral principle
and character; uprightness; honesty.

We again examine and elaborate upon the word "good" in "good
executive." By good, do we mean useful in overall society, as opposed
to useful in the particular endeavor or enterprise that the executive is
in? The narrower good, applying only to the enterprise, might be well
served by an unscrupulous executive. That is, by some unscrupulous
act, the executive may, indeed, increase the power, prestige, monetary
value, or other attributes of the company. However, from an overall so-

115

ciety viewpoint, the boss is not a "good executive." Even when confronted with seeming evidence of double-dealing, we will make excuses for our bosses because to believe them to lack integrity is to lose faith in dealing with them.

The same is true of executives with their subordinates. They *want* to believe their subordinates are honest and straightforward. It is a major complication to them when they discover that subordinate Miller will lie if it suits Miller's purpose. "If Miller lied in order to get the new building approved, is he lying on this issue? How do I know he's not lying to me?" I use the word "lie" deliberately. Mistakes are always tolerable. One "lie" kills forever the trust that is essential in dealing with others. It shows a lack of integrity and destroys trust.

A recent poll conducted by the *Washington Post* found that the public wanted integrity in their elected leaders more than they wanted competence. This was a result of the Watergate scandal. And that should surprise no one. Who wants to be led by someone who is dishonest, and perhaps lying to us, when giving us reasons and explanations? Better a less competent honest leader than a supercompetent scoundrel! Indeed a *competent* unscrupulous leader is *more* dangerous than an incompetent unscrupulous one.

Washington Star columnist Mary McGrory comments on Sunday, May 27, 1974:

> "I lost my ethical compass," Magruder told Judge Sirica in his statement before the sentence was pronounced.
>
> None, of course, was provided by his superiors at the White House. Apparently Magruder expected none. Whatever he brought with him from his middle-class boyhood, Williams College, and his career as a cosmetics executive was smashed in that atmosphere of hatred and fear. Like the other handsome young men who now or soon will be in prison drab—Egil Krogh and Dwight Chapin—he gladly, even eagerly, broke the law for the team. They never expected to be caught. They all seemed to understand they had been chosen for their looks and their loyalty, not for judgment or conscience.

When interviewing for a job, one never tells the interviewer that one of the job seeker's assets is integrity. In our society, that is assumed. Integrity is usually not noticed until it is missing. *Then* it becomes all important. Integrity is standing up for what's right, even though doing so may cost dearly. Going along with the crowd because you agree with their sentiments is not integrity.

It is no great thing at all to "have integrity" when there is no issue to be debated and *all* are in agreement. It is when there is danger in standing up for your principles that integrity shines forth.

> When Neville Chamberlain in 1939 came back from Munich with the deal with Hitler, the English people were delirious with joy.
>
> It took integrity for Winston Churchill to tell the House of Parliament that they had "suffered a total and unmitigated defeat."
>
> He was thunderously booed.

> In matters of principle, stand like a rock; in matters of taste, swim with the current.
>
> *Thomas Jefferson*

Matters of Principle

An organization gets confronted with a matter of principle, and one person must make the decision.

> A settlement to a law suit was offered; instead of $2.2 million the contractor offered $2 million. The company was a $1.5-billion-per-year enterprise, and they had already written off the entire $2.2 million. The $200,000 wasn't important and everyone was willing to forego it. But everyone also felt that the other company was really dead wrong and should pay back everything; to yield the $200,000 was "wrong." Yet, to go to court would cost at least another $200,000 in legal fees. What to do?

Who is to say what is right or wrong here. It is a judgment call, and a close one.

Sometimes the decision is a personal and private one.

> A large company had a program where a young employee could attend graduate school at full pay to attain a doctorate degree. The individual signs an agreement that he will stay with that firm for five years after attaining his degree. One individual broke his "contract" and quit six months after attaining his degree.
>
> The law was clear; the firm could force him to stay. But the vice-president wouldn't press the case, even though his subordinate,

117

the defector's manager, wanted to do so. The vice-president didn't want the fuss.

It was easier to just ignore the matter; the president never did find out, and no one really knew what the vice-president had done—except his one subordinate. The president never knew.

What is right to do in this situation? To pursue the legal remedies is messy and maybe bad publicity will result, and certainly the president will see that the vice-president (or his subordinates) made a mistake in choosing the candidate for the Ph.D. But if the matter is just dropped, then all future Ph.D. candidates will feel a little more free to "jump ship."

What to do? There is no easy answer. One thing that is fairly clear is that the vice-president should not choose to let the matter drop *solely* for the reason that he doesn't want his boss to find out!

Individuals can lose their reputations for integrity in many ways. It can be lost by bluffing too often, in difficult situations. When one is caught bluffing too often, it is difficult not to wonder whether or not that individual is bluffing on the next issue.

They were in deep trouble on a project, and the general manager and the project manager were expecting the president any moment. The general manager said, "Let's just admit we don't know the answers and we are working on it."

The president arrived. The project manager gave a confident presentation what the problems were, and how they were going to fix them.

The general manager knew that the project manager didn't know what he was talking about, but he sure sounded and looked confident. "I wonder how many times he's done this to me," thought the general manager.

Afterwards, he told the project manager, "Don't do that! You'll lose your reputation for honesty. It would have been better to confess." He never again trusted the project manager quite as much as he had before that meeting. (He also told the president that things weren't as good as they sounded.)

Reputation is an idle and most false imposition, oft got without merit, and lost without deserving. . . .
William Shakespeare

Some people have commented that the general manager was not justified to conclude from this incident that he should not trust his

118

subordinate quite as much after the incident. Whether the general manager was justified in this conclusion is beside the point; he *didn't trust* the project manager as much after that incident.

It is sometimes ridiculously easy to hide errors and failings in the hurly-burly of the ongoing business struggle. Some high-level managers argue extensively and adamantly that problem A is the biggest, worst, most awful problem to ever be seen. They then go out and solve one-half of it and look good. But should they have been able to solve three-fourths of it? Or all of it? Only they know. But the technique works very well at times. Magnify the problem; then do what you can.

> Courage without conscience is a wild beast.
>
> *Robert G. Ingersoll*

Negotiating versus Integrity

If you will settle a dispute over costs on a contract 50-50, should you start by stating so? Or should you argue for 75 percent and bargain? Most people will start higher than they are willing to settle at (or even want). Is this a violation of integrity?

When you say, "I can afford to put only six people on this job," when you can really afford ten—and expect to bargain with your customer by putting on eight—are you "lying" or are you "negotiating?"

The boss can often be an adversary who intends to manage you by results only, and if you arrive at the wrong quota, you may be out of a job!

Dilemma! Negotiate or be open? I wish I had an answer! The answer (nonanswer) is: It depends. It depends on the boss, the situation, the goal.

Many find negotiation distasteful and therefore are too open (not realistic). Such people tell the boss "I can sell $1,500,000 worth of goods this year." The boss, a negotiator, thinks, if they start at $1,500,-000, they expect to sell $2,000,000, so I'll ask for $2,500,000.

Problems ahead here! There is a beliefs gap and these two are going to miss each other badly.

On the road to the top, climbers must expect to pass through many negotiators and negotiations. They must do so with as little yielding to expediency as possible.

Integrity is put to the test when one is "wheeling and dealing," compromising, negotiating, or "staying loose." Ambition will often pull in the opposite direction from integrity.

In his book, *Johnny, We Hardly Knew You*, Kenny O'Donnell tells about the time John F. Kennedy had him call a political rival in Massachusetts and tell him a flat lie, denying a conversation that indeed had taken place.

A recent *Washington Post* story reports that a state governor saw nothing wrong in publicly stating that he supported a bill, while at the same time sending his aides to sabotage the bill.

When does dissembling become deceit? This is a matter of judgment. These practices are, of course, not limited to politicians. One often encounters them in superiors and subordinates. All the facts may be there, but an implication is contained between the lines (that is hard to trace) that is not quite true.

My old father used to have a saying: If you make a bad bargain, hug it all the tighter.
Abraham Lincoln

Shading is very difficult to recognize when performed by a very intelligent individual. For example, consider this conversation between a vice-president and his subordinate:

"Did you get Kheun from the commercial division?"

"Yes. This was a trade, you know. We gave up Schwartz."

Now the vice-president knew that Schwartz had demanded to move over to the commercial division and was going to quit if he was not allowed to go.

For his subordinate to go to the commercial division and use Schwartz as a trade to get Kheun was acceptable to him, and even smart husbanding of top people resources.

But the vice-president was miffed because his subordinate did not tell him that Schwartz had demanded out. The subordinate wanted the vice-president to think that a true trade had occurred. This impression would help the subordinate on another problem that he was trying to get the vice-president to change his mind on.

The subordinate was speaking the truth but not the whole truth.

Without integrity a person is not believable, not trustworthy, not dependable. With it, a person is. Without integrity an individual will serve society well only by accident.

You may have integrity, but lose your reputation for it by sloppy communications. Because integrity is so valuable, you as an upward climber should go to great lengths to build and guard your reputation for integrity. You should state the truth as you see it even if it hurts your argument. In the long run, your reputation for integrity is more important than the battles along the way.

120

Some day, in years to come, you will be wrestling with the great temptation, or trembling under the great sorrow of your life. But the real struggle is here, now, in these quiet weeks. Now it is being decided whether, in the day of your supreme sorrow or temptation, you shall miserably fail or gloriously conquer. Character cannot be made except by a steady, long-conducted process.

Phillips Brooks

The only tyrant I accept in this world
is the still voice within.

Mahatma Gandhi

He is not great, who is not greatly good.

William Shakespeare

It is not given to human beings, happily for them, for otherwise life would be intolerable, to foresee or to predict to any large extent the unfolding course of events. In one phase men seem to have been right, in another they seem to have been wrong. There again, a few years later, when the perspective of time has lengthened, all stands in a different setting. There is a new proportion. There is another scale of values. History with its flickering light stumbles along the trail of the past, trying to reconstruct its scenes, to revive its echoes and kindle with pale gleams the passion of former days. What is the worth of all this? The only guide to a man is his conscience; the only shield to his memory is the rectitude and sincerity of his actions. It is very imprudent to walk through life without this shield, because we are often mocked by the failure of our hopes and the upsetting of our calculations; but with this shield, however the fates may plan,
we march always in the ranks of honor.

Winston S. Churchill

The moral flabbiness born of the exclusive worship
of the bitch-goddess Success.

William James

He that loses his conscience has nothing left worth keeping.

Walton Caussin

I desire to so conduct the affairs of this administration that if, at the end . . . I have lost every friend on earth, I shall have one friend left, and that friend shall be down inside me.

Abraham Lincoln

121

Beloved Pan, and all ye other gods who haunt this place, give me beauty in the inward soul; and may the outward and inward man be at one.

Socrates

We ought always to deal justly, not only with those who are just to us, but likewise to those who endeavor to injure us; and this, for fear lest by rendering them evil for evil, we should fall into the same vice.

Hierocles

He who is false to the present duty breaks a thread in the loom, and you will see the effect when the weaving of a lifetime is unraveled.

William Ellery Channing

INTELLECT

Mark this well, ye proud men of action! Ye are, after all, nothing but unconscious instruments of the men of thought.

Heinrich Heine

Intellect is the power of mind. Not all high-level people have a first-class intellect. Some reach their positions by having a high number of the qualities and a high level of knowledge in particular areas.

Intellect should not be overvalued. Given a choice between an executive with a first-class intellect and with all other qualities of second class, or one who had second-class intellect and is first-class in all the other qualities, I would not hesitate for a moment to choose the latter.

Obviously the brilliant have an advantage over those of average intellect, but that advantage is not as great as one might think.

> Only once in seven years of observing and managing high-level executives have I seen a failure of intelligence. To this day, I am not positive that it was a lack of intelligence. The man had *all* the other qualities. His quick mind and communications ability led all to believe that he had all the intelligence needed. But he did not ever have in his mind the key parts of the intricate problems he was trying to solve. He seemed to rely totally on advisors. He would get five minutes into a meeting and then be out of gas. He did not control his smart advisors.

Intellect is something one is born with; it can't be added to. Individuals can use it to gather more and more knowledge, but cannot add to their intellect.

Psychologists do not agree on what intellect is. Most agree that it is more than one quality of mind and *not* able to be labeled by a single number, such as an Intelligence Quotient, or IQ score.

Intellect cannot be measured, and often a genius is rejected for lack of mental power! Churchill just squeezed into Sandhurst, the British West Point. It took him three tries.

Einstein was very "slow" in his early years, having difficulty learning to speak. At nine, he was still not quite there. One schoolmaster told his father that it did not matter what field of endeavor he chose, he would not succeed in any. His family at one point thought he was subnormal. He flunked the entrance exam to the Zurich Polytechnical Institute. Einstein had an incredible memory for scientific knowledge, a poor memory for facts of personal life.

Einstein said of himself that perhaps his slow development was one of the reasons *he* formulated the Theory of Relativity. Perhaps it was because as an adult he was still viewing phenomena through the eyes of a child, he theorized.

> I am in love with our era. This is the first time when supremacy of the intellect is total. Nothing can beat brainpower.
>
> *Jean-Jacques Servan-Schreiber*

Intellect is important but not measurable. It is also not improvable. Lack of intellect can stop you from gaining power, but possession of great intellect does not assure you an executive position.

We won't spend much time on intellect because it is of secondary importance and one cannot do much about improving one's intellect. Yet the executive selecting a subordinate for a key job must take it into account.

However, logic and nimble-mindedness are more easily recognized and more important to success.

> The most intelligent living person might well be Kim Ung-Yong of Seoul, South Korea (born March 7, 1963). By the age of four, he could speak Korean, Japanese, German, and English, and at four years, eight months, he performed integral calculus on a Tokyo television program. On the Terman Index for Intelligence Quotients, 150 represents genius, and indices are sometimes immeasurable above a level of 200. Ung-Yong's IQ is estimated to be 210. Both his parents are university professors, and both were born at 11:00 A.M. on May 23, 1934.
>
> From *Harper's Magazine*

A man of genius knows what he is aiming at. No one else knows, only he alone knows when something comes between him and his object. In the course of generations, however, men will excuse you for not doing as they do, if you will bring enough to pass in your own way.

Henry David Thoreau

Indolence is a delightful but distressing state; we must be doing something to be happy. Action is no less necessary than thought to the instinctive tendencies of the human frame.

William Hazlitt

Speech is the gift of all, but thought of a few.

Cato

I do not know what I may appear to the world; but to myself I seem to have been only like a boy playing on the seashore, and diverting myself in now and then finding of a smoother pebble or a prettier shell than ordinary whilst the great ocean of truth lay all undiscovered before me.

Isaac Newton

LOGIC

It is clear that certain people have a logic ability superior to others. They are able to get to the heart of matters very quickly. They are able to separate the problem into important and unimportant aspects. They are able to diagnose and pinpoint the area that must be studied or fixed. Some problems must be boiled down to find the nub, the key, to the problem. The problem must be stripped.

Logic is hard to describe, but what I mean by it is the ability to get at the nub of things. It means being able to recognize the causes and chronology of events and to strip away the accidental hangings on.

Logic is not raw mental power; that is intellect. It is a quality of the mind which can be improved by practice and education.

Logic is problem solving, not brainstorming, not inventing.

Logic, combined with good communications skills, enables an individual to deal effectively even in areas where personal knowledge is slight. It will take more time, but by skillful questioning the individual will be effective.

Logic has evolved and grown over the centuries. Graham Wallas (1858–1932) writes in *The Great Society*:

It is a historical fact that human thinking has been enormously improved by the invention of logical rules in the past. Aristotle's

124

formal syllogistic scheme seems to us now so poor and clumsy that any insistence upon it is a hindrance rather than a furtherance to thought, but that is because we have already absorbed its main results into the words and implications of our ordinary speech. How could we think to any effect about the complexities of modern life if we had no words like "principle" and "instance" or "proof" or "disproof"? The repetition of such formulas as "All A is B" wearies us now, but they stood at one time for a passionate new conviction that nature is uniform, and that the same conditions might always be trusted to produce the same results. To understand what the invention of the syllogism gave to mankind we must compare it with that world of thought which it helped to supersede, the incalculable divinities, the contradictory maxims and proverbs, the disconnected fragments of observation and experience which make the apparatus of the primitive mind. Bacon's *Organum* itself, and even the Four Methods of Experimental Enquiry in Mill's *Logic,* seem inadequate and almost irrelevant to a modern man of science, simply because he takes the need of testing hypotheses by experiment for granted.

Yet today logic is taught in our higher education system as either philosophy or mathematics—or law. This most practical of skills, this everyday tool, is grossly neglected by universities and corporate management training programs!

> I told him it was low logic—an artificial system of reasoning, exclusively used in courts of justice, but good for nothing anywhere else.
>
> **John Quincy Adams**

Are there really many kinds of logic or only one? When we separate logic into "kinds" we are applying logic to logic.

Stewart Chase names seven kinds or levels of logic:

1. Common sense
2. Formal logic (Aristotelian-syllogisms)
3. Mathematics
4. Modern science
5. Legal procedure
6. Winning arguments
7. All-out propaganda

All of these kinds of logic are practical; they *work!* They produce results; they solve problems or dilemmas; they motivate people to act.

Logic in Persuasion

He that will not reason is a bigot;
He that cannot is a fool;
He that does not is a slave.

William Drummond

Logic is the backbone of persuasion, of sales ability. It is ordering facts and ideas in order to convince, to lead someone to a conclusion.

The first someone is one's self! Logic is the internal operations of the mind leading to conclusions. It is the opposite of faith. I might believe in a religious "mystery," but it is a mystery because it is not supportable, (i.e., arguable), logically.

From the Greeks and Romans of old we get a list of arguing strategies:

- *argumentum ad hominem*—appeal to personal prejudice:
  "Those people are ruining the neighborhood!"

- *argumentum ad populum*—appeal to public opinion:
  "Everyone agrees. . . ."

- *argumentum ad misericordiam*—appeal to pity:
  "You've got to help me, or I'll lose my job."

- *argumentum ad ignorantiam*—stress on ignorance:
  "Magic ingredient P-122. . . ."

- *argumentum ad crumenam*—appeal to the purse:
  "Save 20 percent with our product"

- *argumentum ad verecundiam*—appeal to prestige:
  "Buy a Cadillac; buy the best"

- *argumentum ad captandum vulgus*—any dishonest argument.

- *argumentum ad baculum*—appeal to brute force:
  "Let's make them pay for this!"

In *Zen and the Art of Motorcycle Maintenance,* published by William Morrow, Robert M. Pirsig points out several ways to confront the horns of a dilemma, which he represents as a bull. He says:

1. Take one side or the other and argue,
2. Say that there is a third possibility,
3. Throw sand,
4. Sing the bull to sleep,
5. Refuse to enter the arena.

These approaches are seen in our everyday work life and are not restricted to dilemmas! Which approach to be used is a function of logic.

To "Think and Talk Net"

Logic enables the executive to "think net." It is possible for people with little logic ability to think net, but it requires much more time for them to do so. Time is management's least available resource.

To "talk net" is to state the essential facts and logic of a case succinctly, avoiding elaboration or details. It is a great time-saver. It forces one to think through what *is* essential, and what is just surrounding facts and information. It is very difficult, obviously, to talk net effectively and intelligently unless one is able to think net.

> A middle-level manager ran a group of 30 people. His job was to sell $30 million worth of computer equipment to a certain customer. For extremely complex reasons, his group failed. A competitor got the business.
>
> The manager spent six straight hours one day with his two managers going over the reason they failed. At first they listed the obvious reasons. Then they added the not so obvious. Then they discussed each one. Gradually they narrowed the list to two main reasons, with all the others—about six—being subsets of the main two.
>
> That same evening, the manager had dinner with the regional vice-president of sales and his top management team. Without prior notice, he was asked to explain to the group the reasons for the loss. He put on a brilliant performance, laying out in beautiful logical sequence the causes of the loss. He spoke for 35 minutes without a note. The logic was breathtaking. Dozens of pieces of the story dovetailed precisely. He left that meeting with his reputation and stature significantly enhanced. He had made the very complex understandable!
>
> He had "lost" $30 million of business—but his stock was higher than ever. The exercise in logic with his managers paid off a thousand-fold.

> [The brain is] an enlarged loom where millions of flashing shuttles weave a dissolving pattern, always a meaningful pattern though never an abiding one.
> *Sir Charles Sherrington*

Without getting into a formal course on logic, we should look at conditionals briefly. They play such an important role in our communications ability; yet many people either don't know or don't think about them. There are necessary conditionals, sufficient conditionals, and necessary-and-sufficient conditionals. A necessary conditional says that unless condition A exists, then a result R cannot occur. A is necessary to R.

But R, while needing A, may also need other conditions, e.g., B. Therefore, A is a necessary but not sufficient cause of R. Or, A can be a sufficient but not necessary cause of R. That is, R can occur without A, but will occur if A exists. Or A can be a necessary and sufficient conditional for R. Only if A is present can R occur, and A alone is sufficient for R to occur. R can not occur without A, and it will occur if A is done.

Let's consider an example:

Project manager Walsh is behind on building a new radar. The schedule will be missed by six months. He goes to the vice-president, Evans, and explains his problem. Since a six-month slip will be very damaging to their reputation and profit, they discuss ways of getting back on schedule, of avoiding the six-month slip.

Walsh: If you give me an additional $700,000 for overtime and additional people, I can get back on schedule. This amount is sufficient for Original Schedule, OS.

V.P. Evans: Can you get back to the scedule if I get you the new transistors next month?

Walsh: Yes.

V.P. Evans: Is there any other thing that can be done so that we get back on schedule? People? machines? space?

Walsh: No. I've studied them all. There is no other way but either $700,000 or new transistors.

Had Walsh said no to the new transistors, enabling him to make the schedule, then the $700,000 would have been th*e only* way to get back to schedule, and it would have been a *necessary* and sufficient condition.

Or if he needed *both* the $700,000 *and* the new transistors, then both would have been necessary, and neither one sufficient.

Therefore a condition can be:

1. Necessary and not sufficient. Both $700,000 *and* the new transistors are needed. Therefore, $700,000 is a necessary and not sufficient condition. The money alone is not enough to get the schedule back.

2. Necessary and sufficient. Only the $700,000 will do it, and it will do it. Guaranteed. It is enough. But there is no other way to do it.

3. Sufficient and not necessary. The $700,000 will do it, guaranteed, but there are other conditions that would do it also, such as having new transistors. "We have a choice."

4. Not necessary and not sufficient. Other conditions will do it, and the $700,000 is not enough, by itself, to do it. "I need the $700,000 plus the transistors, and there are other ways to solve the problem."

Numbers 2 and 4 bear close analysis. If number 4 were known in advance to be not necessary and not sufficient, few managers would choose it as an option. But since we are dealing with predictions, we often have managers state the facts as number 2—necessary and sufficient—only to find in closer examination, either before or after the fact, that that statement of the conditions is not correct.

Why all this about conditions? Because managers should explore the options available and understand the combinations of sufficient and necessary conditions *before* they authorize a $700,000 expenditure.

Many experienced managers go through the necessary and sufficient condition drill without ever having heard the phrase "necessary and sufficient." They do it because they are careful and smart. But unfortunately other managers jump too quickly at the first formulation of the solution, ("Give me $700,000 and I can fix the problem."), and lose the chance at a better decision.

A good way to drive out conditionals is to formulate ridiculous hypotheses and ask if that would solve the problem.

> *V.P. Evans:* If I gave you all the engineers in the company for 2 months (or 4, or 6, etc.) could you get back on schedule?
>
> Evans knows he can't put *all* the company's engineers on this job; five other projects will fall apart. But it forces out unrecognized assumptions that may be embedded in a hasty compilation of needs.
>
> *Walsh:* I hadn't thought of that. Hmmm? Maybe . . . maybe I could do it. . . .
>
> *V.P. Evans:* If I gave you all the automatic test machines for 2 months? (He can't really do that either.)
>
> *Walsh:* No, that will not help.

Some managers resent such questions, especially if they are bright and competent, but often even these are surprised to find that new alternatives are found—or already formulated ones are scrapped.

By going through a series of ifs, the necessary and sufficient conditionals are exposed and understood, even if not by the name "necessary and sufficient."

Impediments to Logic

> Life is not an illogicality; yet it is a trap for logicians. It looks just a little more mathematical and regular than it is; its exactitude is obvious, but its inexactitude is hidden; its wildness lies in wait.
>
> Gilbert K. Chesterton

Francis Bacon pointed out in his *Novum Organum,* published in 1620, that "there are four Idols which beset men's minds." He calls them

1. Idols of the tribe—man thinks within the framework of his humanity.
2. Idols of the cave—he thinks within his own individuality.
3. Idols of the marketplace—he thinks using words.
4. Idols of the theater—he is prone to the thought of his predecessors *and* their philosophies and logical structures.

Bacon elaborates on these traps to human thought:

Perceptions accord to the measure of the individual, not to the measure of the universe.

Human understanding supposes more order and regularity than it observes.

Human understanding, not content with singlular things in nature, invents parallels and relatives for them.

Once the human mind has adopted an opinion, it bends all else to support it.

The human intellect is more excited by positives than negatives.

The human understanding tends to associate things that strike the consciousness at the same time.

There is a tendency to believe what one wants to believe.

Some dwell on differences; some on similarities.

The human race is beset by the use of words. And often the discussions of great men end in disputes about words and names. And definitions use words so that definitions do not solve the problem.

Bacon warns that whatever a person's mind finds peculiarly satisfying should be suspect.

Logic is the quality of mind that is often heard about under a different name, "getting to the heart of the matter."

It is a great time-saver in this respect. It enables the executive to ignore the nonessential trappings of the issues and concentrate on the critical items.

In Chinese philosophy, there is no such category as logic! The Chinese are extremely subtle, intelligent, intuitive, changeable, but often inaccessible to our reasoning.

Jacques Guillermaz

The great end of life is not knowledge but action.

Thomas Henry Huxley

> Whatever resolves uncertainty is information. Power
> will accrue to the man who can handle information.
>
> *R. Buckminster Fuller*

Another subset of mental power is nimble-mindedness. Some people have one idea per day. This is not to say that they are not intelligent. The idea which they work on that day may be a brilliant innovation or brilliant interpretation. Their contribution to society over the long run may, indeed, be tremendous.

However, in the executive suite such individuals are not very successful or effective. Confronted with a variety of problems that call for decisions our one-idea-per-day individuals continue to think about their one thought or give only cursory and too little attention to decisions.

The opposite of one-idea-per-day individuals are the one-hundred-ideas-per-minute individuals. At this end of the spectrum these individuals also have their problems as executives. They find it difficult to concentrate on any item for more than 15 or 30 minutes, and they find it extremely hard to absorb details.

However, if we had to choose we would clearly pick our executive from individuals at this end of the scale. They can always hire people to worry about the details, and they can try to arrange their time in such a way that they need not spend more than a half hour on any given problem.

Almost all executives are nimble-minded and are able to switch subjects instantly. It is exciting to watch a good executive, in the course of a day, go from a difficult customer situation to an investment decision in a technical field, to a choice of a key subordinate, to a legal problem, to a sales strategy session, to the design of the parking lot, to another sales situation—and never be befuddled or confuse one situation with the next.

Without nimble-mindedness one is usually not effective in sales. Nimble-mindedness means being quick on your feet and having the ability to think rapidly in an unstructured environment. Some very intelligent and knowledgeable people can be thrown completely off their stride and be unable to communicate because a key executive or customer has quickly changed direction or subject matter. Being unready for this new subject matter these individuals are unable to continue the discussion. They are flustered and in disarray.

An example of nimble-mindedness at its best occurred in a sales practice situation in a marketing organization. A student, the salesman, was trying to convince the instructor, the customer executive, that he should buy data-processing equipment. One of the favorite selling techniques of equipment of this complexity is to point out that other corporations are using such equipment effectively. The sales trainee went on at great length about all the different companies that were using equipment. "The ABC company," he said, "has had the equipment installed for six months."

"But the ABC company is going broke," said the instructor.

Without blinking an eye, the sales trainee said, "Aha, but they *know* they're going broke."

This simple example may mask a very key point—that nimble-mindedness is absolutely vital to selling ability! Salespersons cannot dominate the customers; they must listen and react. They must take objections—some of which defy prediction—and react immediately. They must let customers dart off in any direction (how can sellers stop them?), and then concoct on the spot the strategy and facts to move the customers to the point where they get back on the logical path.

Nimble-mindedness allows you to keep up with fast moving meetings. It allows you to keep pace and to participate when events take sudden and unexplained turns. It allows you to dredge up the factual material from memory that is relevant to the present problem.

I now watch and test for nimble-mindedness. I used to think it was part of intellect and that if persons were "smart," they would be fine in sales and "quick on their feet." I found out by experience that I was wrong. A vice-president made the following remarks:

> A high-level manager was outstanding in just about all areas,
> so it came as a shock to me that he just about "became unglued"
> when a customer surprised him with a claim of poor performance
> on one of our products.

> He just didn't know what to say; he babbled! The other man
> with him jumped into the conversation and by quick thinking
> ended the meeting or it would have been even more embarrassing.

> After that I watched my man in technical meetings. For the first
> fifteen minutes he'd be in the thick of it, giving and taking in the
> flow of ideas. Then, suddenly, he'd retire to be a spectator and
> his subordinates would carry the argument. He just watched.

> I realized he was not "nimble-minded"—smart, yes; nimble-
> minded, no.

KNOWLEDGE

Knowledge is distinct from intellect. It is acquired, rather than inborn. The finer one's intellectual power, the faster one can acquire knowledge, but the harder working, less intellectually gifted individual can acquire equal or more knowledge. Knowledge of a company, its practices and policies and culture, is usually critical to one's success and upward movement. Knowledge of a technical field, such as computers, is critical to success in the computer industry.

There are many kinds of knowledge. There is knowledge of organization, knowledge of history, of the corporation, and of disciplines.

When we say knowledge of organization we mean knowing whom to call, knowing who has the authority and/or the power to make decisions, who is likely to exercise that power and who is not.

The knowledge of history is important, because what will happen can be to some extent foretold by what has taken place in the past. The same is, obviously, true for the history of a corporation. Clearly, if a corporation has passed through similar trials and/or successes in the past, one can foretell to some extent its actions and its predilections by studying those past events.

A great deal of time can be saved if a person in an organization knows where the pressure points are and where the active executives are. This knowledge comes only through experience with the organization.

> There is nothing more frightful than ignorance in action.
> *Johann Goethe*

Many executives cannot succeed if they move to a new company because they don't know whom to call, who are the doers, what is the company's history. Some executives may be outstanding, but they don't have the time to find things out. The corporation should provide them with a capable aide who knows these things.

One vice-president I know has in his notebook a list of all his predecessors, a record of their tenures in office, and their subsequent career paths after they left that office. Most of the paths were downward, showing that the job was a very high personal-risk job. He had that all mapped out *before* he took the job. He has no illusions!

Another example of knowledge is the young man in management school who said to the president: "All but two of the top seven executives have had careers in marketing. Is that a prerequisite to a top-level job?

Such knowledge is power!

The knowledge of discipline is the knowledge of mathematics, of engineering, of computers, of accounting, etc. These knowledges are not raw mental power, but something which has been acquired and gained by individuals as they progress through life. Clearly, the possession of such knowledge makes them more effective. The executive who can avoid stumbling on a legal, or on a technical barrier, is more likely to succeed as an executive than the one who does not have such knowledge.

Vocabulary

The power of words is immense. A well-chosen word has often sufficed to stop a flying army, to change defeat into victory, and to save an empire.
Emile De Girardin

Knowledge of vocabulary is probably the single most reliable guide to future achievement. The better the vocabulary, the more achievement.

Business executives have surprisingly high vocabulary scores, and they are executives because of the vocabulary, and do not gain the vocabulary because they are executives.

By vocabulary we do not mean mastery of the arcane, five-syllable jawbreakers that are rarely used, but the exactness with which one uses one-, two-, and three-syllable "everyday" words.

We will explore at length the critical role that communications ability plays in the rise to and performance of the executive role. Much of this ability depends directly upon one's command of vocabulary. Happily, vocabulary can be acquired rather easily by study and effort.

And ye shall know the truth and the truth shall make you free.
John 8:32

Wise men say, and not without reason, that whoever wishes to foresee the future must consult the past; for human events ever resemble those of preceding times. This arises from the fact that they were produced by men who have been, and ever will be, animated by the same passions, and thus they must necessarily have the same results.
Niccolò Machiavelli

History is lived forwards but it is written in retrospect. We know the end before we consider the beginning and we can never wholly recapture what it was to know the beginning only.
C. V. Wedgwood

A SUMMARY OF THE LESSONS OF HISTORY
Whom the Gods would destroy, they first make mad with power.
The mills of God grind slowly, but they grind exceedingly small.
The bee fertilizes the flower it robs.
When it is dark enough, you can see the stars.
Charles A. Beard

Ignorance is bold, and knowledge reserved.
Thucydides

Everybody is ignorant, only on different subjects.
Will Rogers

The work of progress is so immense and our means of aiding is so feeble; the life of humanity is so long, that of the individual so brief, that we often see only the ebb of the advancing ways, and are thus discouraged. It is history that teaches us to hope.
Robert E. Lee

All history becomes subjective; in other words there is properly no history, only biography. Every mind must know the whole lesson for itself, must go over the whole ground.
Ralph W. Emerson

It isn't what we don't know that gives us trouble, it's what we know that ain't so.
Will Rogers

4
The Six
Abilities

We now come to abilities. They are:

Judgment	Selling ability
Communications ability	Leadership
Political astuteness	Foresight

Each ability is the sum of several of the individual qualities. If persons have great knowledge, for example, they are more likely to have a good amount of foresight. If they have little knowledge, then it will be hard for them to have much foresight.

The quality of empathy is vital to political astuteness; and emotional maturity is essential to judgment.

If persons lack empathy completely, they may still possess all the other traits to excel in sales, but they will not be good in sales.

There are a great many appraisal forms and executive quality lists that treat these combined abilities as though they were single qualities.

Judgment and communications ability are most important to managerial success, so we discuss them rather extensively.

JUDGMENT

Wisdom is the right use of knowledge. To know is not to be wise. Many men know a great deal, and are all the greater fools for it. There is no fool so great a fool as a knowing fool. But to know how to use knowledge is to have wisdom.

Spurgeon

Judgment is the most important ability. It is made up in an individual by a combination of the following qualities:

Beliefs
Integrity
Intellect
Logic
Knowledge
Emotional maturity
Independence
Realism
Ambition

What is judgment? The dictionary gives the following definitions: (1) the act or an instance of judging; (2) the ability to judge, make a decision, or form an opinion objectively, authoritatively, and wisely, especially in matters affecting action; good sense; direction.

Judgment, when used in the selection and evaluation of executives, is used in the second sense. "Some managers have good judgment" means that a good percent of the time their judging of what is to be

138

done, and *how* it is to be done, is right. Right? Meaning it is effective? Yes, but also meaning in line with the beliefs of the society and the organization.

When does "cutting a corner" get to the point that it becomes shady? When does "cunning" (skill employed in a crafty manner) become deceit? When does "dissemble" (to put on the appearance of, to feign) become deceive?

No one can state an absolute answer to the questions above. They are matters of degree and are judgeable by people, and will often be judged differently by two different persons.

It is when you *always* dissemble that your reputation will be ruined. Should you *never* dissemble? No, not never. Sometimes it would be all right. When? Well, that's hard to say. And we begin to see why judgment is important.

Beliefs are the underpinnings of judgment. Your beliefs may be in concert with those of the general society, but can you effectively put those beliefs to work via your judgment?

Beliefs are internal; judgment is bringing them into contact with the everyday world. Judgment is the outward expression of the inner beliefs.

Belief is a mental position which each person arrives at. Judgment is the act of putting that mental position to work in given circumstances, at a given time, and in a given place. There are far more people whose beliefs are in concert with society than those whose judgments are in concert with society.

Judgment is based on a hierarchical set of values and beliefs. First what is good for the country, for the company, for me, for my family, for the public, for the customers, for the world. Each company sets these in its own sequence of importance. All executives have their own sequence. Based on those sequences they make decisions. A wrong sequence is bad judgment.

What is good judgment in one company may not be good in another. Company beliefs make a judgment right or wrong.

> All the wise men were on one side, and all the fools were on the other. . . . And, be damned, Sir, all the fools were right.
>
> *Duke of Wellington*

Do not confuse judgment with knowledge. Knowledge is a contributor to judgment, but knowledge without judgment can be very dangerous. The old saying is true; "There's no fool like a knowing fool."

Judgment is three-tiered. It first has to do with goals, second with means, and third with degree.

First, your ends and goals must agree with the goals of your society and the organization for which you work. If this is not the case, your actions will be pushing in a different direction. But even if your beliefs are different, you can still have "good judgment" by recognizing and conforming to the beliefs of your society and business organization.

Second, the means you employ to achieve the ends must be socially acceptable, and acceptable to the organization. The ends do not justify the means.

Third, your implementation of the means must be in moderation. The *degree* to which you employ the correct means must be acceptable.

A Choice of Goals

The choice of the goal is critical. If you set out to maximize profit, and the board of directors has chosen to maximize growth at the expense of profit, you are in trouble—or at least in difficulty.

How do you manage the choice of the goal?

First you must continuously attempt to define it. It is often enmeshed or confused with other secondary goals (excellence of product is often a secondary goal *after* profit; sometimes it is ahead of profit). Often your superior and your superior's superior can't tell you what the *goal* is; they know the process, the how-to, but the goal is known somewhere higher up.

To a major extent, the goal(s) is a thing parallel to beliefs, and you should find the goal(s) the same way you study an organization's beliefs.

Changes in top management portend changes in beliefs (and often produce great exhibitions of continued support for the old beliefs).

The rising executive should be alert for mistakes attributed to other factors that are in truth mistakes of choice of *end*, of goal. One can fix most mistakes; one may not want to fix a difference in goals.

A Choice of Means

"Means" usually is taken to signify an action, such as borrowing money, selling stock, cutting costs, etc. But the qualities themselves are also means.

I may choose to be *independent* on an issue and use the independence as the means to an end. By disagreeing with my boss, I am being

140

independent and I may convince the boss to reconsider and adopt my solution or recommendation.

I may choose to be *bold*, to *insist* on seeing the senior vice-president without an appointment, in order to dramatize the criticalness of the problem.

I may choose to be *patient* with subordinates in order to motivate them or I might choose to be *impatient* in order to motivate them.

In all cases, the idea of opposites in qualities is at play. Should the quality I am to employ be patience or impatience; should I be independent or a follower, bold or meek?

A major part of judgment is the choice of one of the opposite qualities to use as a means. Choosing the *right* quality of the two is good judgment!

The end versus the means trade-off must be watched carefully to see that it doesn't get out of control.

The Management of Opposites

> I do not admire the excess of virtue, such as valor, unless at the same time I see an excess of the corresponding virtue; as in Epaminondas, who combined extreme valor with extreme gentleness. For otherwise there is not a rise, but a fall. A man does not show his greatness by going to one extreme, but by reaching both extremes at once, and by filling up all between.
>
> *Blaise Pascal*

The opposite of a positive trait is another positive trait—not a negative trait. The opposite of a virtue is another virtue, not a vice. The opposite of a plus (+) is another (+), not a minus (−), and not a zero.

Patience is the opposite of impatience. There are times in business affairs when the absolutely right thing to do is to be patient. And there are times when the absolutely right thing to do is to be impatient. Each quality is *good*, but they are opposites.

For example, the situation may seem to call for impatience. Subordinates have not done what they clearly agreed to do. But you decide to be patient. You *choose* the quality to exhibit.

The act of *choosing* is essential. If you merely happen to use the right quality, you are not using judgment; you are simply lucky.

It may look to others as though the executive is too nice, perhaps afraid to be strong and demanding. But the others may not know as much about the situation as the executive.

The use of a positive trait at the "wrong time" may look like a weakness of the opposite quality, when it might well be in reality (1) a failure of judgment or (2) loss of equanimity (loss of intellectual control of emotions). For example, if the situation calls for impatience (making demands) and patience is exhibited, it may appear that the executive is no good at demanding. But the executive may be very good at making demands; and may simply have misjudged what was needed.

It is up to the executive to make the decision. The executive probably has more knowledge about the situation and should choose which of the opposites to exhibit.

Let's look at some of these opposites in detail.

Not often in the story of mankind does a man [Abraham Lincoln] arrive on earth who is both steel and velvet, who is as hard as rock and soft as drifting fog, who holds in his heart and mind the paradox of terrible storm and peace unspeakable and perfect.
Carl Sandburg

Pride and humility. It is good to be proud, to have pride, to believe in your worth and efforts. It would be awful to have no confidence in yourself. Pride is self-respect.

To always be proud is a stumbling block. To always be humble is the same. You must be proud when it is right to be proud and humble when it is right to be humble.

When you have made a mistake or have not done your best, you should freely admit it and go on with business. When you have done your best you should hold up your achievements for your superiors and peers to see.

Humility is not often found on an executive quality list, yet a person without shortcomings is hardly bearable. A perfect person can become too inhuman and too uncomfortable to be with. It is too easy for people to seem to be tyrants, or know-it-alls.

Persons with pride and humility are complete and acceptable individuals. They are proud of the things they should be proud of, and also humble because they are not perfect.

Humility and objectivity are indivisible.
Erich Fromm

Without some humility, it is difficult for people to be followers, to take directions.

In a recent survey by W. A. Delaney sent to 97 general managers, vice-presidents and presidents, the question was asked, "Can you easily admit to making a mistake?" Ninety-six percent said yes.

142

"Ah," you say, "they can admit a mistake because they're at the top." A chicken-and-egg type of question. Can they say easily yes because they are general managers or are they general managers because they have the humility to admit mistakes? The latter, I contend, is more often the case.

> It is no great thing to be humble when you are brought low; but to be humble when you are praised is a great and rare attainment.
>
> *St. Bernard*

Patience and impatience. Patience springs from your inner beliefs. It is closely coupled with emotional maturity. You either believe in being patient with people or you don't. Without patience you cannot be an effective people manager, and without being an effective people manager, it is unlikely that you can be an effective executive.

There are many times when the executive should exhibit the opposite of patience. There are times in human affairs when the right, correct, and just action of superiors is to be impatient with their subordinates. To never exhibit impatience is to fail to teach the others the value of time and to fail to point out to them their mistakes, errors, or lack of achievement.

> Gentleness is a divine trait: Nothing is so strong as gentleness, and nothing is so gentle as real strength.
>
> *Ralph W. Sockman*

Fierceness and meekness. Should you be fierce, or meek? You must be both—at the right times. Fierce is the same as intense, and earlier we saw that quality described. Here we want to focus on the fact that the opposite of fierce also needs to be present and used by the executive.

Individuals who are always fierce are unbearable. They make poor subordinates, poor followers. But they should be fierce more often than meek. Judgment decides when.

Let's leave opposites for a while; we'll discuss them again later.

> Tenderness is passion in repose.
>
> *Joseph Joubert*

> It is hard to be strong and not rash.
>
> *Japanese proverb*

Beware of people who don't know how to say "I am sorry." They are weak and frightened, and will sometimes at the slightest provocation fight with the desperate ferocity of a frightened animal that feels cornered.

Thomas Szasz

The Management of Degree

Perhaps the best and easiest way to describe degree is to show the following from *The Double Task of Language* by S. I. Hayakawa:

> Bertrand Russell, on a British Broadcasting Company radio program called the "Brain Trust," gave the following 'conjugation' of an 'irregular verb':
>
> I am firm.
>
> You are obstinate.
>
> He is a pig-headed fool.
>
> The *New Statesman* and *Nation,* quoting the above as a model, offered prizes to readers who sent in the best 'irregular verbs' of this kind. Here are some of the published entries.
>
> I am sparkling. You are unusually talkative. He is drunk.
>
> I am righteously indignant. You are annoyed. He is making a fuss about nothing.
>
> I am fastidious. You are fussy. He is an old woman.
>
> I am a creative writer. You have journalistic flair. He is a prosperous hack.
>
> I am beautiful. You have quite good features. She isn't bad-looking, if you like that type.
>
> I daydream. You are an escapist. He ought to see a psychiatrist.
>
> I have about me something of the subtle, haunting, mysterious fragrance of the Orient. You rather overdo it, dear. She stinks.

Any quality that is used too often or too strongly will tend to overpower the opposite quality, and will be viewed as a fault. "That person is strong" is usually an accolade. But let's put some adverbs in front of "strong."

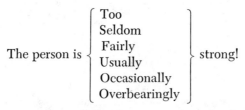

The person is { Too / Seldom / Fairly / Usually / Occasionally / Overbearingly } strong!

Strength is good—if it is not abused. The "choice" of abusing it or not is judgment at work.

We now get to the idea of a vice. If the opposite of a virtue is another virtue, what is a vice?

A vice is a virtue out of control. It is a strength too strong. It is an overpowering, either in degree or frequency, use of a virtue.

$$
\text{A person who is too}
\left\{
\begin{array}{l}
\text{humble} \\
\text{proud} \\
\text{fierce} \\
\text{meek} \\
\text{patient} \\
\text{impatient}
\end{array}
\right\}
\text{is}
\left\{
\begin{array}{l}
\text{abject} \\
\text{arrogant} \\
\text{frantic, manic} \\
\text{timid} \\
\text{uncaring} \\
\text{despotic}
\end{array}
\right.
$$

> Both absolute power and absolute faith are instruments of dehumanization.
>
> *Eric Hoffer*

Any quality of a person can go too far. Now, combine the idea of opposites with the idea of degree, and you can construct a table as follows:

Opposites and Degrees

Unacceptable vice	Acceptable virtues Opposite of		Unacceptable vice
Timid	Meek	⟷ Fierce	Cruel
Uncaring	Patient	⟷ Impatient	Despotic
Fanatic	Determined	⟷ Easy-going	Uncaring
Manic	Dynamic	⟷ Steady	Plodding
Zany	Colorful	⟷ Steadfast	Dull
Impetuous	Energetic	⟷ Calm	Asleep
Unprepared	Extemporaneous	⟷ Prepared	Unchanging
Docile	Faithful	⟷ Independent	Exotic
Overreactive	Fast	⟷ Careful	Leaden
Foolhardy	Fearless	⟷ Cautious	Frightened
Inflexible	Firm	⟷ Flexible	Spineless
Dogmatic	Opinionated	⟷ Open-minded	Wishy-washy
Machiavellian	Politic	⟷ Natural	Naive
Arrogant	Proud	⟷ Humble	Abject
Tyrannical	Relentless	⟷ Compromising	Uncaring
Carefree	Independent	⟷ Loyal	Fawning

> Valor lies just half-way between rashness and cowardice.
>
> *Miguel de Cervantes*

> There is a mean in everything. Even virtue itself hath its stated limits, which, not being strictly observed, it ceases to be virtue.
>
> *Horace*

The degree's border is obscure. Where is the line between proud and arrogant; humble and abject? "It is not enough to just point out that there is a crossing from good to bad," you might say. "Tell us how to see where the border is!"

Unfortunately, this cannot be done. Each situation is unique, therefore the border must be set "on the wing" at the moment of the action.

When to be proud? How proud? How much to resist? How long? It depends! It depends on:

you	your competitors
your boss	your home life
your boss's boss	your health
your subordinates	the situation
your peers	your goals

And on, and on, and on. This doesn't help much, but there is no way to qualify good judgment.

Courage is always greatest when blended with meekness.
E. H. Chapin

From bad judgment to terrible judgment. We have already shown how exhibiting the wrong virtue of the pair at a given time could look like weakness, when it may be just poor judgment. You shouldn't be proud when the situation demands that you be humble.

But you can compound the error by not only being on the wrong end of the spectrum but by being beyond the acceptable range on the wrong side. It is *never* good to be beyond the acceptable range; it is doubly wrong to be beyond it on the wrong side. See Fig. 4.1.

Sometimes the strengths people possess are often their weaknesses, not only in the sense that the strengths become so comfortable that they are loath to leave them, to rise above them to a higher strength but also in the sense that strengths become such ready, reliable, and easy-to-use tools that they are often used without thinking. They spring into use from habit, often before their users even know they are using them. The strength's very success make it more popular to the user.

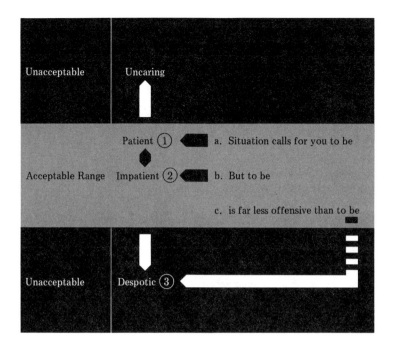

Fig. 4.1   Bad judgment.

The easiest and most often seen example is an overuse of fierceness, a mixture of insistence and willpower. So many successful executives have found that if they yell and stomp and threaten, two things happen.

First, subordinates will exhaust all possible solutions before coming forward with a problem. This is good and bad. It keeps out of fire-breathers' offices problems that can be solved without them. It also brings late to their offices problems that need them.

Second, it will motivate—by fear, admittedly—subordinates to perform. They'll perform—or else. This is effective—the question is would executives be more effective if they were to exhibit fierceness a little less often and meekness a little more often?

> The test of a first-rate intelligence is the ability to hold two opposed ideas in the mind at the same time, and still retain the ability to function.
>
> *F. Scott Fitzgerald*

Opposites everywhere. The qualities are pulling in opposite directions. Ambition pulls against integrity. Cheerfulness pulls against willpower. Empathy pulls against insistence. Willpower pulls against realism. Independence is the direct opposite of loyalty!

147

All men are bizarre and inexplicable composites of
contraries; that is what those fellows who turn out novels
. . . refuse to understand. Their men are all of one piece.
There are no such creatures. There are ten men in
one man, and often they all show themselves within
one hour, under certain circumstances.

Eugène Delacroix

The conflict between loyalty and integrity. Sometimes the only way to
be loyal is to refuse to go along with the team on a project or course
of action that violates your principles. At those times, despite the fact
that your action will be mighty unpopular, you must follow *your own*
values, and refuse to go along.

Look at the following report from the *Los Angeles Times:* The
district judge is sentencing the ex-attorney general. Had Kleindienst
"answered accurately and fully [to the FBI] . . . it would have reflected
great credit on [him] but would have reflected discredit on another
individual." Like Kleindienst's boss. The judge said that Kleindienst
was motivated by "a heart that is too loyal and considerate of others."

Loyalty versus independence. Mr. A. is loyal; he follows the boss,
supports him, and doesn't go off on his own. Obviously the boss appre-
ciates him.

But suppose the boss quits tomorrow. Would you want to follow
Mr. A? For years he's followed, been loyal. He has shown no leadership on his own. Obviously independence, a primary quality, is in conflict with loyalty, a secondary quality.

Loyalty is a "masked" word, the meaning of which we can pick as
we choose. Leaders can't be *all* loyal, or else they will *not* be leaders.

I think what has chiefly struck me in human beings is
their lack of consistency. I have never seen people all
of a piece. It has amazed me that the most incongruous
traits should exist in the same person and, for all that,
yield a plausible harmony.

W. Somerset Maugham

The conflict between ambition and integrity. One of the tugs that goes
on constantly within the individual is the opposite pulls of ambition
and integrity. Not that all ambition is pulling in the opposite direction
from integrity; not at all. But it pulls in that direction often enough that
it deserves special attention.

Read the statement made by Jeb Magruder to the judge as he was
being sentenced for his part in the Watergate affair: "I know what I
have done, and your honor knows what I have done. . . . Somewhere
between my ambition and my ideals, I lost my ethical compass."

148

The better is the enemy of the good. Many development engineers will just not stop improving the new gizmo, so it never gets produced as a stable, steady project.

The future and the present are enemies. We put money in the bank for a *future* purchase. We spend profits today to build a plant for seven years from now. Or we delay a research project so that this year's profit will be as high as that of last year.

The present is the enemy of the past. We all tend to interpret the past, write our history, select our heroes, in such a way as to maximize our present endeavors. Propaganda does this. Totalitarianism requires the rewriting of history to take care of the present (and the future).

> Men love liberty because it protects them from control and humiliation by others, and thus affords them the possibility of dignity. They loathe liberty because it throws them back on their own abilities and resources, and thus confronts them with the possibility of insignificance.
>
> *Thomas Szasz*

Freedom and order are at odds. We are not free to run our automobiles through red lights. To do so would be disorderly.

> Gravity is a mysterious carriage of the body, invented to cover the defects of the mind.
>
> *La Rochefoucauld*

Form and essence. Many organizations place too much importance on form, or image. In a company run by salesmen, appearance alone is enough to make some significant progress up the ladder of success. Actual accomplishments are secondary, especially if the company is very successful.

Brilliant, independent individuals who join this organization but do not fit the image, mold, and culture pattern have their effectiveness immediately and dramatically reduced. They are outsiders and are never welcomed into the in-group.

This is a situation with losses on all sides. Clearly, the individuals lose who do not fit and who do not have the personality or looks to fit the pattern of the new group. They are losers because they cannot get ahead in the organization. The bigger loser, however, is the organization. It has so structured itself that it cannot accept new ideas and criticism unless it is presented by its own kind of person and in the manner and form which is acceptable.

149

Thunder is good, thunder is impressive; but it is the
lightning that does the work.
Mark Twain

On the other hand, an absence of form is not excusable just because the essence is there. Individuals have no right to completely ignore form just because they are brilliant competent individuals. They should try to "fit" into the flow of the organization to some extent.

Perhaps brilliant inventors can be allowed to get away with eccentricity, but not rising executives. They must *conform* to a major (not total) extent to the formal conventions of their society, industry, company, and division.

Form can be very important. Many use it to awe and to impress. And it does awe and impress, and so it is a usable tool of the manager.

Beware of all enterprises that require new clothes.
Henry David Thoreau

To care and not to care. The line, "Teach me to care and not to care," from T. S. Eliot's poem *Ash Wednesday,* speaks volumes. For, indeed, effective executives must care, and yet must not care. They must care, for from this caring comes their drive, their energy, and their willpower. They must care that things go correctly and that the endeavor succeeds.

They also must not care too much. If a strange twist of fate destroys their plans and their year-long activity, they must be able to take that in stride and not become upset and irritable. They must have resilience.

The story is told of a follower of Mahatma Gandhi (the leader of India's struggle to rid itself of British rule in the 1940s) who said to him that India would be free only if the Mahatma authorized violence.

The Mahatma answered calmly, "Then I guess India will never be free."

The Mahatma cared very deeply about India's goal to free itself from British rule, yet he would not authorize violence. He cared and yet he did not care. He had emotional maturity.

Said another way, it is the difference between being "end-oriented" or "means-oriented." Gandhi was both. He wanted India free, but he also cared very deeply about the means.

Teach us to care and not to care; teach us to sit still even
among these rocks, our peace is in His will.
T. S. Eliot

150

Professionalism and amateurism. It is not clear that it is always best to have all the important things handled by the professional. Often amateurs bring a new spirit. Often they bring a fresh approach, unencumbered with conventional wisdom. They don't know "it's impossible."

> Never tell a young person that something is impossible. God may have been waiting for centuries for somebody ignorant enough of the impossible to do that thing.
>
> *Dr. J. A. Holmes*

Finesse or force? One can solve a problem by "selling" all the participants on an agreed solution, making compromises where necessary. On the opposite side of the scale one could demand, insist, threaten, and bully the participants into agreement.

Sometimes force is required. Hopefully not too often, but sometimes. To think it is never required is as wrong as to think it is always required.

For rising managers to be all one-sided, i.e., all force or all finesse, is an indication that they will not go too high.

> A very capable manager was being told by his boss that he was very effective in resolving problems. "But let me tell you, your reputation is Joe Brown, Street Fighter. Whenever there is a street fight, you'll be thrown in and that is not all bad, because you are very valuable in that role.
>
> "But if you want to be a vice-president, you have got to soften the strength of your image. You've got to be much more than just a street fighter. You must show diplomacy and judgment."

If there is a "time for every purpose under heaven," then there is a time to be fierce and a time to be meek; proud and humble; patient and impatient; bellicose and pacific; aloof and involved. There is no *rule* that covers all situations; the only rule is to *select* a quality from a set of two opposites to use, and to manage your expression of that quality to the just-right degree, tuning as you go and the situation unfolds.

> My policy is to have no policy.
>
> *Abraham Lincoln*

> After a year-long, bitter, internal struggle, a young manager finally succeeded in winning a large new contract. His boss's boss's boss, a marketing vice-president, called him in. "Joe, I want to congratulate you. You have done a super job. And I know it has not been easy. You have a great future."

"Thank you, Al."

"There is only one area I would say you can do better in—and that is that you seem to have a tendency to fight rather than negotiate. Everything in this program seemed to be a battle."

"Yes, that's true."

"And I think at least some of that is due to your style."

"Oh."

"But that is not *the* key—you won the thing. That is the important thing. Well done."

"Thank, you, Al."

The young manager went back to his office and thought for ten minutes about the meeting. He called and asked to see the vice-president.

"Al, I thought about what you said and you may be right, but I don't think you know how bad the opposition was in this effort. There is a little episode I never told you about that demonstrates how bad it was.

"I had been trying to get a new coordinator for the proposal from the engineering division. They had one who was not experienced enough to carry the load. I asked the vice-president. To a gruff "Why?" I explained the inexperience. 'Write me a letter,' was his reaction.

"A week later, late in the afternoon, I was meeting with several of the vice-president's subordinates. He came in and asked what was going on. His right hand explained that I was complaining about the lack of progress, which I was.

" 'Have you met our new coordinator, the one you wanted?' the vice-president asked.

" 'No,' I said, pleased to hear that one had been appointed. 'I'd like to thank you for naming him.'

" 'Well, you should meet him fast,' the vice-president said, 'because he's going to get you. He's going to put your neck in the wringer and squeeze.' He twisted the neck of an imaginary chicken as he said this.

"It was bitter, Al, bitter and personal and all-out war. I had no choice."

Al looked sober. "You're right. I take back what I said earlier."

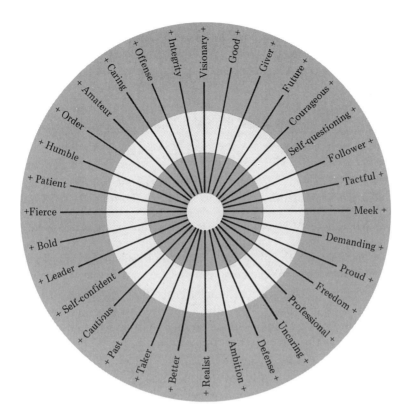

Fig. 4.2   At any given time in a given circumstance, it is *the* right thing to be on one side of the opposites, and at another time, the other side.

"There is a time for every purpose under heaven," and the opposite of a positive is yet another positive. Avoid becoming too fond of either side of the balance shown in Fig. 4.2.

> Do I contradict myself? Very well then I contradict myself. (I am large, I contain multitudes.)
> *Walt Whitman*

Common Sense

Many rising managers are so eager to please their bosses that they seem to take leave of their senses at times. They will "jump off the bridge" if the company says that is what is right. They do not want to fight error or outdated methods; they want to belong, to support.

This is especially true of managers in large companies. Bureaucracies are not tolerant of criticism from within (or from without).

Rising executives should use their common sense to decide whether or not the company policy is right or wrong, to be followed, or to make an exception.

Common sense in an uncommon degree is what the world calls wisdom.

Samuel Coleridge

Nonthinking bureaucrats will always argue against exceptions. Yet the real world demands exceptions. Consider the following example:

A sizeable plant had two start-stop work times in order to reduce the traffic jam each morning and evening. When a new business opened nearby, the plant had to move both start-stop times by ten minutes to avoid jams.

The general manager put out a letter to all managers, giving them their new times. The letter stated that no exceptions would be made and that any requests for an exception was to be brought to the director of personnel.

After a few weeks, a young woman of about 30 asked to visit the general manager. She stated that for three years she had been coming to work 15 minutes late and leaving 15 minutes late because she had to transport her children to school. This arrangement had seemed to be satisfactory to all. Now, with the new start-stop time she would have to be 25 minutes late starting and stopping.

Her manager had told her that this was unacceptable, and that she either had to come to work on time or leave the business. She stated that she believed her manager wished he could let her come in 25 minutes late; but that he had been overruled.

The general manager investigated. Her facts were all correct. In addition, she was a good employee and performer and was well liked by all her fellow workers. The different start-stop time she had been following had caused no trouble or resentment. The decision to not allow her to start 25 minutes late had been made by the third-level manager (her manager's manager's manager) and the personnel director, and was based on the desire not to "set a precedent."

The woman's manager and his manager both wanted to let her start late. They had been overruled.

The general manager could get no more reason from the personnel director or the third level manager than that they did not want to "set a precedent."

154

He overruled them, pointing out to them that the precedent had been set three years before, that it had caused no trouble and had not set off a flood of similar requests.

> The executive exists to make sensible exceptions to general rules.
>
> *Elting E. Morison*

The willingness to follow the policy—in this case the general manager's letter—had interfered with simple common sense. (A check five years after the decision still revealed no problems and no similar requests.)

Personnel people often tend to become, like lawyers, lovers of the written law, in this case, company policy. In large companies, the policy book can run to a thousand pages, covering every kind of eventuality. The personnel people must have fine minds to gain the knowledge of the policy, but that is not enough. They must guard against making the policy sacred. They must also use judgment and let policy be a guide rather than an absolute. The personnel staff who does not do this is only one-half a staff. "Tell me what is right; not just what the policy says," states the wise manager.

> We must never throw away a bushel of truth because it happens to contain a few grains of chaff.
>
> *Dean Stanley*

A vice-president spent 45 minutes listening to a third-line manager argue with the personnel director over how long a maternity leave an employee could take. The policy said six weeks. The employee had been told by her doctor that the baby would be more emotionally stable if it were nursed. She wanted an 18-week leave of absence (without pay) so that she could nurse the baby.

Personnel didn't want to set a precedent; management (bless them) wanted to accommodate the employee, who was an excellent performer, needed in her group, and anxious to come back to work.

After 45 minutes of detailed medical argument—was it or was it not better for a child's emotional health—the vice-president came to his senses. "Nonsense. Give her the 18 weeks."

No adverse results occurred. The employee came back to work after 18 weeks.

> He not only overflowed with learning, but stood in the slop.
>
> *Sydney Smith*

Common sense is vital. Ask yourself the question, "If I were on the other side, is what I would be asking reasonable?" If the answer is yes and the policy says no, fight the policy. Something is wrong with it.

It is easy to see why judgment is so important. Without it, virtues are called into play at the wrong time—and therefore become vices. Or too much of the right virtue is exhibited, and therefore a vice is exhibited!

When one's strengths can become weaknesses so easily, it is easy to see why the control of the qualities—judgment—is more important than the qualities themselves!

Good judgment is (1) selecting the appropriate ends (goals), (2) choosing the correct quality to attain those goals; and (3) implementing the quality within acceptable bounds.

Bad judgment can be:

- A choice of goals different from those the boss would choose. (Instead of bad judgment this divergence may be more accurately labeled different beliefs.)

- A choice of the wrong virtue of a pair of opposites for the situation. To choose to be bold when the boss thinks you should be meek is bad judgment.

- The choice of the right virtue of a pair but the display of too much of it! The situation, the boss agrees, demands impatience, but you exhibited intolerance and tyranny by going too far along the virtue scale (the boss judges).

Whether you are judged positively or negatively depends on the judge's base of information and judgment. But only you can judge yourself. Only you know whether you were patient or permissive; or impatient or domineering.

To everything there is a season, and a time to every purpose under heaven;
A time to be born, and a time to die; a time to plant, and a time to pluck up that which is planted;
A time to kill, and a time to heal; a time to break down, and a time to build up
A time to weep, and a time to laugh; a time to mourn, and a time to dance;
A time to cast away stones, and a time to gather stones together; a time to embrace, and a time to refrain from embracing;

A time to get, and a time to lose; a time to keep, and a time to cast away;

A time to tear, and a time to sew; a time to keep silence, and a time to speak;

A time to love, and a time to hate; a time of war, and a time of peace.

Ecclesiastes 3:1–8

It is the stretched soul that makes music, and souls are stretched by the pull of opposites—opposite bents, tastes, yearnings. Where there is no polarity—where energies flow smoothly in one direction—there will be much doing but no music.

Eric Hoffer

Knowledge is proud that it knows so much; wisdom is humble that it knows no more.

William Cowper

Never be haughty to the humble; never be humble to the haughty.

Jefferson Davis

There is a determinable difference between the apparent casualness of mastery and the carelessness of ignorance.

Charles B. Rogers

Great men never make bad use of their superiority; they see it, and feel it, and are not less modest. The more they have, the more they know their own deficiencies.

Jean Jacques Rousseau

Many would be cowards if they had courage enough.

Thomas Fuller

The arrogance of the learned—that degenerative disease which destroys knowledge and deprives it of beauty and effectiveness.

Peter Drucker

Anyone aware of the imperfections inherent in human affairs is hardly capable of total commitment. Part of him will inevitably remain uncommitted. It is this perch of uncommitment which makes an act of self-sacrifice sublimely human, and distinguishes the man of faith from the fanatic.

Eric Hoffer

Gentleness is a divine trait: Nothing is so strong as gentleness, and nothing is so gentle as real strength.

Ralph W. Sockman

In many people's lives, the need for attention is the dominant motive. This explains why people often espouse one opinion one time, and its opposite soon after: it does not matter what they say, so long as it draws attention to them. Tolstoy was a dramatic example.

In his biography of Tolstoy, Henri Troyat remarks that Tolstoy's family and friends "... could not understand how he had married an upperclass girl after declaring that 'to marry a woman of society is to swallow the whole poison of civilization.'"

Psychoanalysts interpret this sort of behavior as the expression of ambivalence. Moralists call it hypocrisy. It may be both of these things. But it often is simply the result of a passion for attention, which cannot be as easily satisfied through consistent behavior.

Thomas Szasz

A man should never be ashamed to own he has been in the wrong, which is but saying in other words, that he is wiser today than he was yesterday.

Alexander Pope

It is better to be both right and consistent, but if one must choose, he must choose to be right.

W. S. Churchill

The bravest are the tenderest.
The loving are the daring.

Henry W. Longfellow

Humility and objectivity are indivisible.

Erich Fromm

The person who cannot accept his ignorance cannot learn.

Thomas Szasz

Human relations are problematic because men are driven by opposing but often equally powerful needs and passions, especially the needs for security and freedom. To satisfy the need for security, people seek closeness and commitment, and the more they attain these, the more oppressed they feel. To satisfy their needs for freedom, people seek independence and detachment, and the more they attain these, the more isolated they feel. As in all such things, the wise pursue the golden mean, and the lucky attain it.

Thomas Szasz

[People] range from animals to gods. They pray for you and they prey on you. They are bears for punishment and brutes for revenge. They want to be Everyone, Everywhere, Everything. Their rest-

158

lessness fills them with wonderings and spurs them into wanderings. They are creatures of moods and modes. They try to look different, but deep down underneath they are all alike. They are hero-worshippers and idol-destroyers. They are quick to take sides and quick to swing from side to side. They like individuals who can appraise and praise them. People must be taken as they are and still they want to be taken as they aren't. They have their ways and want to get away with them. They cry for the moon and wail for a place in the sun. They are happiest in the hurly-burly, giving and taking, making and losing, to the tune of a hurdy-gurdy. They try everything once and seldom stop to think twice. But they are blessed with nine lives and often strike twelve at eleventh hours. With people all things are possible; without them, all things are impossible. They must forever be felt and dealt with. To lose contact with them is to lose contact with life.

P. K. Thomajan

COMMUNICATIONS ABILITY

Communications ability is essential to achieving *and* using power at a high level. The following qualities combine to form a person's communications ability:

Emotional maturity	Cheerfulness
Independence	Logic
Courage and boldness	Knowledge
Willpower	Intellect
Resilience and durability	Nimble-mindedness
Empathy	

Communications ability is absolutely essential. The higher you go, the more important it is that you communicate extremely well.

Communications ability is a combination of qualities and skills. Clearly, intellect and vocabulary are a part of communications ability. Perhaps not as clearly, emotional maturity, courage, and empathy are also very important to communicating.

What do we mean, "communicate?" To give or receive information. Notice that the definition does not restrict the act of passing information by stating it is done "verbally" or "in writing" or any other way. It is simply "giving or receiving information."

Communications is much more than words, be they written or spoken. Physical gestures can completely change the meaning of the words, as can tone of voice, inflection, intensity, or pitch. A court case years ago was settled when the judge quoted the title of a popular song, "Your lips tell me no-no, but there's yes-yes in your eyes."

To See the Real World

Management must be able to "see things as they really are," and not to see them as they would like them to be, nor as others would like them to see things.

How well you *must* communicate will depend on your level and scope of command, but your level and scope of command will depend directly on how well you can communicate. The higher you go, the broader your scope, the more people under your direction, the more things you must understand and control. As your scope grows, the hours in the day do not.

You must get information and give information. If your ability to communicate is poor, even though your subordinates and peers and superiors may be giving you good information, you yourself may distort the good information to the point where only a portion of it comes through correctly and some is received garbled but not recognized as garbled. The likelihood of your making correct decisions is greatly lessened.

Conversely, if you are giving directions to your subordinate and the message is not clear (or you do not see that the message is not received clearly), then it is likely that your instructions will not be carried out, or worse, be misinterpreted and carried out.

Purpose—The Reason for Communicating

Speech was given to man to disguise his thoughts.
Talleyrand

"People communicate to tell us what they think." This may be true, but all too frequently there is quite a different reason for communicating. When Winston Churchill spoke it was to tell others what he was thinking. It takes a certain amount of courage and self-security to always tell people what you think. It exposes to them your thoughts and invites their criticism. Unfortunately, too many people do not communicate in order to state what is on their minds.

Think like a wise man but communicate in the language
of the people.
William Butler Yeats

You communicate in order to:

- Let people know what you are thinking.
- Keep people from knowing what you are thinking.
- Give directions and information.
- Find out what other people know or are thinking.

160

- Impress people with your knowledge.
- Help your own thinking process.
- Pass time.

Many people communicate in business situations in order to have time pass. Franklin Delano Roosevelt would filibuster a visitor and use up the allotted time so that the visitor was not able to ask him about things that he did not want to discuss.

Many subordinates will go on at great length and in great detail about matters that are not pertinent in order to keep the boss from finding out the shallowness of their grasp of the subject. This may be categorized as "cowing." Cowing means to present evidence of hard work as a substitute for understanding.

> A project wasn't going well, and the boss suspected it. The project manager presented a report to the boss that was beautifully drawn with artwork, and lists of figures to three decimal points. The figures were meaningless. For example, 196 visits were made. These were broken into a long series of items, stating that 14 had been made on state agencies. The list looked like this:
>
> | | |
> |---|---|
> | 14 state agencies | 7.14% |
> | 22 city agencies | 11.22% |
> | 43 charitable agencies | 21.93% |

All this was "puffing"; it was all superfluous. What the boss wanted was the *results* of the calls, the conclusions. Unfortunately, there weren't any. But instead of admitting this, the project manager tried to bluff his way through the meeting. He failed, and took several steps backward on the ladder.

Unfortunately, the opposite of cowing can also be a problem at times. Let's label it "bulling." Bulling means to present evidence of understanding as a substitute for hard work.

> The task force had agreed that the gamma product should be introduced, but wanted to "prove" it to the general manager. Each member of the task force was assigned to research one section of the marketplace, to do a survey, and report the results. One member of the task force presented his results in a brilliant logical postulation of why that section of the marketplace needed the product. Brilliant though it was, it was simply a better restatement of premises already agreed upon. It accomplished nothing. It wasn't what was wanted. A simply "I'm not finished yet" would have been better.

There is an old saying that goes, "Always speak the truth, but do not always tell it."

A certain vice-president is incapable of telling a lie, regardless of how severely the truthful information may damage the cause which he espouses. However, I have seen him go through meetings without bringing up certain information that was detrimental to his cause. On a few occasions I have seen peers, superiors, or subordinates finally pin him with direct questions which, try as he might, he could no longer avoid. The truth then came out.

When thou art obliged to speak, be sure to speak the truth; for equivocation is half way to lying, and lying is the whole way to hell.
William Penn

Another reason for speaking is to parade one's knowledge and intelligence. Many times in meetings people ask questions, usually with a lot of detail contained in the question. The direction in which the question leads often appears to be tangential to the purpose of the meeting. I always wonder whether the question is being asked in order to gain information or in order to show the assembled audience how smart the questioners are, how much knowledge they have, or how perceptive and incisive they are.

Shape the Communications Depending on Its Direction!

Too often descriptions and write-ups on communicating assume that communicating in one direction is the same as communicating in any other direction. It is true that there are basic communicating skills and techniques that will work in all directions. However, you must realize that there are at least five different directions in communicating, and that you must choose your manner, scope, and technique of communicating based upon which one of the five directions you are engaged in. The five are:

- Upward to one's superiors,
- Sideways to one's peers,
- Downward to one's subordinates,
- Outward toward one's customers, and
- Sideways to the experts.

The experts are the lawyers, doctors, financial and/or technical experts that one comes into contact with. Each direction calls for some different skill or attitude. What will work well for communications with peers may or may not work well for communicating with subordinates or customers.

162

Upward? Be Pertinent

It is usually important in upward communications to be pertinent, to talk about what the boss wants to talk about.

Often I have, with great fervor, pressed my views on some important subject on my superiors, only to be frustrated by their inattention. In many cases, my views have turned out to be correct, only doubling my frustration. The superiors in these cases had their minds on other things, and chose not to communicate on my subject. Try as I might, I could not reach them. In upward communication, it is often more important to be pertinent than to be right.

> Language is the armory of the human mind, and at once contains the trophies of its past and the weapons of its future conquests.
>
> *Samuel Coleridge*

Let's look at various aspects of communicating and we will break them into different groups. One will be *skill*, which covers vocabulary, delivery, techniques, and some communicating "tricks."

The others will be *content* and *emotions* which cover demeanor, appearances, and "tricks."

Skill. No survey exists showing how the world's people communicate, but none is needed. Almost all communication is verbal, exchanging information by the spoken *word*.

The most important single thing affecting the ability to communicate is one's ability with words. Ideas and facts lay safely in the harbor of the mind. In order to transport them into the mind of another, people use words and the trouble begins. What a word means to one it may not mean to another.

The fact that the meaning does not arrive intact in the other mind should not surprise us. We should expect this! And it often would be better that no idea arrive at all, for when only half the idea reaches its destination, and the two parties believe they have communicated, then the greatest misunderstandings will occur!

The greater your array of words, that is, your vocabulary, the better your chances of getting your meaning across.

An independent research foundation, the Johnson-O'Connor Research Foundation, states that the one key to measuring potential achievement is to measure a person's vocabulary. They also point out that it is not one's grasp of "five-dollar, six-syllable" words, but the grasp, and the precise use, of the one-dollar, two-syllable words that measure a vocabulary.

Vocabulary is something that we can learn. Yet too few managers continue an effort to improve their vocabulary.

Words are the voice of the heart.
Confucius

Let's look beyond vocabulary to the use of language and some techniques to improve communications.

Communicate in triplicate. If a subject is important, repeat yourself least twice, using slightly different words each time, watching carefully the other's reaction to your words. Amazingly often the first or second set of words is "understood" and agreement is expressed, only to find that the third set of synonyms cause trouble. No agreement is reached; a problem exists.

This technique has saved me from bad misunderstandings. The better your vocabulary, the better you can use this triplicate technique.

Shorthand. A recent study group I participated with had a very complicated task. In order to communicate with each other, they packaged great meanings into labels such as:

Plan A	*Plan B*
Invest $1 Million	Invest $3 Million
Two Years to Pay Off	One Year to Pay Off
Slow Start	Fast Start
Small Risk	Big Risk

"Plan A" to each work group member spoke volumes. Whenever a new person was told about the alternate plans, much time was spent describing the plans.

People who have worked together for a long time also speak to each other in shorthand. One method of gaining information is to observe which people in a meeting speak to each other in shorthand. I have often been surprised to find unlikely and unguessed-at close working relationships between two people. I saw these people communicating "in shorthand," and changed my strategy in some debates.

Don't overdo shorthand. Empathy must come into play in communicating in shorthand. To talk in shorthand is fine, as long as the participants in the conversation understand the shorthand. If one of the group does not, it is rude for the others to continue to use the shorthand. It is akin to whispering.

If you speak to an audience and use shorthand or jargon, you may be thought arrogant. To think that the burden is on the audience to figure out the message is just arrogance.

Many brilliant individuals struggle hard to put their work into intelligible form. "I've decided," an inventor once told me, "that the burden of making the work understandable is on the inventors, not the listener. And if inventors cannot make it understandable to an intelli-

164

gent person who will take the time to listen, then they just don't understand what they are talking about."

He's right, of course. (The intelligent executive takes the time to listen to the inventor.)

Delivery. Any message is sent more effectively if it is sent with fervor, with emotion and gestures. Simply to choose even the exact words and to state them without emotion is not effective communication.

I've listened to many very capable managers who deliver their messages in a strict monotone. Their messages get across only if the listeners are keenly interested in them. Once the listeners get what they want, the communication usually ends. The sender is not in control. Unless the message content is captivating, the speaker loses the listeners' attention.

Conversely the speaker who is always dramatic, even when the subject is not, loses the listener who has witnessed the dramatics on many occasions. The dramatics must match the content, or they will hurt, not help, the message.

Inflection. Words are like vessels in which we place our ideas, send them off across the seas between individuals, and hope that they will be received at the port of some other mind, still bearing the exact meanings which we put into them. However, it is not enough to merely send the ideas off to sea in words. We must send them off with fervor, with conviction, with anger, with sincerity, with humor. These emotions give greater speed to the vessel, greater durability and/or greater delivery power with which to reach the port of the other's mind.

Take a very simple sentence, "I do not want to do that." Said in a very relaxed way the sentence is a statement of fact. However, change the emphasis on words and one gets a very different meaning from the sentence. A sharp ringing "*I* do not want to do that," clearly conveys the impression that many others do want to do it and that I, the speaker, am aware that they want to do it, but that I am willing to brave the censure of the others and choose not to do it.

A wailing "I do not *want* to do that" would lead the listener to believe that although I do not want to do that, I indeed may be forced by circumstances (apparently beyond my control) to do the things that I in truth do not want to do.

If we change the emphasis of the sentence and put all the emotion and ring into the last word, that, then we get a sentence, "I do not want to do *that*." Once again this changes the meaning of the sentence dramatically, and indicates to a listener that, although I do not want to do this particular thing, it's clear that I do desire to do something.

Listen to yourself. Do you listen to yourself? Do you *hear* the words and decide whether they are "right," i.e., the words, inflection, tone, and volume *you* want?

If you do not listen to yourself, try to. It can be done and it is an excellent check. Time after time I have heard myself coming through in the wrong tone, or at the wrong level. Midway in a meeting with a senior vice-president, I suddenly realized that I was "whiney." I had a why-are-you-all-picking-on-me tone. I was not aware that it had crept into my speech (probably because I had lost an important dispute in the meeting immediately prior to this one). A combination of the reaction of the listeners and hearing my own tone alerted me. I changed tone the next time I made a point, switching to a more belligerent, righteous delivery.

I don't remember if I won the dispute; I just remember vividly the act of hearing myself conveying the wrong tone of voice!

Language was invented to ask questions. Answers may be
given by grunts and gestures, but questions must be
spoken. Humanness came of age when man asked the
first question. Social stagnation results not from lack of
answers but from the absence of the impulse to ask
questions.

Eric Hoffer

Questioning. The ability to ask the precisely right question and to follow it with succeeding detailed questions on the critical point is an attribute of the good executive. Without this questioning technique, many meetings and communications are aimless and haphazard. Information is gained or exchanged at a very random rate, if at all.

It is a pleasure to watch a capable executive, after listening patiently (or impatiently) to a presentation, penetrate with precise and clear questions to the key points that have been left fuzzy and/or unexplained.

Asking the right question is a result of:

- knowledge—what to probe, what is important,
- verbal skills—which words to use,
- courage—I'm willing to accept the answer, even if it hurts,
- willpower and logic—get to a result, not just information,
- insistence—insist on an answer; don't let the point slip by.

This last point is very vital when stakes are high; too many let the unpleasantness of a confrontation stop them from driving home to a conclusion—and weeks or months later this failure to "force the issue" will be seen as a glaring mistake; not always, but often enough, and that is too often.

On her deathbed, Gertrude Stein was said to have been
asked if she had any answers to the great problems of
life. She allegedly replied, "Answers? What I need
are the questions!"

166

Listening. Listening is, of course, a critical element in communicating. One of the key secrets to being a good listener is to *not* be thinking of what you are going to say when the talker finishes. If the speaker is long-winded (and happens to be the boss), he'll cover many points before you get a chance to rebut them. Take notes, put the keywords down to remind yourself of what they are and then cover them one by one after he has finished. Then, *indicate that you heard what he said.* People get a psychological lift just to have someone listen—so listen, show that you have listened—then rebut if you wish. This takes self-control and maturity, more than good ears. But it's essential.

> **There is only one rule for being a good talker: learn to listen.**
>
> *Christopher Morley*

By taking notes in any long conversation or meeting, one can check the drift of ideas that start off in a certain direction and, perhaps by sloppiness, tend to drift off to another direction. By noting down the keywords and phrases and checking them as one listens to the ideas and directions being repeated later in the conversation, one can find nuances in meaning. These nuances can be very important and can often mean the difference between success and failure.

Try to notice what people have mentioned more than once. When in a conversation persons repeat a phrase or idea two times, it usually means that they believe it very firmly, especially if the wording is the same each time it is repeated.

One should listen very carefully for "Freudian slips." Many times people will wish to soften the blow of an idea that they are going to get across, yet their words will expose their true meaning!

> I had been employed but untasked within a large company for some period of months. Luckily, I was then put on a task force working for a man who worked for a senior vice-president. As the task force neared its conclusion, the man I was working for became very interested in seeing to it that I was put into a good position within the company. Without my knowledge, he had talked to the senior vice-president, and I was told the vice-president wanted to discuss with me my future.
>
> "Bob would like to talk to you, Joe, about what it is you're going to do in the future. I mentioned to him that you have had nothing to do before this task force for several months. He can't understand why a person of your capability has not had a job. Bob is very interested in cases like . . . I mean, in your situation."

That little "Freudian slip"—"cases like"—on the part of my friend told me a great deal about the interview that I was about to have with the senior vice-president. It told me that the senior vice-president was interested in a "case" and in the mechanisms of a large company that could produce temporary unemployment. He might be interested in finding me the proper job, but he was more interested in the overall kind of problem than he was in me as a person.

Armed with this knowledge, gained by a very slight slip of the tongue quickly corrected by my friend, I approached the interview with the senior vice-president on a much different basis than I would have if I had thought that he was primarily interested in placing me in the right job. Slips like this are extremely important.

> My colleague was talking with a customer. We were behind schedule in a project but we believed that we could catch up. We saw no reason at that time to worry the customer and, as it turned out, we did indeed recoup the lost time. He explained to the customer the fact that we were somewhat behind schedule but that there was really nothing to worry about.
>
> "We'll dig ourselves out of this hole," he said.

By using the expression of "digging out of a hole," he was stating the problem more seriously than he desired to. He made a careless and perhaps Freudian slip of the tongue, and he quickly shifted the emphasis to the correction program that we had underway and assured the customer that things were under control. An alert and sharp listener would have caught the slip of the tongue and realized that perhaps there were more problems than were being freely discussed.

A man cannot utter two or three sentences without
disclosing to intelligent ears precisely where he stands in
life and thought, whether in the kingdom of the senses
and the understanding, or in that of ideas and
imagination, or in the realm of intuitions and duty.
Ralph W. Emerson

> Another inadvertently revealing word pops up in the following:

> We have three subcontractors. Company 1 is working hard to fix the front end. Company 2 is working to fix the control unit problems. Company 3 is working on the software problem. The whole system will be about one year late. But Company 3 is genuinely concerned with fixing the problem.

The speaker kept talking, but the general manager's sensitive ears had hung up on the word "genuinely." Implied in that word could be the unstated judgment that Companies 1 and 2 were *not* "genuinely" concerned or that Company 3 is in much more trouble than Companies 1 and 2. The general manager interrupted and by questioning determined that Company 3 had problems of far greater magnitude than Companies 1 and 2.

Precision

Misunderstandings are the worst of all communicating failures. When both parties *think* they have communicated, and they haven't, it may take months and many actions in the wrong direction before the mistake is caught. It may be too late by then.

One very easy way to fall into this problem is to think in the "plus or minus" manner. "If he doesn't say no, he says yes." That's plus or minus thinking, but it doesn't fit the real world. Many times deciders aren't ready to hand down a decision. So they listen to the evidence and decide to take the matter under advisement. "They say, "OK," *meaning* "I understand." The people leave the meeting, and I have heard the proponents state, "We won. He agreed with us." In truth he did not. He took the evidence under advisement.

The best way to avoid this problem is to repeat, as boldly, clearly, and completely as you can, what you understand the decision to be. "OK, I will state that you have authorized us to spend up to but not beyond $50,000, beginning March first." This is almost guaranteed to get a yes or no, and it makes it difficult for anyone to later claim that the decision was otherwise.

Logic is absolutely essential to good communications ability.

I do not agree = I disagree. These statements mean the same thing.

I agree ≠ I do not not agree.
I agree ≠ I do not disagree.

These statements do not mean the same thing.

"I do not disagree" means that I do not have enough information to not agree. It does *not* mean that I have enough information to agree. Perhaps if we see the sentence in a context it will help:

> A space program project manager was asking the executive of each major contract, "Do you agree that we are ready to launch?"
>
> An answer "I agree" is interpreted to mean "I have looked over the data from *all* the contractors and if I were you I would launch."
>
> The answer "I do not disagree with launching" means that I see no reason within my scope of responsibility to recommend against a launch. I do not know about the other parts of the system, so I can not agree in view of this lack of knowledge. I do not know enough to make that decision myself so I can't agree with your decision; what I do know shows me no reason to recommend not launching; so "I do not disagree."

Therefore, an exchange; "Do you agree?" "I do not disagree," is not wordsmanship, it is meaningful communications.

A critical proposal item was clearly in need of changing. The customers, a government agency, pointed out the items inconsistency to the sales manager, *but* they did not request a change. To request a change could be viewed as favoritism.

The sales manager briefed his boss, the vice-president of sales. He, in turn, needed approval from the president. It was a complicated matter.

The vice-president kept stating that the customers were requesting a change, which was just what the customers did not want said.

The sales manager kept reminding the vice-president (in private) that the customers were *not* asking for a change. The vice-president exploded. "Damn it, I can recognize nuances."

"Well," replied the sales manager, "I know that, but for some reason you keep saying it wrong."

The vice-president got it straight after that.

Sign in a college cafeteria: "Shoes required to eat here."
In pencil below: "Socks can eat anywhere."

The sharpness, that is, the precision, of the communicating process is so vital it cannot be overemphasized.

Look at the following example of precision.

From *The Reader over Your Shoulder*, by Robert Graves and Alan Hodge

From the Minutes of a Borough Council Meeting:

Councillor Trafford took exception to the proposed notice at the entrance of South Park: 'No dogs must be brought to this Park except on a lead.' He pointed out that this order would not prevent an owner from releasing his pets, or pet, from a lead when once safely inside the Park.

The Chairman (Colonel Vine): What alternative wording would you propose, Councillor?

Councillor Trafford: 'Dogs are not allowed in this Park without leads.'

Councillor Hogg: Mr. Chairman, I object. The order should be addressed to the owners, not to the dogs.

Councillor Trafford: That is a nice point. Very well then: 'Owners of dogs are not allowed in this Park unless they keep them on leads.'

Councillor Hogg: Mr. Chairman, I object. Strictly speaking, this would prevent me as a dog-owner from leaving my dog in the back-garden at home and walking with Mrs. Hogg across the Park.

Councillor Trafford: Mr. Chairman, I suggest that our legalistic friend be asked to redraft the notice himself.

170

Councillor Hogg: Mr. Chairman, since Councillor Trafford finds it so difficult to improve on my original wording, I accept. 'Nobody without his dog on a lead is allowed in this Park.'

Councillor Trafford: Mr. Chairman, I object. Strictly speaking, this notice would prevent me, as a citizen, who owns no dog, from walking in the Park without first acquiring one.

Councillor Hogg (with some warmth): Very simply, then: 'Dogs must be led in this Park.'

Councillor Trafford: Mr. Chairman, I object: this reads as if it were a general injunction to the Borough to lead their dogs into the Park.

Councillor Hogg interposed a remark for which he was called to order; upon his withdrawing it, it was directed to be expunged from the minutes.

The Chairman: Councillor Trafford, Councillor Hogg has had three tries; you have had only two . . .

Councillor Trafford: 'All dogs must be kept on leads in this Park.'

The Chairman: I see Councillor Hogg rising quite rightly to raise another objection. May I anticipate him with another amendment: 'All dogs in this Park must be kept on the lead.'

This draft was put to the vote and carried unanimously, with two abstentions.

The following test that measures your "precision ability" in communications points out how easy it is to be imprecise:

The Uncritical Inference Test[*]

William V. Haney

Instructions: This test is designed to determine your ability to think *accurately* and *carefully*. Since it is very probable that you have never taken this type of test before, failure to read the instructions *extremely carefully* may lower your score.

1. You will read a brief story. Assume that all of the information presented in the story is definitely accurate and true. Read the story carefully. You may refer back to the story whenever you wish.

2. You will then read statements about the story. Answer them in numerical order. *Do not go back* to fill in answers or to change answers. This will only distort your test score.

3. After you read carefully each statement, determine whether the statement is "T," "F," or "?."

---

[*] © W. V. Haney, 1975.

a. "T"—meaning: On the basis of the information presented in the story the statement is **definitely true.**

b. "F"—meaning: On the basis of the information presented in the story the statement is **definitely false.**

c. "?"—meaning: The statement **may** be true (or false) but on the basis of the information presented in the story you cannot be definitely certain. (If any part of the statement is doubtful, mark the statement "?".)

4. Indicate your answer by circling either "T" or "F" or "?" opposite the statement.

A businessman had just turned off the lights in the store when a man appeared and demanded money. The owner opened a cash register. The contents of the cash register were scooped up and the man sped away. A member of the police force was notified promptly.

1. A man appeared after the owner had turned off his store lights. T F ?

2. The robber was a man. T F ?

3. The man did not demand money. T F ?

4. The owner opened a cash register. T F ?

5. The store owner scooped up the contents of the cash register and ran away. T F ?

6. Someone opened a cash register. T F ?

7. After the man, who demanded the money, scooped up the contents of the cash register, he ran away. T F ?

8. While the cash register contained money, the story does not state how much. T F ?

9. The robber demanded money of the owner. T F ?

10. The robber opened the cash register. T F ?

11. After the store lights were turned off a man appeared. T F ?

12. The robber did not take the money with him. T F ?

13. The robber did not demand money of the owner. T F ?

14. The man who opened the cash register was the owner. T F ?

15. The age of the store owner was not revealed in the story. T F ?

16. Taking the contents of the cash register with him, the man ran out of the store. T F ?

17. The story concerns a series of events in which only three persons are referred to: the owner of the store, a man who demanded money, and a member of the police force. T F ?

18. The following events were included in the story: someone demanded money, a cash register was opened, its contents were scooped up, and a man dashed out of the store.   T   F   ?

Just a few answers will give you the gist of what is at play here.

Number 2 "The robber was a man" is questionable. Nowhere is it stated that a robbery took place. The owner could have been sending money out to the bank and the whole transaction may have been hurried. The owner may have notified a policeman for protection, if the owner was the one who notified the policeman.

Number 5 points out that it *may* have been the owner who ran away with the money. But maybe someone else did. Finish the test; it is good practice!

Such precision is vital to many business transactions. The precise communicator avoids many embarrassing and career-hurting misunderstandings.

One may think, "This is too much! How can anyone be so precise?"

For you as the person on the way up, this precision is a key "winnowing-out" factor. You probably spend little time with the top executives, and you must be supereffective when you do. You often will be told in a hurried fashion what is desired. You must understand what was *not* said. If you are precise, you may look very good, depending on your capacity to implement. If you are not precise, even if you implement well, you are wide open to chance—are you doing what was desired?

Answer the questions! One of the most frustrating things an executive encounters is the person who simply will not answer the question. Here are two actual examples, one of a conversation between a high-level manager (who was making a presentation with two dozen people looking on) and a division president:

Katz: We are very strong in the problem analysis.

President: Does the customer view you that way?
(Pause.)

Katz: Let me answer. Customer two years ago gave us two million to study the area. Last year they gave us one million.
(Pause.)

President: Is that yes or no?

And one of a conversation between president and vice-president.

The president asked, "Was our lawyer aware of this problem?"
The vice-president tried to protect the lawyer and change the subject.
"Well," he said, "he was moving from Buffalo to here and. . . ."

The president cut him off. "The question can be answered yes or no."

Anonymity. Having heard hundreds—perhaps thousands—of explanations, I now am attuned to the indefinite answer. It is often a dodge, a way of avoiding an answer. It is always vague.

"With whom in sales have you checked this?" I asked.

"We have checked this with sales and they stated it cannot be done. . . ." comes back a positive and confident answer.

In my earlier days as a manager, I'd have let it pass. But the key is that the question was not answered. "*With whom* in sales . . . ?" was the question, ". . . with sales . . ." was the answer. Often this is not just sloppiness on the answerer's part, but deliberate evasion!

How many times I have refused to accept a vague answer and pursued with question after question to finally find that either the answerer didn't know (someone had told the answerer so and so) or that the "checking with sales" amounted to a three-sentence conversation at a cocktail party with a salesman from a small office who happened to state "sounds OK."

These indefinite answers should be red flags to the good executive. They are *at best* sloppy communications on the part of the speaker. Another example:

A key proposal was going out, and something was amiss. Calling a meeting, I asked one of the sales managers, "Who is responsible for putting out this proposal?" "We are," he replied, meaning sales.

"Who? What person?" I pursued.

"We are" he evaded, intentionally or unintentionally.

"Who? What's the person's name?"

"Me!"

"Full-time?"

"Well . . . no, but. . . ."

Now I knew the problem. There was no full-time, high-level (assuming that high-level means competent) person running the proposal. To have accepted the "we are" would have meant failure. I could have later blamed it on the speaker—but why fail at all? We appointed a proposal manager and I listen to that speaker very carefully now.

The great enemy of clear language is insincerity.
George Orwell

174

One of the most frustrating things to read is a directive from management which is written in the passive voice. Search as one might, it is almost impossible to find a subject who is performing the actions mentioned. For example, "It has been decided to reduce the investment in product A by 20 percent." Such statements only tend to frustrate the perceptive reader. Who decided? The author? management? the general manager? the local manager? a visitor? the wife of an employee? the signer?

To state that "it has been decided" weakens one's argument. It appears that the writer doesn't know who.

When I read sentences like those above, it convinces me of one of two things. First, that the writers do not know what they are writing and have therefore resorted to the trickery of the language. They call in expert witnesses without naming them, and they hope that the reader is impressed by "it is said." Or, I believe that the writers indeed do know their facts, know who their expert witnesses are, but are sloppy writers who have not taken the time to put the message forth plainly.

In either case, the writers are guilty.

> There is no requirement that all official correspondence be written
> in the third-person impersonal passive style. This is occasionally,
> but rarely, a good style; because the effect in some cases is to make
> the bureau seem to try to evade responsibility by anonymity and
> in almost all other cases to make the officers of the Bureau seem
> pompous and affected. Wherever possible, use direct statements
> and active verbs. Such phrases as *It is thought, It is requested,*
> *It is desired,* etc., should be avoided generally. When appropriate
> to the subject, the addressee, and the signer of the letter, there
> is no objection to the use of the first or second person. Indeed,
> all three grammatical persons may be used in the same letter if
> the transitions are made perfectly clear.
>
> *Admiral E. W. Mills*

Notes. How about communicating with ourselves? All of us have fallible memories and yet, for some unknown reason, most of us are adverse to taking notes; that is, writing down points of a person's communication as we listen to a speech.

I have listened to presidents of companies speak to managers. They will speak for perhaps an hour; they will cover several different subjects. They will give their views on many topics; they will respond fairly candidly to certain questions.

Whether the listeners agree with the answers being given (or even judge them to be intelligent), the fact is that the speaker is the boss. Whether the boss's view is right or wrong, it is going to carry weight and be a force to reckon with.

In these meetings I have watched twenty managers sit with their arms folded and listen for an hour or two. Rarely does anyone make a note of what has been said.

After such sessions, I have seen the rare person who has taken notes in discussion with some of the others who have not. It is very clear that those who have not taken notes generally have not remembered crisply what was said. What they have done is slightly changed it, modified it, shortened it, or lengthened it, apparently inadvertently. The communication is already garbled, one-half hour after it has taken place. Obviously, the note-taker is ahead of those who do not take notes.

Why don't more people take notes? Perhaps people resist taking notes because doing so is a throwback to their school days and an outward sign that they are not at the same level as the speaker. That is the only reason that I can see that justifies such a flagrant waste as listening to a speaker for over an hour and taking no notes. Only in rare instances of exceptional memory capacity is this justified.

We should all take notes copiously and unashamedly. It is extremely effective to read back to a superior, peer, or subordinate the exact words of a speech.

"I didn't say I wanted to, I just said that I might."

"No, let me read back to you your exact words; here are my notes; you said 'I would prefer to go.' 'Prefer' is your word."

I have seen many managers, when confronted with such clear-cut recollections of what was said, (a) accept that they probably did say that or, (b) remember that indeed that was what they had said. The effect of the exact phraseology does wonders for jogging the memory.

It is often interesting to go back in time and look at the notes and identify changes in your own attitude, knowledge, ambition, or perception. Often you will be surprised. Your memory plays tricks at times, and you find that you have been remembering things the way you want to remember them, and not as they were truly happening in the real world. This reviewing of old notes is a very rewarding practice.

Put it in writing. Many people think this is "padding the file" and that it is offensive to the other party, but it's just helping the memory, and forces everyone to look at the same words and to agree or disagree once again. Putting it in writing, "We agreed yesterday that. . . ." has saved me many, many disputes. When a conversation long past suddenly becomes important, pulling out the letter helped. Often I found I had "misremembered." The human mind remembers what it wants to remember, so send a memo.

> The senior vice-president called me and told me to go ahead with the Schlu project. "Tell them we'll twist 3, twirl 4, and settle 5 if, etc."
>
> "OK," I said. I started to implement this and found that the seemingly simple instructions could be tricky.

I decided that we—the senior vice-president and I—had skipped a lot of levels of management and that I had better put what he'd said in writing. We were dealing with an expenditure of several million dollars, and another division had to do the work.

It took me several passes before I got the memo to state *exactly* what he had said—no more and no less. It took me four hours. It was worth it.

Two days later I was with the senior vice-president on another issue when the door flew open. In stormed an angry division president, waving a memo and glaring at me. He had a copy of my memo which I had sent him. "It's *wrong!*" he yelled, glaring at me.

"If it's wrong, then that is exactly why it was written," I threw back at him, defiantly.

The senior vice-president jumped up from behind his desk, told the division president to sit down, and glanced at the memo. He didn't read it, but merely looked at the first paragraphs.

He grimaced at me and stated, "I should have written this, not you." He called his secretary in and began to dictate. My hours of care were paying off; he stated things exactly as I had recalled he had stated them.

The division president protested time and again. "I didn't agree to that!" he'd state. "Oh, but yes you did," the senior vice-president would answer. A 10 to 20 minute discussion would ensue. The secretary, who was still taking dictation, and I watched the struggle.

The division president was morose. Finally, after 45 minutes, the senior vice-president read my letter. "This is almost exactly right. I should have written this." He sent his own version.

My memo had avoided a much nastier conflict. Had no memo been written immediately, weeks or months could have elapsed before the conflict took place—and memories would have been fuzzy—and tempers more frayed. I, being far junior to the others, would have been the big loser.

Whenever someone is unwilling to put it in writing, be careful! Something is wrong.

> I don't care how much a man talks, if he only says it in a few words.
>
> *Henry Wheeler Shaw*

Brevity. "Talk net" is a saying that means, "Tell the essence; skip the nonessential."

To talk net is a relatively rare ability and the lack of it holds back many people from rising to higher management levels.

To talk net, one must be able to "think net." Some can do this quickly; some must struggle and sort out laboriously the essential points. Mental ability is vital to this "talking net."

Some will not talk net because they lack courage or independence. They fear that if they "talk net" the superior may miss the subtleties of an issue. They insist on giving the *whole* story. They fear the superior may act without *all* the information, and they fear that a mistake may be made.

This is *usually* fatal to career growth, because the executives usually understand that there are subtleties, that "talking net" eliminates them, and that caution is in order if an important issue is at stake.

But the executive also usually knows better than the subordinate the true importance of the issue (it is often bigger in the eyes of the subordinate than in the eyes of the superior) and often knows many of the subtleties. The executive should judge if more time should be spent, not the subordinate.

> One of the finest managers I ever saw in action had his upward chances ended because he would never talk net. I hated to get a phone call from him because it *almost always* lasted 30 minutes. He insisted on telling me *every* detail, *every* conversation, word for word. He would not accept the direction to talk net.

To speak much is one thing, to speak to the point
is another.
Sophocles

At the end of a conversation "tell everything" subordinates can justifiably feel that if anything goes wrong now, the boss is in it with them. The boss can never say, "You didn't tell me." But the boss should worry about the independence of such a subordinate.

[Franklin] made the first pair of bifocal spectacles ...
because he could not follow French at Court unless he
could watch the speaker's expression.
Joseph Bronowski

Facial expressions. Shorthand isn't just with words; it can be even more effective (and more private) with glances and facial expressions. I can communicate quickly, accurately, and easily with people I've worked with for extensive periods. As a third party speaks, a squinting, doubting look flashed in silence means "I'm not sure I buy what he's saying." Doubt, incredulity, rejection, anger, agreement, etc. can be communicated to the initiated in this way.

The face is the artless index of the mind.
Horace Mann

178

A good communicator not only uses these tricks, but watches for others using them. I have often changed my strategy in a meeting because I've detected visual shorthand between my opponent and my superior. This is information; it should be recognized and used.

> Your face is a book, where men may read strange matters.
>
> **William Shakespeare**

In his fine book, *The Effective Executive,* Peter Drucker points out that some people receive communications very selectively. Readers like to read things, and talking to them on complicated matters doesn't communicate nearly as well to them as a letter will. Conversely, listeners won't get much from your letter; they like to hear information.

Then, Drucker points out, there is a small number constituting a third type, talkers. They talk and watch the reaction to their words. From facial expressions, etc., they can tell what the listener thinks. Franklin Roosevelt was a talker. This close scrutiny of a listener's reaction is a very powerful tool! Drucker states, in *The Effective Executive* published by Harper & Row:

> It is, I submit, fairly obvious to anyone who has ever looked that people are either "readers" or "listeners" (excepting only the very small group who get their information through talking, and by watching with a form of psychic radar the reactions of the people they talk to; both President Franklin Roosevelt and President Lyndon Johnson belong in this category, as apparently did Winston Churchill). People who are both readers and listeners—trial lawyers have to be both, as a rule—are exceptions. It is generally a waste of time to talk to a reader. He only listens after he has read. It is equally a waste of time to submit a voluminous report to a listener. He can only grasp what it is all about through the spoken word.

Drucker is not advocating that one should be a "talker." He is just pointing out that some executives are very adept at *getting* information by talking. This information is gained even when the listener is trying not to show reactions.

If the listener were trying to give information the talker would not need to talk and watch.

> When a thought takes one's breath away, a lesson on grammar seems an impertinence.
>
> **Thomas Wentworth Higginson**

Content. So far we have been treating communications independently of its content. In real life we don't do this. What you say is often more important than how you say it. William Jennings Bryan, one of the great orators of history, once said that "eloquence is ninety percent content."

It is usually difficult for speakers to be eloquent, or to communicate effectively, if they have no ideas, meanings, or directions to communicate. Unfortunately too many people go on and on at great length about nothing. Content will often make the difference between a fine communication and a bad one. If what you want to communicate is not clear in your own mind, it will be very difficult, if not impossible, to communicate it clearly and place it in someone else's mind. The best way to persuade others is to know what it is you yourself believe, to have reduced that belief to words before you try to convince someone else.

Many people feel that when they have little content they should make up for that lack in length. They will discourse at great length on a trivial subject. If you do this often, you will be quickly excluded from future deliberations. Your superior will be asked to present the facts or ideas for you.

The level of the communication. The level of detail of communication is a stumbling block to many. It is sad to see eager persons with good verbal skills and good messages lose their audiences because they either cannot shift levels, or don't even recognize that there are levels.

What do we mean by "level?" An example is easier to provide than an explanation. Imagine a presentation to a group about a new resort community. Your company is creating it, and you are giving the presentation.

You can say:

1. "Our new community will be in northern Florida and will open in 1978."
2. "We'll have four types of houses and two sizes of condominiums."
3. "The beach will comfortably handle 250 people."
4. "The beach will be developed by bringing in 502,100 tons of used sod. This will take four and one-half months, etc."

Each statement is factual and informative. But clearly the person interested in the first statement will be far less interested, if at all, in the fourth. The fourth statement is to be used with the construction company, the planners, the auditors, the first, is with investors, bankers, and the fourth isn't to be used with them. The second is to be used with bankers, and the second and third will be used with planners or prospective buyers.

The point of all this is that there is a *level* of information that is to be communicated. If you try to communicate a fourth level to people who are interested in a first level, *you* are in trouble. They either can't

180

absorb it, (you're "over their heads"), or they aren't interested. In either case, you are wasting their time.

Almost all subjects are capable of being communicated at different levels. It is a very pleasant experience to watch fine communicators shift levels, up or down, as they watch the effect of their words on the listener, or listen carefully to the questions and select the level the question deserves in response. Conversely, it is very unpleasant to suffer through a communication where speakers insist on speaking at the fourth level, despite repeated clues, or even *demands* from the audience, that they avoid such detail. (I step into these communications and usurp the floor, if I can.)

To be able to shift levels demands a good knowledge of the subject, but even without such a knowledge, you should always recognize when you are wasting the listener's time. Better to say "I'm not familiar with that level of detail, but I'll get John to come and see you" than to keep fumbling at the fourth level. Better to say "I'm familiar with the engineering details only, and I'm not conversant with the overall scheme. I'll get Bill to talk to you about the overall."

Many people don't realize that these levels exist. They erroneously think that everyone wants to communicate at their level. Not everyone does.

Atmosphere

> Nothing more enhances authority than silence. It is the crowning virtue of the strong, the refuge of the weak, the modesty of the proud, the pride of the humble, the prudence of the wise, and the sense of fools. To speak is to . . . dissipate one's strength; whereas what action demands is concentration. Silence is a necessary preliminary to the ordering of one's thoughts.
>
> *Charles de Gaulle*

The demeanor of superiors, their personalities and their approach to a communication are perhaps the most important factors in determining whether or not the communication will be effective. Assuming an angry, aggressive, or abusive demeanor is one of the fastest ways of terminating effective communication. Unfriendliness dries up any urge to communicate and makes the exchange a question-and-answer, let's-get-it-over-with-as-soon-as-possible situation. Conversely, the person who is willing to listen, patiently and understandingly, and perhaps most importantly, without seeming to be sitting in judgment on the person talking, will receive a great amount of information.

People normally like to talk and like to express their ideas; however, they are reluctant to express these ideas if they feel that the person receiving them will be judging them, be it a peer, superior, or even a subordinate. In many ways it is safer not to expose one's thoughts and knowledge and therefore not be judged.

It is the executive's responsibility to set a climate for the communication that puts people as much at ease as the situation permits. If it is a situation fraught with possible severe consequences, all will be more guarded in what they have to say. Conversation in such meetings usually is slow and halting and needs constant stimulation by questions from the executive.

Emotions. Communicating is between people, and people are emotional. Therefore, speakers with outstanding vocabularies, technique, and content still may be thwarted by the emotions, either their own or those of the listeners. The higher up managers are the more attuned to people they must be, the more alert they must be to the emotions and desires of their subordinates.

People who make us like them will get away with more sloppiness in thought and/or communication because we want to help them, we want them to be right. Therefore the friendly approach, the ease-up-to-the-criticism-or-attack approach, is much more likely to get the desired result.

> An executive had made a decision to spend $100,000 for a project. He had carefully considered it and checked it with his superiors.
>
> The controller, who worked for the executive, asked to see him. The controller started the conversation curtly, challengingly. "Project W! Why are you doing it?" The executive, treated as though the roles were reversed, was angered. "Damn," he thought, "who works for whom here?"
>
> Now the controller had every right to ask the question. As a key executive, he had the right to know the logic behind decisions, but he had *attacked*—and he had angered, needlessly. And the key word is—needlessly.
>
> He should have said either: "I'm curious about Project W. Would you tell me about it?" or "We're running low on discretionary funds. If you do Project W, you'll be down to $50,000. Have you made a final decision? Is it critical?"

How easy to change the result from an irate superior—who now wonders about how the controller treats peers and subordinates—to a superior who wants the controller to know the logic behind the decision, to have the controller's opinion, to find out that there are money problems. The superior who does not want to disclose the reason can gracefully say so to the soft question. There is no way to gracefully avoid the head-on attack.

There are times for blunt challenging questions, but they should be used as the *last* resort. The gentle friendly approach is always best. It doesn't always work, but it should be tried first.

The use of emotions to help get the message across is a powerful technique. Conviction, sincerity, fear, enthusiasm, and even anger, are great aids to speakers. They power their words. Conversely, the listener must be wary of feigned emotions. If emotions lend power, they lend power even if they're not real, unless they are obviously fake.

Too often one see deference, and even fear, exhibited by the junior people toward the higher level executives. They are afraid to ask questions of their superiors, or to request explanations and reasons for decisions that are handed down. As a result, these decisions are often not accompanied with the proper explanation and background.

How often I have sat in meetings and, although questions were encouraged, have withheld my questions because I feared that I would show everyone that I did not understand. So the meeting goes forward, leaving me further and further behind.

Demeanor speaks so much to us without words, we must be on guard that it not speak too much. Beware the simple "I'm concerned" look. Grave and sincere, the speaker uses emotions, real or feigned, to cover a paucity of ideas, facts, or solutions. Persons who sit solemnly and say nothing often gain a reputation for wisdom based solely on their facial expressions. Such are the traps of communications.

Sincerity is another misleader. After a meeting filled with contention, I told my cohort, "Mr. X didn't know what he was talking about. But he's so sincere, he's so committed, maybe we ought to try to do it his way." My friend killed this weakness in me with "Hitler was sincere, too."

Simulated anger is another ploy used by speakers.

Boy, I'll never do that again. The boss was really angry." How often one hears that. And how often is the anger feigned? I have watched executives turn their "anger" on and off at will, in order to power home a message.

Too much anger, or anger too often, is bad judgment and overkill. Faked anger is dangerous. Once it is known that the boss fakes it, the power of the "anger" is greatly diminished. Genuine displeasure can be displayed without anger.

Conviction. Stating things very positively usually helps get the message across. It inspires confidence in the listener. It says "this person knows this subject." As a speaker, show your conviction.

The listener, however, must be wary of a person who states *everything* with conviction. I have seen executives who do this. I now completely ignore these people's "conviction." I have counseled them that they have lost a communicating power and have hurt their credibility.

A fellow manager—a peer—called me one day to state that one of my technical advisors had refused to attend a meeting at a local branch office, had flown in, been difficult, refused to do such and such. Would I chastise the man? The fellow manager was very outraged and positive. "I will indeed," I said and called my man.

His story was much more reasonable. His plane had been very late; he had an important meeting the next day in a different city *and*—this is vital—he had explained all this to the local manager, and they had agreed that one of his two meetings was not necessary.

I called back my fellow manager and told him these new facts— expecting to be told that the local manager didn't agree with them.

"Well, that's right, but the meeting he did go to he did very poorly at. He didn't understand the X or the Y and didn't. . . ." I interrupted him.

"Look. You were very sure of your first set of accusations. I wonder if these are as faulty. Write me a letter and *state* specific things he did wrong. Then I'll talk to you."

I never got the letter. From then on, I never believed anything based on my fellow manager's say so.

Certitude is not the test of certainty.
Oliver Wendell Holmes, Jr.

Communication is almost synonymous with life. We *must* communicate. This short chapter gave only a few of the aspects of communications. You can improve your communications ability continuously— and if you don't, you are ignoring a great opportunity.

The art of conversation is to be prompt without being stubborn; to refute without argument, and to clothe great matters in a motley garb.
Benjamin Disraeli

The way a man speaks lays bare the texture of his mind, the goodness of his heart, the inner pain or the sweet serenity that are his companions in solitude.
Harriet Van Horne

Words have ruined more souls than any devil's agency. It is strange that the word which is a chief ingredient of human uniqueness should also be a chief instrument of dehumanization. The realm of magic is the realm of the invisible and the domain of the word.

Eric Hoffer

Well-timed silence hath more eloquence than speech.

M. T. Tupper

SALES ABILITY

Sales ability is the ability to sell, to persuade, to convince someone of something. It is more than just glibness plus determination, and it is in constant use. You "sell" your superiors, subordinates, peers, friends, customers—in short, everyone.

The following qualities combine to form a person's sales ability:

Ambition	Resilience and durability
Logic	Empathy
Nimble-mindedness	Cheerfulness
Knowledge	Courage and boldness
Willpower	

Persuasion: Logic and Empathy

> It is the man who is cool and collected, who is master of his countenance, his voice, his actions, his gestures, of every part, who can work upon others at his pleasure.
>
> *Denis Diderot*

People who are superior persuaders use empathy and logic. They start with logic, laying out the flow of argument, progressing step by step to the desired conclusion. Each step supports a future one, and several steps lead to a subconclusion. Then perhaps a completely separate set of facts and assertions lead to an independent subconclusion. A number of subconclusions support a main conclusion. This ordering is essential and, when done well, is beautiful to see; its order and its interlocking pieces resemble a work of art in many respects.

But all this superior work is wasted if it is simply poured out to listeners without monitoring its effects. No matter how good the flow, the whole structure comes crashing down if the listeners don't understand a key step, a key jump in logic. They may just need to think about the step for a minute, or they may need extra intermediate steps to support a subconclusion. After all, everyone's logic is not the same, and everyone's knowledge base is different. Persuaders who *see* that the persons to be persuaded don't yet grasp the particular conclusion go into a question-and-answer interaction with those they are trying to persuade.

"Do you follow me up to Step 2?"

"Yes, I'm with you that far."

The critical thing is to know where the persuaded person *is* in the process. And the persuadee will often not tell you because of embarrassment, confusion, or even a deliberate desire *not* to be persuaded.

Persuaders must use all five senses to *read* persuadees—their facial expressions, their finger movements, their posture, etc. Empathy is the quality that enables persuaders to do this.

Persuading can be a most exciting endeavor, especially if fine minds are at work and the subject is important.

Nimble-mindedness is vital, as we must come up with supporting logic paths "on the fly" as the discussion progresses and the persuadee goes off on tangents.

Style Adaptability

Executives find themselves with a great many different types of people, some of whom are rather cultured, some of whom are not; some of whom are very action-oriented, some not; some scientific, some not; some abrupt, some slow. If rising managers can adapt their style to the style of the individuals that they must influence, they stand a much better chance of influencing those individuals. I have seen excellent sellers change their style at will. They match the other's wavelength. In the morning, they may be with a forceful, overly aggressive, abrupt, outspoken customer. The seller adapts by also becoming abrupt, forceful, and blunt. In the afternoon, the same seller will call upon another customer who is quite the opposite from the morning customer; urbane, witty, charming. The seller changes the entire approach and exhibits the same traits as the second customer.

A lack of this adaptability causes "cultural clash." Cultural clash occurs when individuals come up against a superior who comes from an entirely different background. The subordinates have risen to a fairly high level within an organization on the basis of many of the qualities above, but their cultural styles are set. Let's for the moment assume that they are suave and controlled. The superior, however, is abrupt and tough. The subordinates and the superior are excellent executives, but they will never get along because the cultural gap between them is too great. Usually this is a failing on the part of the superior because of failing to take advantage of very fine subordinates. Be that as it may, these subordinates have talent and ability and are being held down because of clashes with superiors. Subordinates should see the problem and *change their cultural pattern* so that they may continue on the road up. Hard to do, but most executives can do it.

Some people see style and adaptability as conflicting with integrity. The following is from David Halberstam's *The Best and the Brightest* published by Random House:

> The reporters sat there writing it down, all of it mindless, all of it fitting McNamara's vision of what Vietnam should be. Vietnam confirmed McNamara's preconceptions and specifications.
>
> One particular visit seemed to sum it up: McNamara looking for the war to fit his criteria, his definitions. He went to Danang in 1965 to check on the Marine progress there. A Marine colonel in I Corps had a sand table showing the terrain and patiently gave the briefing: friendly situation, enemy situation, main problem. McNamara watched it, not really taking it in, his hands folded, frowning a little, finally interrupting. "Now, let me see," McNamara said, "if I have it right, this is your situation," and then he spouted his own version, all in numbers and statistics. The colonel, who was very bright, read him immediately like a man breaking a code, and without changing stride, went on with the briefing, simply switching his terms, quantifying everything, giving everything in numbers and percentages, percentages up, percentages down, so blatant a performance that it was like a satire. Jack Raymond of the *New York Times* began to laugh and had to leave the tent. Later that day Raymond went up to McNamara and commented on how tough the situation was up in Danang, but McNamara wasn't interested in the Vietcong. He wanted to talk about that colonel, he liked him, that colonel had caught his eye. "That colonel is one of the finest officers I've ever met," he said.

Halberstam clearly is critical of the colonel and McNamara. I think the colonel was right on target, doing a superb job at communicating. (This assumes that the facts were presented honestly, which Halberstam points out the military people were not doing on all occasions. If that were the case here, integrity is being violated, but *not* because of the style adaptability.)

Demeanor

Demeanor is vital to persuasion. An assured presentation, calm and secure, has merit without even any content. There was a comic strip in the Freddy series by Rupe that ran a few years ago that makes the point. Freddy, a youngster of about 5 or 6 years of age, is arguing with a friend. In four frames, the argument is finished.

Frame 1
Freddy: "I know it is true; my mother told me."
Friend: "Ha."

Frame 2
Freddy: "I know it is true; my teacher told me."
Friend: *"Ha!"*

Frame 3
Freddy: "I know it is true, my preacher told me!"
Friend: **"Ha!"**

Frame 4
Freddy (walking away crestfallen): "Boy, is he a good arguer."

Writing in the magazine, *Human Behavior* (October 1974) Ann Nietzke points out dramatically how compelling and persuasive good demeanor in presentations can be:

> Last year, when I read the popularized accounts of the first "Dr. Fox" experiment, I felt pretty smug. The fact that a professional actor could masquerade successfully as an academician made me feel superior—especially since the people he duped were supposedly discerning educators.
>
> When "Dr. Fox" first appeared on the scene, he lectured to these academic "peers" as part of an experiment conducted by Donald Naftulin and Frank Donnely of the University of Southern California and John Ware, Jr., of Southern Illinois University. Although his subject matter was derived from a legitimate article on game theory, the actor was coached to employ double talk, non sequiturs, neologisms, contradictory statements, irrelevancies and meaningless references—and to convey all this nonsense in a dramatic way, with humor, warmth and enthusiasm. Eleven psychiatrists, psychologists and social-worker educators heard the one-hour talk by "Dr. Myron L. Fox," introduced rather impressively as an authority on the application of mathematics to human behavior, and then participated in a 30-minute question-and-answer session that was hardly more substantive.
>
> Later, a videotape of the introduction, lecture and discussion was shown to two more groups of educators and administrators, bringing the total number of subjects to 55. All participants anonymously filled out an eight-item questionnaire about their attitudes toward the lecture, and their responses were overwhelmingly favorable. These findings appeared to confirm Naftulin's hypothesis that "given a sufficiently impressive lecture paradigm, even experienced educators participating in a new learning experience can be seduced into feeling satisfied that they

have learned, despite irrelevant, conflicting, and meaningless content conveyed by the lecturer. . . .

But a few weeks ago, I saw for myself a videotape of the USC lecture and discussion, and now I'm not sure I could have responded much differently than the subjects in the study.

What none of the accounts of the experiment had prepared me for was the brilliance of Michael Fox's acting performance (he has often played "doctors" of various sorts, including a veterinarian on "Columbo").

Fox is gifted with a very solid stage presence that, of course, many teachers (and not a few actors) lack. From the moment he stepped to the front of the room and began his "lecture," every gesture and movement of his body, every facial expression, every emphatic syllable he uttered helped create the image of an authoritative professor who had full charge of the context in which he was operating. Even though I knew the lecture was a phony, I found that Fox's delivery—his intensity, his emphasis, his appropriate and authentic-sounding intonations—kept giving me the *feeling* that he might have just said something important or that he was *now* saying something important or, at least, that he was *about* to say something important any second and that I'd better listen and listen good so as not to miss it. I'm sure that an examination of the lecture's script would readily have revealed the circuity and emptiness of its phrasing, content and structure, but in the oral presentation, "Dr. Fox's" performance unquestionably reduced the likelihood of anyone's perceiving it. This, of course, has always been the talent of "confidence men," who are able to present themselves so assuredly in their assumed roles that they inspire the confidence of their "marks."

Lest you think that this could happen only in the classroom, look at the following real life example:

Some important designers were visiting the Y Company to hear about a new idea in building radars. The Y Company's key designer was late, and his superiors were frantic, stalling the visitors and searching for Adams. Suddenly, Adams was there, in the conference room, giving his presentation.

His superiors relaxed, and settled back to listen. After a few minutes, they were uneasy. Something was wrong with Adams' presentation, but what? Several more minutes of listening, and they realized that what Adams was saying didn't quite make sense.

Now Adams was the giant brain of the Y Company and even his superiors at times had difficulty understanding him. But they had heard him give this presentation many times!

A few minutes later, and it was clear to his superiors that Adams was drunk!

The visitors never realized it. Weeks later one of the top visitors told a Y Company vice-president that the Adams' presentation was one of the finest he had heard in 15 years in the radar business!

"I didn't understand some of it, but it was really new!"

It is a thing of no great difficulty to raise objections against another man's oration—nay, it is a very easy matter; but to produce a better in its place is a work extremely troublesome.

Plutarch

Until there is understanding, there is no real basis for motivation. I believe management must seek consent.

T. J. Watson, Jr.

LEADERSHIP ABILITY

Leadership, distinct from sales ability, is simply the ability to lead others. The following qualities combine to form a person's leadership ability:

Beliefs	Independence
Courage	Willpower
Knowledge	Ambition

The single item you must have to be a leader is a deep belief in something—almost anything—and the courage to so state. You need not be eloquent, although that helps. You need not be vigorous, dynamic, nor even outgoing, although those qualities help. You just need to believe deeply.

It seems as though there are millions of people in the world who are looking for someone who believes strongly in something so that they can follow. They seem to get a sense of belonging by following someone else's lead. To a certain extent it is not even clear that the people really believe what the leader is stating or, indeed, even *understand* it. The mere fact that the leader is stating a position will draw

190

people. People want a leader. If you doubt this, recall the American Nazi Party of the 1960s.

> **You will never be a leader unless you first learn to follow and be led.**
>
> *Tiorio*

Time magazine (1974) had an issue devoted to leadership. Its reporters interviewed many prominent people and asked them about leaders. Many answers were really talking about leadership *and* management, and the two are worlds apart. We'd like our managers to be leaders and vice versa, but reality intrudes and we find that often the two capabilities are not present in the same person. We know dozens of competent managers that are not leaders. They have attained their present positions through quiet, steady competence—but they are not leaders.

A leader leads. It is not sufficient, however, to leave it at that point and not bring in the folklore that has grown around the world "leader." In the United States, to be a leader is *good*. Leadership is admired and a leader is respected regardless of whether or not those who are being led are being led in the right direction. Certainly Hitler was one of the great leaders of all times, yet he led to untold misery.

Hitler was no manager. He squandered resources recklessly (deliberately losing 500,000 troops at Stalingrad rather than withdraw) and decided great issues capriciously. That is not management.

The *Washington Post* reported on Secretary of State Henry Kissinger, speaking at a gathering to honor the memory of Winston Churchill:

> "Cathedrals were not built by saints," said Henry Kissinger, the Secretary of State. The splendor of mankind is not always accomplished, in other words, by glorious folk, but by faithful ones. In his extemporaneous words, all the more moving for not being deliberately grand, Kissinger asked himself aloud what leadership consists of and how it happens that Churchill, dead these 10 years, still seems to people "more relevant than most of their contemporaries."
>
> Surely, he went on, the thing "is to have a vision of the future and the courage to walk to it." And yet "if he is too far ahead, he will be isolated; if he is not out in front at all, he will be irrelevant. Churchill was never irrelevant."
>
> Leaders are mortal men, as the occasion well reminded everybody listening, and fallible in the nature of things, but leaders like Churchill "must act as if they had intuition of the future and as if their vision were true."

Let's look at some of the people interviewed by *Time* magazine (1974) and what they said:

■ Mortimer Adler, United States philosopher: In Aristotelian terms, the good leader must have ethos, pathos, and logos. The ethos is his moral character, the source of his ability to persuade. The pathos is his ability to touch feelings, to move people emotionally. The logos is his ability to give solid reasons for an action, to move people intellectually. By this definition Pericles of Athens was a great leader. Winston Churchill, Thomas Jefferson, or almost any of the founding fathers—Adams, Madison, Washington. Perhaps Lincoln, Franklin D. Roosevelt, and Woodrow Wilson as well.

■ Correlli Barnett, British military historian: Greatness has nothing to do with morality. A leader gets people to follow him. Napoleon led the French to catastrophe, but they followed him almost to the end. Marlborough and Wellington had greatness, and Hitler, unfortunately. Al Capone was a leader in a primitive environment.

■ Alexander Heard, United States educator and Chancellor of Vanderbilt University: No concept of leadership is complete without the element of zeal and fervor, an almost spiritual element. Martin Luther King, Jr., had it. Adolf Hitler had it, so did Gandhi and Nehru. The Old Testament prophets had it. It's commitment, it's a kind of self-confidence which can be egotistic and arrogant. But a degree of it has to be there. The leader must have a belief in what he is doing, almost a singlemindedness.

■ Archibald MacLeish, United States poet: In my own experience, the man who most obviously possessed the equality of leadership was General Marshall. He was a man of enormous moral authority.

■ Golo Mann, West German historian: Marcus Aurelius, emperor and philosopher, valiant pessimist and warm philanthropist, was good for his own age. In our time, vacillating between two very different types, Franklin Roosevelt and Konrad Adenauer, I choose the former because his achievements had greater significance for world history. His demagoguery was tempered by humanity; he could not hate. He was fearless and had humor, two virtues that Bismarck, too, possessed; he radiated hope and meant well by people, which Bismarck did not.

■ Henry Steele Commager, United States historian: Washington and Jefferson. Both had character and intelligence and people had confidence in them. Leadership is intangible. You can't define all the parts.

Nobody should ever look anxious except those who have no anxiety.
Benjamin Disraeli

There is often as much independence in not being led, as in not being
driven.
Tryon Edwards

You have not converted a man because you have silenced him.
Lord John Morley

No man is good enough to govern another man without that other's
consent.
Abraham Lincoln

Your position confers on you only the obligation to so live your life
that others can take your orders without being embarrassed.
Dag Hammarskjöld

Morale is faith in the man at the top.
Albert S. Johnstone

You can employ men and hire hands to work for you, but you must
win their hearts to have them work with you.
Florio

A great leader never sets himself above his followers except in
carrying responsibilities.
Jules Ormont

Nothing more impairs authority than a too frequent or indiscreet use
of it. If thunder itself was to be continual, it would excite no more
terror than the noise of a mill.
A. Kingston

POLITICAL ASTUTENESS

Knowing that there are always other sides and other viewpoints, and
knowing how to recognize and deal with them is political astuteness.
The following qualities combine to form a person's political astuteness
ability:

Intellect	Knowledge
Logic	Courage
Nimble-mindedness	Ambition
Realism	

Rarely if ever is anything good (or bad) for everyone. In all walks of life where are constituencies that desire opposite paths to be taken. The ability to see these constituencies, to weigh between them, to secure their approval or at least tolerance, is absolutely essential to being an executive. The negative opposite of political astuteness is naivete.

Never cut what you can untie.
Joseph Joubert

Some people never seem to be able to realize that there is an opposing view with adherents that must be dealt with. These people go charging forward.

This is not to say that at some point one shouldn't "roll over" some opposition. Indeed, this kind of fierceness is absolutely necessary. But it should be done consciously, premeditatively, and deliberately, with the knowledge that the opposition will be there and will be disappointed or outraged, as the case may be.

"Decide what is right; then decide what is possible. If you don't decide what is right first, you'll never start in the right direction." With these words, the head of a large government agency set the tone for his people who were charged with selecting a contractor for a large satellite program.

He knew that even though Company A might have the better price and product, if Company B were located in a high unemployment area, that might outweigh the other considerations—and often did. He was realistic, and knew that politics often undid the "right" decision.

Another example of political astuteness follows:

A major radar corporation had excellent customer contact with the Air Force and knew that they had to bid a "phased-array" radar to win the big procurement. The problem was that engineering didn't want to build a "phased-array" radar. It was "too new, too radical, too risky," they said.

The engineers raised such a fuss that the vice-president/general manager had to appoint a "czar" to settle the disputes that were arising daily between marketing and engineering in the writing of the proposal.

The new czar, Andrews, told the marketing manager that he would settle the issues as he saw fit, some for marketing but some for engineering. That was all right with Collins, the marketing manager.

"I'd like to call on the Air Force project office," added Andrews. "I want to be sure they want phased array."

"Sure," said Collins.

Collins's subordinate got him alone. "You can't let Andrews call on the Air Force. He's too tough. He'll rub them wrong. Besides, they have told us so many times they want phased array that for us to ask again at this late date will cast doubt on our sanity."

"You're right," said Collins. "But how do I tell that to a czar?" Collins thought a minute. "Leave it to me. Andrews will never see the Air Force." He never did. Collins, by a series of stalls and subterfuges kept him away—*and* kept him happy even though he never saw the Air Force.

The company won the $100,000,000 contract.

And Anthony Jay, in *Management and Machiavelli* published by Holt, Rinehart and Winston, writes:

> Their chief competitor ran into grave cash-flow troubles which they themselves, for special reasons, escaped. But they did nothing. It was not that they did not see the opening; they saw it, and they took action. But the actions were little more than gestures, and the reason was that their real energies were absorbed by a full-blown baronial war. One of the senior managers, with the known sympathy of some members of the board and an important corporate shareholder, was trying to get control of two other departments and some important production resources. Other managers were resisting bitterly. Long passionate memos were being placed before some executives and passed behind the backs of others. The talk in dining rooms and bars was of nothing except this all-absorbing internal conflict. Managers spent the journeys to work and back pondering nothing except the next move in the battle; they talked about it endlessly to their wives, and lay awake half the night thinking about it. Resignations were mooted and threatened, and preliminary secret approaches made to other companies. In short, all the thought and energy and passion that should have gone into the sales and promotion drive were diverted into the baronial war. When it was over, the opportunity had passed.

Another example from my experience:

The senior vice-president had ordered the engineering group to reverse course. They were hurt and angry. As a gesture of conciliation he also criticized their opponents, the marketing people. "You people never made it clear that we needed a computer for this effort. You guys weren't out in front enough."

"You're right," said the marketing vice-president. He was throwing himself on the pyre, so to speak, to ease the pain of the engineers. He was politically astute.

The marketing manager, however, was not politically astute. "Wait a minute," he said. "I wrote you a letter on that three months ago." "Ha," he thought, "I've got him. The letter is in the file."

The senior vice-president fixed him with a glare. "I don't read my mail."

The marketing manager was speechless. The outrageousness of it was mind-blowing. What the hell did he mean, he didn't read his mail?

But the marketing vice-president was quick. "You're still right, Vin, even if we wrote you a letter, we didn't make a big enough issue of it. We should have been more forceful."

The marketing manager was not dumb. At this point, he shut up. He was beginning to learn political astuteness.

True political astuteness is rarely seen. It is done so adroitly that usually it is not noticed at all and just seems to fit with the natural flow of things. On the other hand a lack of political astuteness can be recognized almost immediately. The individual's actions stand out like a sore thumb.

We were about to merge two divisions and I was to head the resulting merger. One of the high-level managers from the other division came to see me. "I have some ideas," he said, "about how you should organize. Would you like to hear them?"

"Yes, I certainly would," I answered. "What do you have in mind?"

He hesitated. "Before I give you my ideas," he said, "I'd like your commitment that you will give me one of the three top jobs in your division."

This was so blatant and raw a thrust for power that it was almost laughable. Indeed if it had not happened to me personally I would find it hard to believe that any high-level manager could be so abrupt and politically naive.

I told him thanks but no thanks, and he proceeded to give me his ideas anyway. However, his clumsiness had made a lasting, negative impression upon me.

Stay on good terms with all sides, if at all possible. Make all conflict ideological and not personal.

Halberstam in *The Best and the Brightest*, published by Random House, comments on Averell Harriman during the Kennedy Administration:

Or was [Averell] Harriman himself too single-minded, too ruthlessly seeking power, too much the outsider wanting to enter the Administration in the early days to bother with the second tier of government, concentrating his affection on the top-level people only, . . . showing his rude and brusque side to the others, such as [Lyndon] Johnson, forgetting that most basic rule of politics: always stay in with the outs.

Earlier in this book under Courage we quoted the review of David Halberstam's book by retired General James Gavin. We cited the incident when, according to Halberstam, General Maxwell Taylor, President Kennedy's military advisor, is discovered to be sending messages to the United States military leaders in Viet Nam telling them how to respond to queries from the White House.

Halberstam makes a very interesting point in the book showing how politically astute some of the White House aides were.

The White House staff is puzzled, Halberstam reports, because a telegram from Viet Nam to the White House refers to a cable of General Taylor's. They find no cable of Taylor's sent from the White House.

So, suspicious, they call the Pentagon and ask for the Taylor telegram by number. But, Halberstam reports, they carefully "call a low-ranking clerk, not someone in the Chairman's [of the Joint Chiefs] Office who might have understood the play."

A person not politically astute may have just called a high-level liaison officer, and been told that there was no such cable, or that it was missing, or something. Or, if they had gotten the cable, the Pentagon people would have at least tipped off Taylor that the White House was aware of his telegram. Being politically astute got the result, the telegram, without showing their hand.

Loyalties

Perhaps the clearest way to show what the politically astute manager must perceive is to describe the reporting relationships in large corporations. On paper and in practice, the staff heads—personnel, finance, legal, public relations, etc.,—report to the division president. But many of these heads see their long-term future at the corporate level. One moves to be head of personnel at the Cement division at Denver, Colorado, but believes that *home* will be at corporate headquarters in Los Angeles. See Fig. 4.3.

Loyalties then are divided. They work for the Cement division, but their long-term goals and careers are controlled more by the corporate headquarters staff heads than they are by the Cement division president. With divided loyalties, confusion, conflict, and intrigue thrive. The division finance head is a check and balance on the division president, as well as being the president's staff support.

Not to recognize these divided loyalties and not to take them into account is to be politically naive—and to risk being hit by poor results in your efforts to move projects forward!

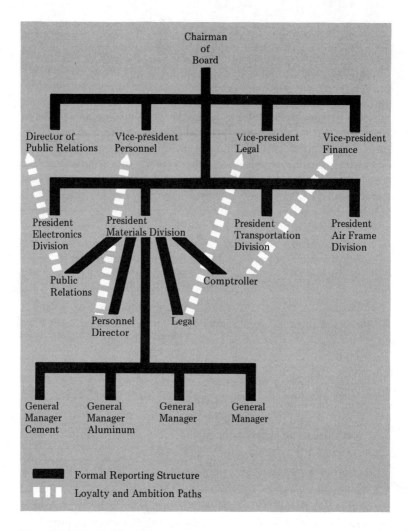

Fig. 4.3   Divided loyalties.

When political administrators change in Washington, D.C. after an election, new heads of governmental departments are appointed such as the Secretary of Transportation, of Labor, of the Treasury. Often political figures are given these posts. The politically astute recognize that the real power resides with the 20-year career civil servant who has headed a branch in say, Transportation, and has connections on Capitol Hill. The long time professional has more real power than the new 'amateur' politician. Either a struggle for power or an accommodation follows the change of administration. Even though all organization charts show the Secretary as holding the power, this is seldom the case in actual fact.

Robert N. McMurry, in a *Harvard Business Review* article, "Power and the Ambitious Executive," has this to say:

The position of a top executive who has little or no equity in the business is often a perilous one, with little inherent security. If things go well, his tenure is usually ensured; if they go badly, all too often he is made the scapegoat. Since many of the factors that affect his performance are beyond his control, he is constantly subject to the threat of disaster. His only hope for survival under these conditions is to gain and retain power by tactics that are in a large measure political and means that are, in part at least, Machiavellian.

Such strategies are not always noble and high-minded. But neither are they naive. From the selfish standpoint of the beleaguered and harassed executive, they have one primary merit: they enhance his chances of survival.

Observation of many politically astute executives in action indicates that most of them utilize supplementary ploys in coping with and influencing owners, associates, employees, and other groups. They know that an executive-politician must:

- Use caution in taking counsel—He may take the views of others into account, but he knows the decisions must be his. Advice is useful but, unless its limits are recognized, it can easily become pressure. (Realism, Independence)

- Avoid too close superior-subordinate relationships—While he must be friendly with his subordinates, he is never intimate with them. His personal feelings must never be a basis for action concerning them. His door may be "open"—but not too far. (Emotional maturity, Insistence)

- Maintain maneuverability—He never commits himself completely and irrevocably. If conditions change, he can gracefully adapt himself to the altered circumstances and change course without loss of face. (Independence, Political astuteness)

- Use passive resistance when necessary— When under pressure to take action which he regards as inadvisable, he can stall. To resist such demands openly is likely to precipitate a crisis. Therefore he initiates action, but in such a manner that the undesired program suffers from endless delays and ultimately dies on the vine. (Independence, Courage)

- Not hesitate to be ruthless when expedient —No one really expects the boss to be a "nice guy" at all times. If he is, he will be considered to be a softy or a patsy and no longer deserving of respect. (A surprisingly large segment of the population has a strong need to be submissive. Hence these people are more comfortable under a ruthless superior. This can be clearly seen in the rank and file of many labor organizations.) (Insistence, Willpower)

- Limit what is to be communicated—Many things should not be revealed. For instance, bad news may create costly anxieties or uncertainties among the troops; again, premature announcements of staff changes may give rise to schisms in the organization. (Realism)

- Recognize that there are seldom any secrets in an organization—He must be aware that anything revealed "in confidence" will probably be the property of everyone in the establishment the next morning. (Realism)

- Learn never to place too much dependence on a subordinate unless it is clearly to the latter's personal advantage to be loyal—Although some people are compulsively conscientious, most are not. Most give lip service to the company or the boss, but when the crunch comes, their loyalty is exclusively to themselves and their interests. (Realism)

- Be willing to compromise on small matters— He does this in order to obtain power for further movement. Nothing is more often fatal to executive power than stubbornness in small matters. (Realism)

- Be skilled in self-dramatization and be a persuasive personal salesman—He is essentially an actor, capable of influencing his audiences emotionally as well as rationally. He first ascertains his audience's wants and values. He then proceeds to confirm them, thus absolutely ensuring his hearer's acceptance of his message. (Empathy, Sales ability)

- Radiate self-confidence—He must give the impression that he knows what he is doing and is completely in command of the situation, even though he may not be sure at all. (Emotional maturity)

200

- Give outward evidence of status, power, and
material success—Most people measure a leader
by the degree of pomp and circumstance with
which he surrounds himself. (This is why the
king lives in a palace and the Pope in the Vati-   (Boldness)
can.) Too much modesty and democracy in his
way of life may easily be mistaken for a lack
of power and influence. For example, most subordinates take vicarious pride in being able to
say, "That's my boss who lives in the mansion
on the hill and drives a Rolls Royce."

- Avoid bureaucratic rigidity in interpreting
company rules—To win and hold the allegiance
of his subordinates, an executive must be will-   (Beliefs,
ing to "bend the rules" from time to time and   Independence)
make exceptions, even when they are not wholly
justified.

- Remember to give praise as well as censure
—Frequently, because he is under pressure
from his superiors, he takes out his frustrations
on his subordinates by criticizing them, some-   (Empathy)
times unreasonably. He must remember that,
if their loyalty is to be won and held, they merit
equal amounts of praise and reassurance.

- Be open-minded and receptive to opinions
which differ from his—If he makes people feel
that anyone who disagrees with him is, ipso
facto, wrong, his power will suffer. Listening
to dissent is the principal means by which he   (Courage,
can experience corrective contact with reality   Emotional
and receive warning that the course he is fol-   maturity,
lowing will lead to trouble. Also, openness to   Realism)
disagreement helps him to use his power fairly
—or, more accurately—use it in a manner that
will be perceived as fair by subordinates.

Are Mr. McMurry's words unnecessarily harsh? I think not. What
he has to say rings true. The idea that Machiavellian means are
not necessary is naive; they are. Idealists may rail against this, but they
are not being realistic.

The politically astute manager *always* keeps in mind that climbing
the ladder of advancement are many climbers, and they are in competition with each other a great deal of the time. And those climbers
include all levels of management. Often decisions are made on the
basis of what is good for a superior's career, as opposed to what is good

for the company. This is discouraging, but true. Often a decision is based on who will get credit for it, or on whether or not a superior and his or her superior are on friendly terms.

The large organization is made up of people, and it has all the people problems that families and societies have. Jealousy, deviousness, rivalry, unscrupulousness, ambition, timidity and all the other human conditions will be found. In order to get things done, effective individuals must be alert to these human traits, recognize them, and work their wills despite them. They must compromise and placate, threaten and cajole, steamroller and finesse.

A politician thinks of the next election; a statesman of the next generation.
J. F. Clarke

FORESIGHT

I hold that man is in the right who is most closely in league with the future.
Henrik Ibsen

The ability to see the end of the road, to be able to predict what will occur, is foresight. The following qualities combine to form a person's foresight ability:

Intellect	Independence
Logic	Realism
Nimble-mindedness	Courage
Knowledge	

Foresight is the ability to foresee and predict what will happen. Obviously, no one has this to an unerring extent. But many are able to foresee the outcome of events in looking at three or four apparently unconnected activities. By being able to foresee, one is able to forewarn and avoid. It is better to foresee too much than to foresee too little. It is better to be ready for things that do not happen than not be ready for things that do happen. Foresight has sometimes been called "having a good nose for trouble."

A young and outstanding engineer from another company interviewed for a job with us. We liked him, made him an offer. He thought it over for a week, then said he couldn't move because he couldn't sell his house. We offered to buy his house. He said, "OK, I'll join."

202

A week later he called. He couldn't leave his old company. A delegation of his friends and subordinates had appealed to him not to leave them. He couldn't refuse.

He was an excellent, but young, engineer. A person with foresight would have thought through the whole process, would have foreseen the possibility of such a delegation, would have taken steps to have either stopped it or explained to it why he had to leave. No foresight!

(Or maybe he just wanted his superiors at the other company to recognize that he was valuable!)

It is a part of the law of probability that many improbable things will happen. The worst does sometimes happen. As human beings we have to count on that possibility, have to arm ourselves against it and, above all, we have to realize that since absurdities necessarily occur, and nowadays manifest themselves with more and more forcefulness, we can prevent ourselves from being destroyed by them and can make ourselves relatively comfortable upon this earth only if we humbly include these absurdities in our thinking. Perhaps the most famous example of foresight in this century is Churchill's predictions of World War II. He predicted it many times, but no one listened. Due in no small part, however, to these predictions, he was quickly chosen to be Prime Minister when the war did come.

Subordinates are not always able to survive until events show their foresight to be accurate. Many managers do not like to hear forecasts that are not glowing in their view of the future. Subordinates can easily get the reputation of being "negative." In some companies, this reputation is the worst one can have. In such companies, one must be negative in a very positive way, which is quite a trick at times, but a very needed one.

> In our time, one has to ask children and the ignorant for news of the future.
>
> *Eric Hoffer*

Time Will Tell

The perspective of time is critical to seeing whether or not your actions are right or wrong. Consider the two words "stubborn" and "steadfast" and try to label persons who refuse to change their minds as stubborn or as steadfast. In one case, if they are being stubborn, they are acting wrongly, and the other case, if they are being steadfast, they are acting correctly. How does one tell whether they are being stubborn or steadfast?

The only way to tell is whether or not the persons are *right* in the position that they refuse to relinquish. Very often it can be several years before it is seen clearly whether they were right or wrong.

It is common for first-line managers to worry about next week; middle managers, the next quarter or next year; and top-level managers, the next decade. This expanding of scope is not difficult, if one has the mental qualities and the personality to think about the next decade. Most important in the mental ability area is knowledge. What happened in the last decade? What are our competitors doing? our government? our customers? Seemingly very difficult to find, this information is surprisingly plentiful and accessible to the top people of a large organization, especially if the organization is set up to collect it and feed it forward.

The further backward you can look, the further forward you are likely to see.
Winston Churchill

Human foresight often leaves its proudest possessor only a choice of evils.
C. C. Colton

The art of living is more like that of wrestling than of dancing; the main thing is to stand firm and be ready for an unforeseen attack.
Marcus Aurelius

We should all be concerned about the future because we will have to spend the rest of our lives there.
Charles F. Kettering

My advice to any young man at the beginning of his career is to try to look for the mere outlines of big things with his fresh, untrained, and unprejudiced mind.
H. Selye

5

Other Qualities;
Other Lists

In this chapter we'll look at other qualities that we did not think warranted being listed as executive qualities, and some other lists of talents that other authors, groups, professors, consultants, and schools have compiled.

OTHER QUALITIES/OTHER LABELS

Qualities not on the list may appear on the list of secondary qualities.

Creativity	Sincerity
Dedication	Enthusiasm
Loyalty	Thoroughness
High energy	

Creativity

It is wonderful to be creative; to have four ideas for every problem. It is decidedly a benefit in getting to be and performing as an executive. But in large organizations, executives manage hundreds of people who produce ideas that they can judge. Creativeness is therefore a secondary quality. Creativeness is much more important to the executive of a small firm than to the one in a large firm. Creativeness can be hired.

Dedication

Dedication springs from belief. If individuals do not believe in what they are doing, it is difficult for them to be dedicated to the effort, but not impossible. They may be dedicated out of a sense of pride, of commitment to excellence, but this dedication is never as great as dedication to a cause. Dedication is usually more important in attaining the top than in performing there. I have known many effective executives who were not dedicated to the task. They were, however, less effective than those with equal qualities who were dedicated.

There will usually be those in your company in competition with you who are willing to work two times the normal workweek. They will probably be intelligent and possess most of the executive qualities. They are indeed powerful competition, especially if you want to spend a "reasonable" amount of time at work.

Loyalty

Many books on management and success stress loyalty as a means of getting ahead. And this is correct. Loyal followers pose no threat to leaders. As leaders rise, they carry along their loyal subordinates.

The very word "loyal" has an emotionalism to it that makes "disloyal" akin to treason in our society. Yet think about loyalty but for just a short time and you can become troubled. Loyal to what? to whom? If you are loyal to your immediate manager, should you also be loyal to your manager's superior? Suppose your manager is being clearly unfair to a co-worker; does your loyalty to the co-worker conflict with your loyalty to your manager? Are you loyal or simply someone with no independence?

Yet clearly almost all "how-to-succeed" books emphasize loyalty. Which is right? Is loyalty a good quality, pure and simple? Or is it a quality that must be managed carefully? To even ask the question can raise doubts about a person, so strong is the American dictum that "to be loyal is good." But loyalty is not always good. Indeed, it is more often not even logical. Persons must be loyal to one thing only—their sets of beliefs. When your boss operates according to that set of beliefs, then you can be loyal.

When the boss operates in conflict with your beliefs (e.g., is unfair to a co-worker) then to be loyal to the boss is to be disloyal to yourself. It is inconsistent.

Many examples can be given illustrating conflicting loyalties. Should I help A, my boss, or B, my boss's opponent, who it happens is correct in my opinion? At this point, the opposite of loyalty—independence—comes to the fore. It is good to be loyal, but it is also good to be independent. Is it more loyal to support the boss in an error; or to state the facts as you see them, even if it hurts the boss's case? Here loyalty is thrown into opposition with integrity! You must choose integrity over loyalty.

Many times I've heard the argument that goes "I said that it was round because my boss believed it was round and I couldn't undermine my boss in front of the vice-president. I had to say it was round, even though I knew it was square." What a sorry excuse. What weakness.

There are many choices of action in the situation above. First, one can say nothing. If it is your boss's meeting, you have the option of keeping silent. (This assumes that you have stated your views strongly to the boss before the meeting, and that they were rejected. You can say, if pressed to state an opinion, that you have nothing to add, or that you can understand how your boss reached that conclusion. You can state that you don't agree with the boss, but point out that the boss has much more experience than you in these matters. Or you can just state your own position. Which of these choices to pick is an interesting question. Unfortunately there is no easy answer. So much depends on the issue and the consequences of the wrong decision. Questions to consider are, "Can the decision be easily changed?" and "What is your boss's attitude toward disagreement from below?"

This obviously evades the issue, but it must be skirted. Each instance must be decided on its own merits. The only absolute is "Don't support bosses *just* because they are bosses." Political astuteness and judgment are the abilities that enable one to make the correct choice!

Loyalty is the opposite of independence. Loyalty should be tempered by emotional maturity and judgment.

For subordinates (or superiors) to be trusted by their superiors (or subordinates) three qualities are necessary: beliefs, integity, and emotional maturity. The beliefs of the two individuals must be in fairly close harmony, or they will approach problems from different bases, and have difficulty communicating. Integrity means living in accordance with one's beliefs; if one does not, one is not trustworthy.

Possessing emotional maturity ensures that individuals will not violate their intellectual beliefs because of emotional instability. No fit of depression or euphoria will cause erratic actions. It is up to the boss to see that you will act as you must, even if you disagree with him.

Sincerity

Sincerity is a natural fallout or expression of emotional maturity. To be always sincere is easy if one is always honest. To be apparently sincere when you are not is deceptiveness. Sincerity is a good and valuable trait, but it is part of emotional maturity.

Sincerity is an openness of heart; we find it in very few people. What we usually see is only an artful dissimulation to win the confidence of others.
La Rochefoucauld

High Energy

Some people have high energy levels and others do not. Most executives have high energy levels. They are continuously on the go and are able to sustain that pace over exhausting hours and beyond the endurance of the average person. High energy is an outflow of ambition, beliefs, and emotional maturity.

Enthusiasm

Enthusiasm is an invaluable quality in selling, but it is listed as a secondary quality because it can too easily be groundless. The seller who is *always* enthusiastic lacks a little credibility.

Enthusiasm is a distemper of youth, curable by small doses of repentance in connection with outward applications of experience.
Ambrose Bierce

Earnestness is enthusiasm tempered by reason.
Blaise Pascal

Thoroughness

Thoroughness is a fine quality. It means being thorough, checking everything, leaving nothing to chance. It is attention to detail. Thoroughness is not on the prime list because it is a capability that is easily found and hired. Nimble-minded people sometimes find it hard to be thorough.

OTHER LISTS

Qualities can be grouped and described in many ways. Howard A. Westphall, Vice-President, J. W. Newman Corporation, Los Angeles, writing in *Industry Week,* January 21, 1974, describes them in this way:

- *Self-esteem* This is the foundation of high-performance behavior. You see yourself as valuable, worthy, and capable. You stand for something that is good. You know you can accomplish just about anything you set out to do. You deserve success, because the decisions you make and the actions you take are good. You eagerly seek out the new and the challenging. And you know that you can change and control the conditions which lead to your success. (Emotional maturity, Independence)

- *Responsibility* You know that you are a self-made person. You have put the events into motion which account for your success, and your failures. When things seem to go right or when things seem to go wrong, when things seem to drift along or when things seem to zoom ahead, you acknowledge your accountability. You reinforce the reasons for your attainments and correct for the errors. (Emotional maturity)

- *Growth orientation* You know it is impossible to stand still in a world of change. You've chosen to grow, rather than sink slowly toward eternal rest. (The "pro" in every field of endeavor searches constantly for more effective ways to grow and develop.) The more you can learn about yourself, the better. You give high priority to the task of getting ready for your future. (Ambition, Willpower)

You welcome the chance to trade old, unproductive habits for new, profitable thought patterns.

■ *Positive response to pressure* When deadlines close in, when a family crisis develops, when a decision is called for, when pressures of all kinds grow severe, you actually function better, more smoothly, more efficiently. You know that pressure and life are synonymous. Because you expect pressure, you've learned how to use it as a trigger to set off constructive responses. You've programmed yourself so that you peak up— rather than cop out—when hostile conditions surround you. You actually welcome times of pressure. Often, when everything is going along smoothly, you will "stir things up" by creating pressure because you know you function better.
(Emotional maturity, Durability, Courage)

■ *Trust* In every area of your life you feel an atmosphere of trust. You believe that people don't, as a rule, deliberately try to do badly. You're comfortable tossing the ball to another member of the team; you trust that person to act responsibly. This feeling of trust gives your communications with others honesty, directness, and openness which set the tone for genuine cooperation throughout all your relationships.
(Cheerfulness, Realism, Emotional maturity)

■ *Optimism* To the degree that your self-esteem and responsibility reach optimum levels, you expect things to be even better tomorrow. Because you know that you guide your destiny and that you are competent and worthy, there's every reason to expect that your future will be bright, good, productive, and profitable. You invest your time and your talents in full measure today because you're certain of harvesting the benefits tomorrow.
(Cheerfulness)

■ *Goal orientation* Many people set goals, and often nothing happens. If you are a high performer, you use your goals differently. It's what you do with your goals after you set them, the way you program your goals into
(Willpower, Foresight)

your system, that counts. You've learned to keep your goals before you continually, to live with them so they motivate you and direct your behavior.

- *Imaginativeness* By habit, you focus your imagination on the positive, constructive images toward which you want to move. You aren't limited to what you have done before. You can imaginatively experience new and profitable situations for yourself before they happen. You dwell in your imagination on all the good things you want for yourself. (High-performance people do not cope with change; they cause it!)

(Secondary quality)

- *Awareness* You absorb more information from what's going on around you. Because you know where you are headed, you are alert to the "road signs," and you are more aware of opportunities which can help you meet your goals. You see and make use of more signals, clues, and cues—in your business, your community, your home life, your leisure activities.

(Foresight, Communcations ability)

- *Creativeness* You're certain there's a better way to do just about everything. This attitude keeps you searching for new opportunities, new approaches, and new ways to implement your new approaches. You have learned how creative ideas flow more spontaneously and more fruitfully.

(Secondary quality)

- *Communicativeness* You know that your success is largely rooted in your ability to get your ideas across and to understand what the other person is trying to say. Thus, you take full responsibility to make sure the message gets through in both directions. You know it is profitable for you to understand how other people look at the world, so you've developed your empathy skills and use them as the foundation for all your communications.

(Communications ability, Empathy)

- *Joyfulness* You feel a real enjoyment in whatever you do; it feels good to work, to relate, to communicate, to achieve. You

enjoy your activities and the people you
work with. Your energy is contagious. It
radiates from you; others pick up your enthusiasm, and they, too, begin to work with
more enjoyment and involvement. You're
proud of your contributions to your own
goals and those of the company.

(Cheerfulness)

■ *Risk-taking* Life is not made up of guarantees. Because you realize and accept the
idea that all activity involves some degree
of probability, you are ready and willing to
reach out and take reasonable risks. Your
objective is excellence, not perfection. And
when you begin a new project, launch a new
product, or diversify your activities, you
weigh the probable gains against the probable losses.

(Courage and
boldness)

■ *Newness* As the high-performance characteristics approach summit levels together,
you feel a sense of nowness. You make decisions now, and you take actions now, not
because you have to, but because you want
to. You enjoy it. There's a continuous excite-
ment, intensity, and urgency in the air. You
reflect a sense of power, motion, accomplish-
ment, and enthusiasm.

(Emotional
maturity)

A chairman of the board of a textile firm listed the following:
An executive:

has absolute integrity
is willing and able to work
is objective
is a leader
has courage
has imagination
delegates and checks
watches his time
knows and props up his weaknesses
shares credit and blame
is a good listener
doesn't take himself too seriously
doesn't get discouraged
does what he says
is careful to state only facts
encourages subordinates to disagree with him

limits his reasons for doing something
does not get mad unless he decides to
sees the unusual and handles it
is not swayed by flattery
is decisive
must like people
has a sense of humor
has an obligation to guard his health

Here is a list that attenders of an advanced management school are ranked against:

1. *Ability to Think Critically and Analytically*
Does he try to get beneath the surface of a problem to discover its full meaning? Does he challenge basic assumptions? Does he have the ability to break up a problem into its essential parts, logically and systematically?

2. *Judgment*
Are his decisions or conclusions based on a careful and balanced consideration of the *facts* available and an awareness of the *values* involved?

3. *Originality*
Does he show creative imagination and resourcefulness in solving problems? in suggesting various alternatives?

4. *Independence of Thought*
Is he willing to stand up for his own convictions? Does he have intellectual integrity? Is he frank? outspoken?

5. *Emotional Maturity*
Does he deal with differences constructively? Can he accept criticism without being unduly upset? Does he remain poised when challenged or when majority opinion is against him? Does he adjust readily to changing conditions? Is he self-confident?

6. *Cooperation with Others*
Is he willing and able to work with others? Does he seem to prefer to work alone? Is he self-centered?

7. *Tact*
Does he know what to say and when to say it? Does he show skill in dealing with people? Is he considerate of others? Is he aware of the effect he has on others?

8. *Aggressiveness*
Is he forceful and assertive? Does he drive hard to achieve his objectives?

9. *Self-expression*

Are his speech and diction good? Are his presentations clear and interesting? Does he speak convincingly? Does he express ideas in logical order?

10. *Leadership Qualities*

Is he a natural leader? frequently consulted by others? sensitive to changing conditions and attitudes of the group? able to coordinate the efforts of others?

11. *Breadth of Business Knowledge and Interests*

Is his knowledge of business problems and practices broad and diversified? Does it extend beyond his speciality?

12. *General Impression*

Considering all of the factors above, how would you rate this man?

13. *Capacity for Advancement*

Indicate your judgment of the potential of this man for the position of *general manager* of a new division or its *corporate staff* equivalent.

William J. Reddin, of the University of New Brunswick, Canada, in his book *Managerial Effectiveness,* McGraw-Hill (Series in Management), describes four styles of management. In the book he lays out the following chart, which not only describes the four styles but cross-correlates them with other management structures by other authorities, such as D. V. McGregor, A. Zaleznik and D. Moment, R. R. Black and J. A. C. Brown, E. Jennings, D. Wallings, K. Horney, and K. Davis.

	Separated	Related	Dedicated	Integrated
(1) Interactional mode	Correcting	Accepting	Dominating	Joining
(2) Mode of communication	Written	Conversations	Verbal directions	Meetings
(3) Direction of communication	Little in any direction	Upward from subordinates	Downward to subordinates	Two-way
(4) Time perspective	Past	Unconcerned	Immediate	Future
(5) Identifies with	Organization	Subordinates	Superior and technology	Co-workers
(6) System emphasis	Maintains procedural system	Supports social system	Follows technological system	Integrates sociotechnical system
(7) Judges subordinates on	Who follows the rules?	Who understands people?	Who produces?	Who wants to join the team?

	Separated	Related	Dedicated	Integrated
(8) Judges superior on	Brains	Warmth	Power	Teamwork
(9) Committee activity	Clarifying, guiding, and channeling	Supporting, harmonizing, and coaching	Initiating, evaluating, and directing	Setting standards, testing, and motivating
(10) Work suited for	Administration, accounting, statistics, and design	Managing professionals, training, and coordination	Production and sales management	Supervising interacting managers
(11) Work not suited for	Nonroutine	Low personal contact	Low-power	High-routine
(12) Employee orientation	Security	Cooperation	Performance	Commitment
(13) Reaction to error	More controls	Pass over	Punish	Learn from
(14) Reaction to conflict	Avoids	Smothers	Suppresses	Utilizes
(15) Reaction to stress	Withdraws and quotes rules	Becomes dependent and depressed	Dominates and exploits	Avoids making decisions
(16) Positive source of control	Logic	Praise	Rewards	Ideals
(17) Negative source of control	Argument	Rejection	Punishments	Compromise
(18) Characteristic problem of subordinates	Lack of recognition	Lack of direction	Lack of information	Lack of independence
(19) Punishments used	Loss of authority	Loss of interest by manager	Loss of position	Loss of self-respect by subordinate
(20) Undervalues	Need for innovation	Needs of organization and of technology	Subordinates' expectations	Need for independent action
(21) Main weakness	Slave to the rules	Sentimentality	Fights unnecessarily	Uses participation inappropriately
(22) Fears about himself	Emotionality, softness, and dependence	Rejection by others	Loss of power	Uninvolvement
(23) Fears about others	System deviation, irrationality	Conflict	Low production	Dissatisfaction
(24) Reddin more effective style equivalent	Bureaucrat	Developer	Benevolent autocrat	Executive

(Cont.)

	Separated	Related	Dedicated	Integrated
(25) Reddin less effective style equivalent	Deserter	Missionary	Autocrat	Compromiser
(26) McGregor (140) equivalent	—	—	Theory X	Theory Y
(27) Zaleznik and moment (194) equivalent	Rational— procedural	Maternal— expressive	Paternal— assertive	Fraternal— permissive
(28) Blake (23) equivalent	3.3	3.7	7.3	7.7
(29) Brown (32) equivalent	Laissez faire plus strict autocrat	Incompetent democrat plus genuine democrat	Incompetent autocrat	Benevolent autocrat
(30) Jennings (103) equivalent	Abdicrat plus bureaucrat	Democrat	Autocrat	Executive plus neurocrat
(31) Walling equivalent	Objective thinker	Friendly helper	Tough battler	—
(32) Davis (42)	Custodial	Supportive	Autocratic	Collegial
(33) Horney (91)	Moving away (detached)	Moving toward (compliant)	Moving against (aggressive)	—

The following lists are from *The Pyramid Climbers* by Vance Packard, published by McGraw-Hill.

Dr. Chris Argyris of Yale states:

1. The successful executive exhibits high tolerance for frustration. He doesn't blow up when provoked.

2. He encourages full participation. He can permit others to discuss and pull apart his decisions without feeling his personal worth is being threatened.

3. He continually questions himself. He is willing to examine himself carefully and ask himself embarrassing questions. At the same time he has a high degree of self-respect.

4. He understands the rules of competitive warfare. (Dr. Argyris cites one executive who explained, "It's not a dog-eat-dog world, but I do get nibbled at.") The good executive is able to play it cool, in the British manner, and he doesn't feel distressed if a colleague shows a little "fight."

5. He expresses hostility tactfully. (Dr. Argyris explained to me: "This executive has a real skill for telling the other man to drop dead without batting an eyelash.")

6. He accepts both victories and setbacks with controlled emotions. (Such a man, says Dr. Argyris, "withholds and hides his own feelings of either pleasure or pain. . . .")

7. He can snap out of defeats without feeling personally shattered and can quickly start thinking of the next goal.

Still from *The Pyramid Climbers:*

Dr. Lyman W. Porter and Dr. Edwin E. Ghiselli of the University of California asked 1000 top-management people and 170 middle-management people to check what applied to them from a long list of adjectives. The results:

Top-management saw themselves as:	*Middle-management* saw themselves as:
capable	discreet
determined	practical
industrious	planful
resourceful	deliberate
sharp-witted	calm
enterprising	steady
sincere	modest
sociable	patient
pleasant	civilized
dignified	intelligent
sympathetic	courageous

Top managers, in contrast to middle managers, saw themselves as active, self-reliant, taking action based on self-belief, risk-takers, candid, straightforward, getting along well with others without having to ingratiate themselves.

Middle managers did not see themselves as reckless, egotistical, disorderly, opinionated, aggressive, outspoken, excitable, self-seeking, shallow, and tense.

In contrast to top managers, middle managers saw themselves as involved in careful planning, thoughtful action, and well-controlled behavior.

Three more excerpts from *The Pyramid Climbers*:

Professor William Gormbley, Director of Harvard's Advanced Management Program, described executives sent by their companies:

1. They are bright men.

2. They know how to get along well with people.

3. They have all got drive.

4. They are men who have goals.

5. They make the most of what they get.
6. They are not content to sit still.

Researchers for Booz, Allen & Hamilton studied forms filled out on 1427 executives to see what commonly distinguished the "promotable" ones from those not recommended for promotion.

1. Position performance
2. Drive
3. Intellectual ability
4. Leadership
5. Administration
6. Initiative
7. Motivation
8. Creativeness

Richardson, Bellows, Henry & Co., a large testing, consulting, and recruiting firm, identified six factors as vital indicators of future executive success:

1. The man matured early.
2. The man of promise rates higher in practical intelligence than most of the people he will ever manage.
3. He is self-confident but not aggressively so.
4. He demonstrates fairly early in life that he has broad interests and knowledge and a considerable curiosity about many things going on in the world.
5. He shows fairly early in his experience as a manager that he is developing more than his share of first-rate people.
6. He is willing to admit his problems and mistakes.

Packard synthesizes all the lists and, in a chapter entitled "Seven Abilities That Seem to Count Greatly," comes up with his own list:

1. The ability to maintain a high level of thrust.
2. The ability to be deft in handling people.
3. The ability to marshal a competent mind against the problems peculiar to executives.
4. The ability to communicate—and perhaps originate—ideas.
5. The ability to respond to provocation objectively and effectively.
6. The ability to enjoy organizing and running large projects.
7. The ability to generate confidence.

6
Executive
Environment

The most important factor in most high-level jobs in any organization is the lack of time. Executives rarely have time to do the things that they desire to do, or have to do. They are constantly putting off, or delegating to other people, things they should do personally. Because time is so critical to executives, communications ability becomes extremely critical, both to executives and to subordinates on their way to the top. The more quickly and directly one can communicate, the more one can accomplish.

The greatest of all sacrifices is the sacrifice of time.
Antiphor

Executives must decide how much time to give to the company, how much to the family, to the church or school or Little League, to themselves. No matter what allocations they make, the time they give to the job will always be too little to do 100 percent of the job. There will always be something else to be done, now.

Almost nothing executives do takes 15 minutes; everything always takes at least an hour. By the nature of their positions, the easy decisions get made at a lower level. Executives get the tough ones; tough in terms of agonizing choice, and tough in terms of being complicated to understand. A lot of executive time is spent just understanding the problem.

The idealized view of executives serenely sitting in their comfortable offices handing down decisions is just that—idealized. Most executives are out of time not because they are bad planners, but because *events* overtake even the best plans. A new product doesn't work the way it was planned, or doesn't sell the way it was forecasted. A key subordinate has a heart attack. The energy crisis springs upon the world. Environmental standards change. A thousand things can go wrong, and they usually do. It is executives' job to keep organizations going. It is to their offices these surprises come for resolution. *All* high-level jobs are time-eaters. Top executives cannot control everything.

Time is
   too slow for those who wait,
   too swift for those who fear,
   too long for those who grieve,
   too short for those who rejoice;
But for those who Love,
Time is eternity.

Henry Van Dyke

The following is by Herbert E. Meyer from *Fortune*, June 1974, on executive vacations.

Indeed any season of the year executives are apt to be forced to cope with unexpected developments in inflation, materials shortages, global political unrest, or government controls.

For example, the big economic surprise of 1971—the Phase One price and wage freeze—was sprung by President Nixon on August 15th, in the middle of the traditional vacation season.

Many executives who listened to that presidential announcement on radios far away from their offices came scurrying back to their desks the next morning. Others who had been planning to get away toward the end of that month quickly abandoned such hopes.

> Time is precious but truth is more precious than time.
> *Benjamin Disraeli*

POWER

Within any large organization today there are basically three sources of power:

1. Executives
2. Competent doers
3. Customers

1. *Executives:* They have power because they can hire and fire; they can promote and demote; they can raise salaries, create organizations, and set directions.

Perhaps not as obvious is the fact that any individuals who have the ear of executives are also powerful. Executive secretaries often have more power than middle-level managers, even though they are not the managers of anyone. Executives often place a great deal of credibility in the opinions that the secretary holds about people and/or business plans. An acquaintance, low in the organization but who knows the executive socially, can exert great power by dropping a word here and there to the executive. It is up to the executive to either accept or reject these inputs. Many executives do accept them, and therefore, these people that are close to the executive in one way or another have executive power, even if they do not have executive position, title, and salary.

2. *Competent doers:* In every organization there are individuals who are the outstanding engineers, or the outstanding printers, or the outstanding mechanics, or the outstanding etc. Although these individuals may not be managers, the organization depends upon them for a great deal of its day-to-day activity, and they are valued. They can look any executive in the eye and say, "I can't do that," and be believed. The executive, disappointed, still accepts the word

221

of competent doers, because they have been right in the past. In large organizations there are, of course, a large number of competent doers. Some of them rise to be executives themselves.

Competent doers who refuse to be promoted have a great deal of fun and freedom. They know what they are doing, and they are respected.

3. *Customers:* The third source of power is the customers. Every organization gets money or "income" from some set of customers. If the customer set consists of a few large customers, then each customer has a great deal of power over the organization. On the other hand, if there is a great diversity of smaller customers, then each customer's power is lessened. (In some cases, the "customer" can be another part of the same organization. The library of a university may have no paying customers, but it is still measured on customer satisfaction.)

Harnessing customer power is a tricky and difficult operation. Clearly, those in sales are the key beneficiaries of customer power if they are capable enough to put that power to work. Large corporations have been "stood on their heads" by competent marketing people handling large customers. The salesperson can become the wielder of the customer's power.

Most corporation executives will listen when a large customer speaks, even if the message coming across is most unwelcome, and even if it means a change in cherished plans.

Negative Power

In today's large organization a simple but bitter truth is that there are hundreds who can say "no," but there are few who can say "yes."

Organizations today are structured so as to check everything to prevent mistakes. Policies, practices, rules, and tradition are upheld—whether they make sense or not. This aspect of the big organization is often simply called "bureaucracy." Bureaucracy is frustrating, often totally so.

Some organizations seem to delight in putting obstacles in the paths of decision makers. (I am not talking about insecure executives asking for more study; we saw them earlier under Emotional Maturity.) The culprit that holds back progress is the system, the rules. It's "you can't."

Negative power sets up "policies" and *"goes by the book."* Any deviation is to be examined carefully.

When the game *Monopoly* was invented in 1933 by an unemployed salesman, he was unable to produce in his basement enough sets to satisfy his home area. He offered the game to Parker Brothers.

The corporation staff played the game and liked it, but it violated 52 basic rules of the company regarding games. It took too long to play. They turned it down.

Luckily for Parker Brothers a friend of the wife of the president called to tell her of the wonderful new game of *Monopoly*. The company bought the game. The rest is history.

Other examples of "great turndowns" abound. Western Union turned away Alexander Graham Bell and his telephone. RCA, GE, IBM and others turned down the basic Xerox patents. Several companies in the 1950s turned down a production-line laboratory machine that has all but revolutionized hospital laboratories. The owners of a small firm who were bold and took it became multimillionaires.

How many corporations today would hire Albert Einstein if he showed up as an applicant with his wild hair?

A chairman of the board of General Electric once challenged his management team, asking "How many of you would hire Steinmetz, the immigrant genius who had hundreds of patents to his—and GE's—credit before he finished?"

Bureaucracy stifles creativity like an immense fog. It is hard to fight because it is everywhere—yet no clear place exists to attack it!

How to ensure a bureaucracy. If you put capable people into jobs that are unimportant, they *will find a way* to make the jobs important. The danger of a large staff is that it will try to *run* the business out of a sheer excess of energy. One executive once said, "When I try to zig slightly off course to pick up a good opportunity or to explore a little, I find that there are seven other hands on the wheel: Planning, Finance, and Personnel,—all steering with me and unwilling to let me turn a single degree. Yet, if I go aground, it's my neck. I'm *supposed* to be sailing this ship." The fault here is with management, not with the staff themselves. They have been allowed to grow too large and they can do their own job in two hours a day. They'll spend at least five more helping someone who doesn't want their help. Thus are bureaucracies made!

Using Power

The natural result of thought is action. Without actions, people would not control their lives. Power is effective action. It is action that gets results. Some people have great power; most people have little. Executives in large organizations potentially have great power; potentially, because at times they fail to use it.

Truly powerful persons will often use all the power points to cause the organization to do the things they want it to do.

Knowledge of the "power points" of a corporation is the key to getting fast results and to resolving issues effectively. Powerful individuals know that Vice-President Jones will not make a decision without consulting his financial advisor. They know that the assistant to the president has great influence on the president in marketing matters. They know that the vice-president of personnel will not make any decision until the president has indicated the direction in which matters must flow. They add to their power if they know who the competent doers are.

These sources of power are often in conflict, going in different directions. One job of the executive is to allow enough conflict and yet keep the enterprise from fighting itself too extensively. Many people do not understand that these conflicting power sources exist. They believe that what the executive says, happens.

Powerful individuals often deliberately pit one faction against the other. They may pit a large customer's desires (which are also theirs) against the desires of their superiors. They pit a doer against the staff. They manage the power sources.

> We were negotiating a major contract and finance didn't want it. They said "you can't" a dozen times. And each time the marketing people took it to the president and won. But the finance people kept saying, "You can't." Energy was wearing out!
>
> Late one evening the marketing manager called the vice-president. "They said we can't agree to Standard Clause 32. We'll have to see the president—again, I'm afraid."
>
> "Should we accept the clause?" asked the vice-president.
>
> "Yes. It's a standard clause in all government contracts."
>
> "Then tell finance that we are going to do it. If they don't like it, let them go to the president."
>
> The marketing manager did. Finance didn't. We signed, and nothing bad ever happened because of Clause 32!

Authority

Let us not confuse power and authority. Power is the ability to get something done. Authority is the legal or organizational approval for one to make certain decisions and give certain directions or commands. That the command is very often not followed is a surprise to too many new managers.

A great many executives have great authority and little power, for they either fail to use the authority or use it badly. Other executives have power far beyond their authority, for they assume and usurp authority as an everyday part of life!

Don't be misled by the trappings of power. There are many vice-presidents with big salaries and offices who *do* nothing or close to it.

A group vice-president had two division presidents reporting to him. He saw them once a month together at lunch, and they never discussed business. The presidents worked directly with the corporation president. The reason for this? The president was piqued at his subordinate, the group vice-president.

The only unusual thing about this is that it went on for years.

David Halberstam, in *The Best and the Brightest,* writes about Lyndon B. Johnson in his early senate years:

Johnson leaned over, grabbed Baker [Russell Baker, *New York Times*], "You want a speech, you go see Lehman and Pat McNamara. They'll make you a speech. . . . You want to find out how things are *done,* and you want to see things done? You come to me."

CONFLICT

Not only is conflict a fact of life but most organizations foster it in order to sharpen the resulting decisions. Executives must be able to accept conflict, handle it, foster it, use it, and stop it. They must not foster it unless it is helpful. Constant conflict will wear down an organization and its people. How executives seek, promote, and handle conflict tells a great deal about them. Without adversity, it is very difficult to tell the true stars from the mass of the employees.

When everything is going right, everyone looks good.

SIZE OF ORGANIZATION

Obviously the president of a company which employs 70 operates on a completely different plane and scope than the president of a company which employs 70,000. The president of one requires a very different use of the qualities than the president of the other. In the large company the upward moving executive must exercise political astuteness much more often than the small-company president. In the small company, some of the secondary qualities become more important, perhaps become primary qualities.

For example, creativity is a secondary quality in a large company because it can be found in abundance in employees and then utilized by the executive. In a small company there aren't that many employees. It is useful for the executive to be creative.

Complexity is an unmeasurable burden the manager struggles with. It is very different from size. It is harder to manage a chemical company than it is to run a bank; it is harder to run a hospital than a school.

The job of the high-level manager in a small organization is vastly different from that in a large one. There is no bureaucracy to block plans, to check and recheck operations. There is no reservoir of creative people constantly sending ideas upward.

DECIDERS AND ADVOCATES

The controller of a large company is usually an executive, but the general manager is almost certain to be. Functional managers (sales, finance, personnel, production, etc.) can be somewhat parochial. They can take a one-sided role; "Let the boss decide. The opponents to my scheme will argue their case well." In many cases, this is precisely what happens.

The burden falls on general managers. All functional managers will be advocates, but they should also be more. They should also lay out for the general managers the consequences of the decision going either way, as the functional managers see those consequences.

Functional managers run the risk that by being constantly one-sided they don't learn to be general managers.

It is much more difficult and demanding to be a general manager than to be a functional manager. The decisions are more difficult, the consequences of them more far reaching.

Ralph Cordiner, Chairman of the Board of General Electric for thirteen years, was asked by *Forbes* magazine in 1967, after his retirement, why it took him so long to evolve the corporation from a functional organization to a decentralized one. His answer:

> For one thing, I thought that a lot of the fellows we took from functional jobs [engineering, manufacturing, sales, finance] and made general managers would respond to the challenge of being measured. I was wrong. I should have realized that you can't expect a fellow who has been running just a part of it to, all of a sudden, be accountable for the whole thing.
>
> In fact, to my surprise, a lot of people who looked good in functional jobs actually asked to be passed by. They didn't want to stick their necks out. A lot of these people and some others came to me and said, "See all the troubles you've caused and the heartaches." OK, but if I hadn't, the company couldn't have gone from $2 billion to $5 billion—and now it's $7.2 billion.

Chief financial officers are certainly high-level managers who make a lot of money and have tremendous influence. But do they make the really tough decisions? Or do they simply recommend to general managers a course of action?

It is the general managers who *make* the tough decisions after listening to the recommendations of their chief lieutenants, of whom the financial vice-president is but one.

The situation is akin to the court trial, where an advocate (the lawyer, or the chief financial officer) espouses a case. The advocate has the luxury of knowing that an opposite case will be made by an opponent—in the court another lawyer; in the case of the financial vice-president, perhaps the vice-president of marketing. In the court case, a judge must *decide*. In the organization example, a president (or the general manager, or site manager, or area manager) must decide.

The emotional weight that the advocate must bear is far less than the weight that the decider must bear. The advocate can go home at night and say "I argued well. My logic was sound. But the boss decided otherwise."

The boss goes home, agonizes once again over both sides of the argument, and thinks, "I wonder if my decision was the best one I could have made."

This emotional burden is a heavy one, and we treat it at length in the section, Resilience and Durability.

A chief executive of a small company told me about the people who gave him advice.

"They split into two classes: those who tell me what I should do, and those who tell me what the key considerations are, but who are careful to *not* tell me what to do.

"The latter are usually people who are on the board of directors, who have had high-level jobs. They recognize the burden the decider bears. They would not presume to tell me what to do; they know how hard it is to be the decider.

"Those who tell me what to do are generally the younger managers who have never had a top-level job."

Direction of Interaction

Too many power seekers do not recognize the fact that in today's large enterprises most managers interact in five different directions.

All are conscious of subordinates and superiors, but many people overlook peers.

When peers are considered, they are too often viewed by some power seekers as nothing but competitors—competitors for the next promotion, for the critical resources, for the time of the boss.

Indeed peers are competitors, but they are also potential supporters, subordinates, and superiors. One never knows which peer will

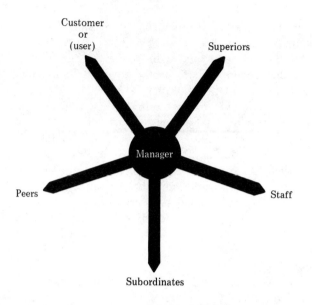

Fig. 6.1   Managers interact in five directions.

become the boss. Even if you become the boss, it will be easier to manage your ex-peers if you treat them with respect and dignity while you are at their level.

Relationships with peers are signposts to superiors.

> A high-level manager got into a feud with a peer. They didn't speak to each other, and made life difficult for all. A position opened up above them both, and the manager asked for the job. He was refused.
>
> "Yes, you have all the other qualities," he was told, "but you were childish to get into a public, demeaning feud. That is not very mature."
>
> The manager explained all the provocations he had been subjected to, how he had had no choice but to lash back.
>
> "No excuse," he was told. "It is just not mature to stoop to that kind of thing."
>
> He didn't get the job and neither did his battling peer.

A fourth group—the staff specialists, such as legal, personnel, and financial experts—are viewed by some rising managers as opponents to be avoided, thwarted, or beaten down.

The astute power-seeking manager realizes that staff members have two loyalties. One is to the profession they serve. The staff careerists develop a loyalty and respect for their calling that is deep and dangerous to attack. Lawyers have a deep respect for the law, no matter who they work for. To try to steamroller a point, to mock a legal principle, can change a potential supporter into an enemy, or into at least a detractor. Personnel people and finance people have the same kind of feelings toward their callings.

The second loyalty is described by the name staff itself. The staff is the staff of the boss. There is a bond between the boss and the staff that many rising managers never seem to understand.

To attack (or worse, to ignore) the staff invites their counterattack or at best their lack of support when their boss—who is also *your* boss—asks, "What do you think of Smith?"

The fifth group with which the rising manager interacts is outside the company. Usually customers make up this group.

Clearly, the relationship here is different from the internal relationships. Power-seeking managers should practice and polish their marketing skills. The general manager must be able to work effectively with customers.

I have seen interesting combinations of effectiveness in these five directions. One particular middle-level manager was very effective with his subordinates and the customers. He was neutral with his peers. And he was terrible with his superiors. They disliked him intensely.

Another young middle-level executive was fine with subordinates, peers, customers and superiors—but the staff couldn't abide him. "He's no good," they'd say.

After talking to this manager, I determined—and he agreed— that he just didn't think that getting along with the staff was important. Once he focused on the fact that his career could be hurt by poor rapport with the staff, he changed his approach and decided to "be nice" to the staff. He stopped treating the staff like servants, and his career prospects were much improved.

Rising managers should work on their relationships to all five groups. A common mistake is to concentrate all efforts toward superiors. Occasionally this will work, but even if it does, it will sometimes last only so long as the particular superior is in power. Once that superior leaves, potential executives are in trouble if they have not been working on the other four groups.

What you tell marketing managers to persuade them can be very different from what you tell staff experts.

A salesman was telling the lawyer why he should be allowed to sell below cost.

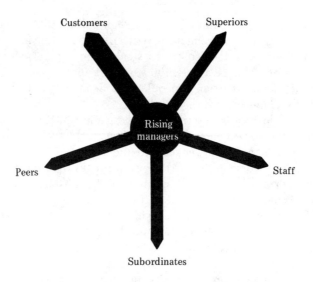

Fig. 6.2 Managers must interact with groups external to the company.

The salesman was telling the lawyer, "We could possibly get a follow-on order for 20 million dollars. If the competition gets in, we'll never get them out."

These two statements had the effect of convincing the lawyer to disapprove. The statements were great for the sales manager, terrible for the legal counsel.

A "Market-Oriented" Society

In the United States today, in virtually every field of endeavor, marketing personnel are paid more than technicians. This is because the United States economy is market-oriented. It is a consumer-driven economy, and the purchase of goods or services is the key starting point the economic cycle. Engineers and scientists resent the fact that those in sales are paid more, get more powerful jobs, and often run the companies. Their resentment often is focused on the company or local executive, but they are missing the point. It is a societal, not an organizational, phenomenon. They must learn the trade of the salesperson.

In such a market-oriented society, the personality of individuals becomes most important. Individuals' personalities mainly shape the result of their interaction with others. Knowledge, intellect, and beliefs become less important (not unimportant, but less important).

A teenager was quite capable, but liked to have a good time.
The woman next door told his mother in a rather rude display

230

of candor, "Your son is very personable, but he won't get far. He likes a good time too much."

He got to be a president. The neighbor didn't understand the society.

He succeeded *because* he was personable and liked a good time, not *despite* that fact.

There are "performance executives" and there are "marketing executives." An executive who can be both is clearly much more valuable than an executive who can be only one.

An organization was so structured that certain high-level managers were totally performance-oriented. They did not have responsibility to *sell* the project but to perform—to make the 1000 gizmos in ten months. Such executives began to ignore the marketing role completely.

Such an attitude usually gets the job done, but it too often means an unhappy customer and no follow-on contract. The customer is not so dazzled by performance, when it is accompanied by an open display of dislike.

The company lost a $15-million follow-on because the performance manager for three years did not think it was his job to "sell" the customer.

The opposite is true also. "Marketing executives" can decide that their jobs stop after they get the order. Then it is up to production (or systems or engineering) to do the rest. They should keep one eye on the performer and ensure that the customer is "happy" with the efforts.

Why do we include this advice here? It's obvious! We include it because it is *so often* violated. Especially by the performance people. They simply do not understand the real world.

Complete executives do the whole job; they are "general managers," even if they are managing only a small project. Their job is to complete the task, with their people intact and eager for the next job, with the customer happy with their company! A tall order, but an everyday one.

Perhaps the reason for the split between marketing and performance can be seen from the different qualities that are needed by the two positions. The list for sales is strikingly different from the list for project management. Obviously the general manager must be able to do both and the combined list (Fig. 6.4) is an almost complete list of the needed executive qualities.

Qualities	Sales	Project manager
Emotional maturity		√
Independence		
Realism		√
Courage and boldness	√	
Ambition	√	√
Insistence		√
Willpower	√	√
Empathy	√	√
Cheerfulness	√	
Resilience and durability	√	
Beliefs		
Integrity		
Intellect		
Logic	√	
Nimble-mindedness	√	
Knowledge	√	√

Abilities

	Sales	Project manager
Judgment		√
Communications ability	√	
Sales ability	√	
Leadership		√
Political astuteness	√	
Foresight	√	

Fig. 6.3 The checkmarks show the difference between the qualities and abilities needed for success in sales and for success in project performance.

Executives are dealing with people constantly. They are paid to keep the organization—the people—effective and moving. They must manage people. They can't delegate this management, they must *do* it.

A "successful" executive quit after setting up a new corporation of which he was chairman of the board. The new firm was doing fine but he didn't like managing the other executives. And he had to do it. He kept the title of chairman of the board, but he stopped running the business.

Many executives must deal with "customers." The "customers" may be truly customers, like the users of the firms and product, or "inside customers," e.g., the marketing vice-president is a "customer" of the production vice-president.

The age of exploiting the worker is over (at least in most societies in today's world). Therefore, today's managers must do two jobs. First, they must accomplish their goals, within the resources—time, money, and materials. Second, they must manage, conserve, and *increase* the *human* resources under their control.

They should motivate their subordinates, leaving them ready and enthused for the next task. They should *train* their subordinates, making them more capable for the next assignment. A manager who *does one but not both* jobs is *not* doing a good job.

VISIBILITY AND EXPOSURE

Visibility is getting the opportunity to see how the organization operates. A choice of a job in New York at Headquarters or in San Diego in a branch is a difficult choice—most people would prefer living in San Diego—but to learn the business, to see how the organization makes decisions and operates, there is no place like Headquarters.

A "task force" or "special committee" can be an excellent way to get a glimpse behind the curtain of the Wizard of Oz and to see how things really happen.

Exposure means being seen by the executives. The trick here is to let them see you in action. Obviously there are risks to this but you might as well find out how you stack up against your competitors. The best way to get exposure is to be in the middle of a crisis. Either have a critical account, or a critical project. The boss will be around to see the problem sooner or later. People who run everything smoothly often get very little attention.

"It's Who You Know That Counts"

This absolutely true saying is true in two directions. First, if you know people in the organization, you can talk to them freely and you know to whom to go for assistance. Second, if you know the executives and have talent, you are more likely to get ahead than if you have the same amount of talent and you don't know the executives.

Some people argue that this is "unfair," and some large organizations try (through reviewing promotions) to make it more "fair."

What to Look For in a Job

There are four things to measure a job by. If you are not getting one of the four, change jobs.

First, enjoyment. If you enjoy your job, it's not work; it's fun. No more to be said; don't change.

Second, learning. If you don't enjoy your job but you are learning, then you are growing by the learning and becoming better.

Third, achievement. If you are not enjoying or learning, but achieving a result, then you are accomplishing, producing. If it is something worth while; don't change jobs too soon.

Fourth, practice. You may not be learning, enjoying, or achieving, but if you are practicing needed skills, sharpening needed qualities, then don't change jobs too soon. This last, practicing, is not as obvious as the first three. We'd like to think we are "natural" leaders, "natural" executives, but the truth is we all learn by doing, by making mistakes, by finding a way to do something more easily, more smoothly.

If your job has all four things, you are indeed fortunate. If it has none, change jobs if you can!

Don't work just for money.

TRANSPLANTS

High-level newcomers have a very tough time of succeeding. Something seems to elude them. Actually at least three things are working against these individuals. The resentment of the subordinates who didn't get the job is obviously a factor to contend with. In addition, the newcomers have a new society and all its beliefs to absorb. Unless they are very fast learners, they will try to base decisions on their old beliefs—which may be disastrous.

Third, they lack knowledge. They don't know where the "bodies are buried." They don't know that a new product was tried three years ago and embarrassed the president who was the proponent of the disaster. They don't know that the workers everyone is so willing to transfer to them are the marginal or weak workers. They accept them in good faith—and suffer.

It is sometimes easy to identify the marginal people. They were the "deadwood" that all the old-time managers will transfer to the incoming high-level manager in an effort to "help the newcomer out."

WORKAHOLICS

Some people are "workaholics." They must work or they are miserable. They are in the office all the time, until all hours of the night and all day on weekends. Such work habits wreak havoc on the home scene *and* havoc on subordinates. There are just three points to be made about workaholics:

1. They are tough competition. If they have the qualities, it is difficult to stay with them because they *know* more because they spend all that time.

2. As the name suggests, they are usually mixed-up people and have some tough problems. If some of your subordinates are workaholics, you should be aware of their problems and the problems they cause, which takes us to number 3.

3. It is usually a miserable experience to work for a workaholic. You spend ridiculous hours at work just to get *to see* the boss. A meeting at 11 P.M. for you to give your presentation is not unusual.

DELEGATION

Delegation is the giving of your work to a subordinate to do. It is more an emotional achievement than an intellectual achievement, although it is both. Effective managers on the rise are on the rise because they have been effective in their past associations and efforts. They know what they can do. In order to delegate, however, executives must not do; they must be content to send others off and have them do. There is an emotional aspect to delegation, because there is worry and uncertainty. The job may not get done, perhaps because of the inefficiency or inability of those to whom it was delegated, or perhaps because the communication in the delegation itself was faulty. Even when the job is done right, there is still an emotional lack. Executives do not get the same direct emotional feedback of success because it was done not by them but by others. Effective executives should learn to get some of the emotional reward from a task done by subordinates that they would get from doing it themselves.

Executives who will not delegate will not rise very high, and usually the reason they will not delegate is emotional. They lack emotional maturity.

INCESSANT COMPETITION

In today's large organization, competition for the next raise, the next promotion, the next assignment is ever present. There are always others who will spend more time, work harder, cut some corners, butter up the boss more, etc., etc., in order to beat you to the next job.

And it never ends. Even if you are the very unusual one who gets to be *the* boss, you must still worry and protect your position. And if you are only a vice-president, you are not secure at all. You must please the boss.

THE QUALITIES GRAPHS

You are an executive whose task is to select a high-level subordinate basing your decision on the following four qualities: knowledge, mental power, beliefs, and personality qualities. You are interviewing four candidates for the position, each of whom lacks one quality. Which would you choose? The candidate who:

a) lacks only knowledge but will be great as soon as the candidate learns the ropes?

b) is a great administrator but lacks mental power?

c) is a superman out of control whose beliefs are "wrong" but who is not beyond hope?

d) is a know-it-all s.o.b. who has no personality quality?

In choosing the candidate you would probably take into account certain facts.

a) A candidate's lack of knowledge can almost always be rectified in time.

b) The candidate who lacks mental power is still a respected, solid, steady performer.

c) The candidate probably doesn't want to change personal beliefs; but it's possible.

d) The candidate's lack of personality qualities is the toughest lack; people don't like the candidate.

Let's look at the following diagrams and characterize the type of individual represented by them. For these diagrams, we'll make knowledge a separate area.

A long arm from the center to the name of the quality means that the person possesses that quality, the absence of the arm indicates a lack of that quality.

236

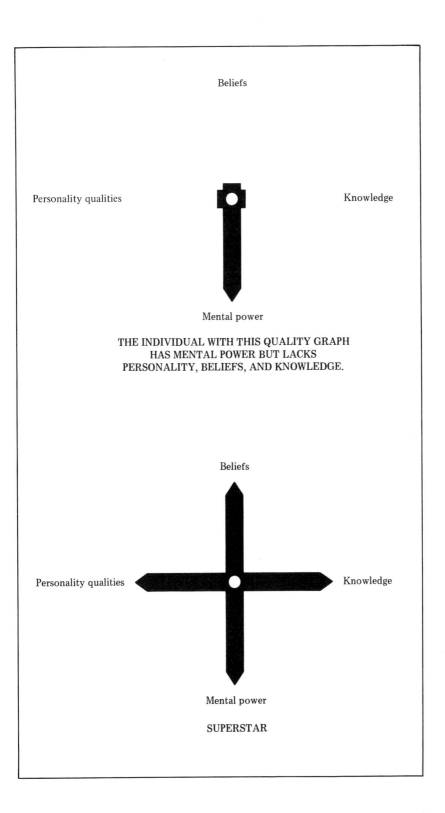

Beliefs

Personality qualities   Knowledge

Mental power

**THE INDIVIDUAL WITH THIS QUALITY GRAPH
HAS MENTAL POWER BUT LACKS
PERSONALITY, BELIEFS, AND KNOWLEDGE.**

Beliefs

Personality qualities   Knowledge

Mental power

SUPERSTAR

237

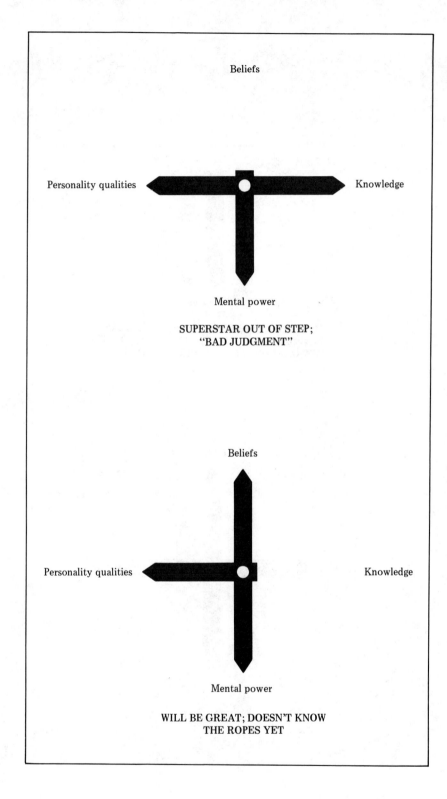

Beliefs

Personality qualities   Knowledge

Mental power

**SUPERSTAR OUT OF STEP;
"BAD JUDGMENT"**

Beliefs

Personality qualities   Knowledge

Mental power

**WILL BE GREAT; DOESN'T KNOW
THE ROPES YET**

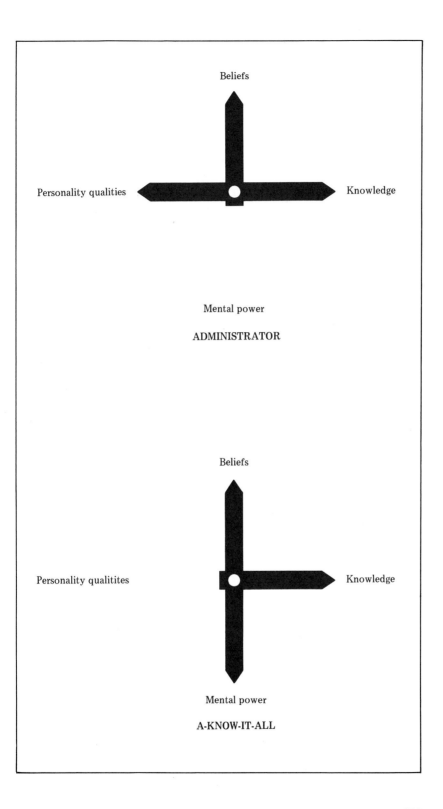

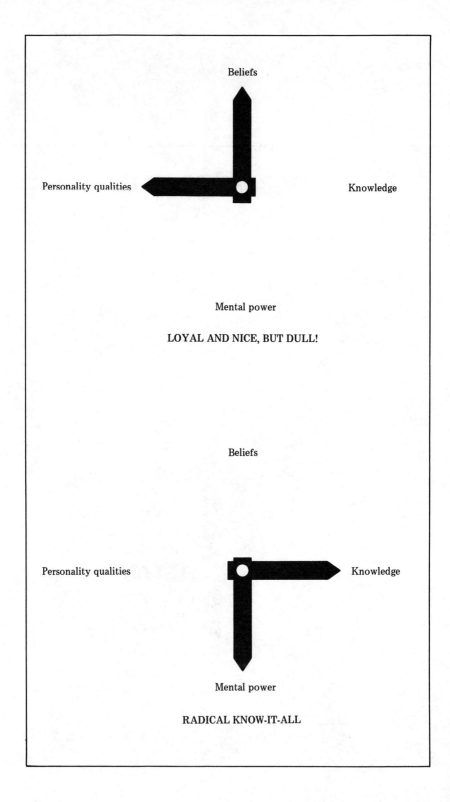

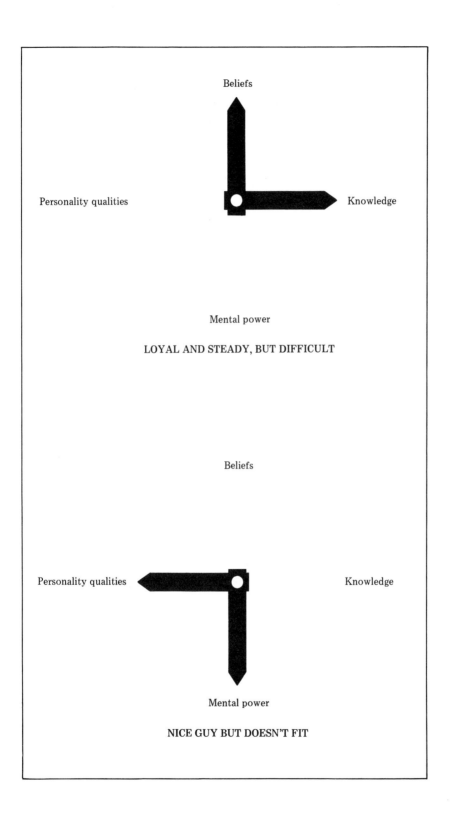

Beliefs

Personality qualities

Knowledge

Mental power

LOYAL AND STEADY, BUT DIFFICULT

Beliefs

Personality qualities

Knowledge

Mental power

NICE GUY BUT DOESN'T FIT

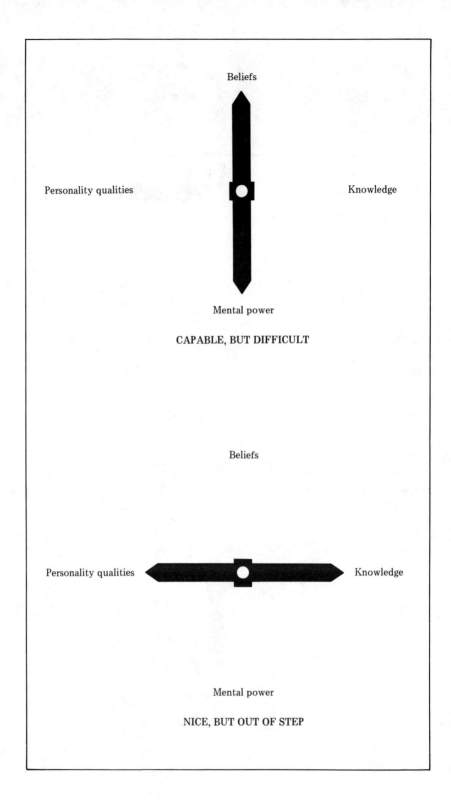

Beliefs

Personality qualities   Knowledge

Mental power

CAPABLE, BUT DIFFICULT

Beliefs

Personality qualities   Knowledge

Mental power

NICE, BUT OUT OF STEP

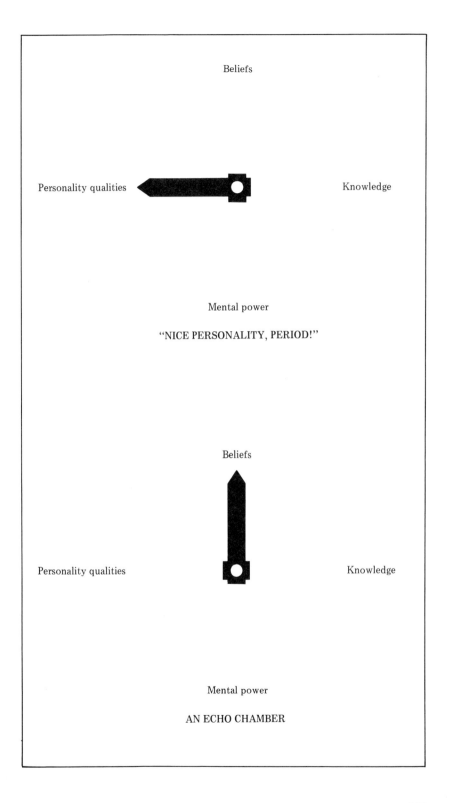

Beliefs

Personality qualities   Knowledge

Mental power

"NICE PERSONALITY, PERIOD!"

Beliefs

Personality qualities   Knowledge

Mental power

AN ECHO CHAMBER

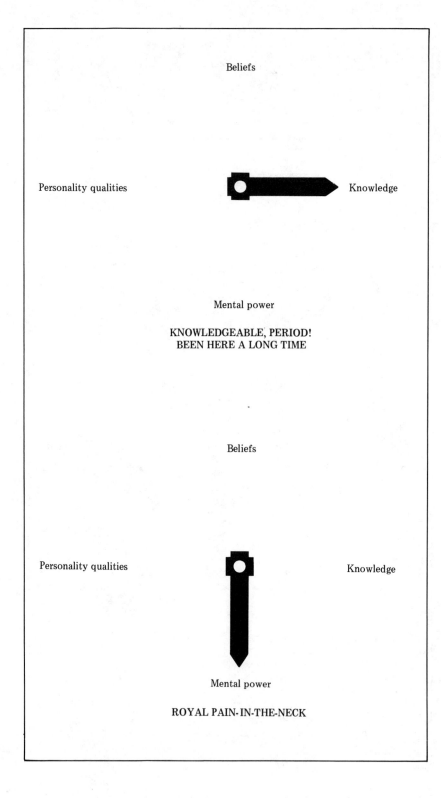

Beliefs

Personality qualities   Knowledge

Mental power

**KNOWLEDGEABLE, PERIOD!
BEEN HERE A LONG TIME**

Beliefs

Personality qualities   Knowledge

Mental power

ROYAL PAIN-IN-THE-NECK

Beliefs

Personality qualities
Knowledge

Mental power

NOT GOING TO MAKE IT

An Epilogue: Success

There are masked words abroad which no one
understands, but which everyone uses, and most people
will also fight for, live for, or even die for—fancying they
mean this or that, or the other. . . .

John Ruskin

This book is about personal qualities. There is an unstated premise that
getting to the top, that being an executive, is *good!* But is it?

Most people find themselves caught up in the race for power without reflecting upon whether it is really what they want. Society tells
them they want it. Let's look at *Success* in depth!

The dictionary says that success "is the gaining of wealth, position,
or other advantage; prosperous, fortunate." Wealth and position is the
way most people understand the word, but they are oversimplifying!
The word has far more meaning than merely wealth or position or other
advantage.

Let us examine some of the common conceptions of the word success and see if we can gain some insight in the process. Such insight
is important, for as Ruskin said, some people are willing to die for
some notion of a word that they have not really understood.

IS MONEY SUCCESS?

Bill Simpson made $35,000 per year. He is 34 years old, but he is no
success. He is in deep trouble with his company. He achieved his
former salary by luck and ruthlessness that finally caught up to him.

His neighbors think that Bill is a success because he has money
and lives well. They do not know that Bill was removed from his most
recent job because his people rebelled. He was too hard a taskmaster,
and too little concerned about his people. One of the fine salesmen in
Bill's office quit, and when management looked to see why, they found
a very unhappy group of people in that office. Bill was taken out of
that job and transferred to a different city, where he is now. His pay
was cut, but he still makes $25,000 per year. But far worse than the
pay cut was the fact that Bill's reputation was in trouble. No one
wanted him. He was assigned a small cubicle at the main headquarters
location. He had no work to do. He read the newspapers and maga-
zines. In time, he did not even come to work on Mondays and Fridays.
The people in the nearby offices ignored him; his manager ignored him.

He started to drink. At 34, he is through in that company. He has
lost his drive and self-confidence. The 31 years until he retires look
grim.

Bill is *not* a successful man, he has been "de-hired."

Sam Williams is rather the opposite of Bill Simpson. He makes
$35,000 per year, but his upward climb on the career ladder is at an
end. He is a "middle-level" manager, with 100 people working for him.

He is respected by all, valued by the company, and at 35 has achieved a fine position. For many reasons (lack of technical knowledge, for one) his upward progress is at an end. His family life is happy and warm.

Is he a success?

It would seem so. But, no, sadly, he is not because *he* believes he is not. His goal (unrealistic) is several steps higher than the level he has achieved. And the knowledge that he isn't going to get there has made him bitter. His anger is hurting things at home.

He believes he is a failure; therefore, he is.

IS MONEY PLUS POSITION SUCCESS?

Have you heard about "de-hired" executives? These are executives, sometimes vice-presidents of very large corporations, who have fallen into disfavor and yet are not fired for one reason or another. Instead, they are given useless jobs to perform, and in the long run, they quit! Fired? No! "De-hired."

One high-up was sent to Europe, supposedly to set up operations there. It was a few months before he realized that no one back home in the States was reading the reports he was sending. He had been sent to Europe to be gotten out of the way!

Others are not so fortunate to be sent to Europe. They are "allowed" to stay where they are, and this is even tougher to take. It is soon obvious in a big company who is not being invited to the board meetings. "But Mr. Smith, you always go to the board meetings," his secretary says before she understands that her boss is no longer an influence. "Yes, but today I have a more important thing to finish," he alibis. But, of course, he has no important thing—and she knows it— and soon so will all the others.

Isn't it much harder to take such a fate if you were once in power, if you once had a big job and were an important man? Why doesn't he quit?

Stock options that must be exercised over a period of time may keep him on the company payroll. Or he can't get another job at the $50,000 salary that he is now getting, and he needs every cent of that money. So he swallows his pride and comes to the office every day and is humiliated.

The number of people making excellent salaries while de-hired is not small. These people surely are not "successful."

And even if you are president of a large, successful, exciting business firm and you have your own jet-powered airplane, and you spend a lot of time in the tropics every year—and your teenage son has just been arrested for drug abuse—are you a success?

Money and position do not bring happiness automatically.

POPULARITY?

If money is not a sure sign of success, then how about great popularity? The people who are cheered by multitudes—are they successful? Maybe.

Let's look at some instances of great popularity. In 1938, when Neville Chamberlain, Prime Minister of Great Britain, came back to England after his meeting with Hitler in Munich, he was hailed as a hero. He had secured "peace in our time." When Hitler invaded Poland less than a year later, Chamberlain was in utter disgrace and driven from office.

Charles Stewart Parnell was the great Irish leader of the 1880s. In the midst of a turbulent, adoring crowd, he was unmoved. When asked why the emotional welcome did not affect him, he replied that the crowd was fickle and that next year they could well be just as emotional in condemning him. The next year they were.

HISTORY: THE TEST OF TIME?

It is sad to hear people, usually when they are in trouble or de-hired, recite their heroic deeds of five years ago. By pointing to past glories they hope to impress upon you their present worth. But life is demanding and the important thing is *today's* worth.

The changing of fortunes, the rise and fall of popularity, leads us to another aspect of success—time. If history declares persons to be successes, then are they?

Many greats are unknown by history.

Many greats are acknowledged great today yet they were not always seen to be great.

Churchill, out of office from 1929 to 1939, was seen as a colossal failure, and was blamed for the World War I Gallipoli failure.

No! A person's "standing" at a point in time does not make that person a success or failure! Even after death.

People are seen in a different light as time passes. Their actions can't change, but their actions can be reinterpreted in many different ways.

Is the verdict of history then the badge of success? If history deems you great, then you are a success? No, for the verdict of history is imperfect and changing. New information is found, and massive social changes now show an individual against a different backdrop than the times of 30 years ago.

FAILURE

Let's look at the word that means the opposite of success—failure. Failure is not losing; it is quitting, it is "not trying." T. J. Watson, the founder of the IBM Corporation, once said that he judged a person not by successes but by failures. You can tell a lot about persons by what they attempt—whether they succeed or fail. The world is sometimes better served by a noble failure than by an easy victory.

Not only may the world be better served but also those who do the failing. They stand out in their failure to be judged—if they have performed in a superior manner, but fate is such that victory is not to be theirs, their efforts stand for all to see.

To boldly dare and not succeed is no failure. It may miss the mark, but it is only a step, not the whole journey.

One must view each episode of life in a somewhat detached way. Life is long, and a failure here and there is nothing to be ashamed of. Indeed, if you have no failures, you ought to worry that you are not thinking big enough, that you are not daring.

Roger Bannister was the first man to run a mile in less than four minutes. He was a thin, almost emaciated man. He spoke of defeat in a way that one would speak of success.

> Failure is as exciting to watch as success, provided that the effort is absolute and complete. But the spectators fail to understand—and how can they know—the total agony through which an athlete must pass before he can give his maximum effort . . . and how rarely, if he is built as I am, he can give it.

All of us should be what we are capable of being; to be less is to fail. To perform the highest tasks that we are capable of—that is success. And a hundred small detours on the journey are not failures. They may even be necessary to the overall journey in that they may show which way is the wrong way.

Leonardo da Vinci, on his deathbed, said, "I have offended God and man because my work has not achieved the quality it should have." Only God and Leonardo know if he was right—maybe not even Leonardo! ! !

Have you failed lately?

WHAT SUCCESS IS

Then what is success? Not popularity, not money, not power, not achieving greatness at a point in time, not historical repute. Then what?

It is being at peace with yourself. It is usually arrived at by doing your best and being satisfied with the results whether that makes you a number 1 or a number 10, or a number 100!

Doing one's best may be being the best police officer on the force, or the fourth best; it may be being the teacher who gets through to the difficult student. Who knows? You—and only you. Or you should.

No one else knows your talents, your capacity, your failings. No one else knows whether you are a success or failure. You must honestly and diligently seek to know your capacities.

Success means managing your expectations to fit your capabilities! Success is success at *life*—not at a career. It is accepting yourself as "OK," in the "I'm OK—You're OK" Thomas Harris sense. A career is just a part of that.

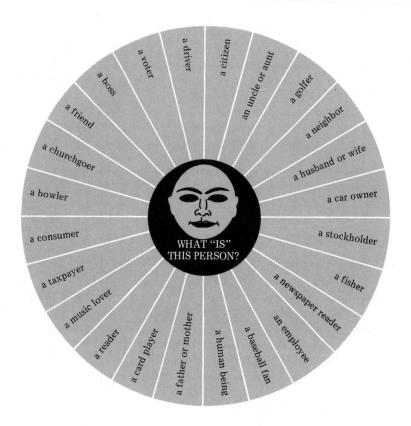

Persons who are "succeeding" (as they judge themselves) in most of these areas should never judge themselves failures just because their job goals are not being met. They should judge themselves failures who succeed greatly at work and fail in all other endeavors.

Success is liking yourself.

The secret of happiness is this: Let your interests be as
wide as possible, and let your reactions to the things
and persons that interest you be, as far as possible,
friendly rather than hostile.

Bertrand Russell

To finish the moment, to find the journey's end in every step of the road, to live the greatest number of good hours is wisdom.

Ralph Waldo Emerson

He that is proud of riches is a fool. For if he be exalted above his neighbors because he hath more gold, how much inferior is he to a gold mine.

Jeremy Taylor

Money may be the husk of many things, but not the kernel. It brings you food, but not appetite; medicine, but not health; acquaintances but not friends; servants, but not faithfulness; days of joy but not peace or happiness.

Henrik Ibsen

A successful man is he who receives a great deal from his fellowmen, usually incomparably more than corresponds to his service to them. The value of a man, however, should be seen in what he gives and not in what he is able to receive.

Albert Einstein

Pleasures, riches, honor and joy are sure to have care, disgrace, adversity and affliction in their train. There is no pleasure without pain, no joy without sorrow. O, the folly of expecting lasting felicity in a vale of tears, or a paradise in a ruined world.

Gotthold

The great and glorious masterpiece of man is to live to the point. All other things—to reign, to hoard, to build—are, at most, but inconsiderate props and appendages.

Montaigne

If thou art rich, thou art poor; for like an ass, whose back with ingots bows, thou bearest thy heavy riches but a journey, and death unloads thee.

Jeremy Taylor

Contentment is a pearl of great price, and whoever procures it at the expense of ten thousand desires makes a wise and a happy purchase.

Balguy

There is a burden of care in getting riches; fear in keeping them; temptation in using them; guilt in abusing them; sorrow in losing them; and a burden of account at last to be given concerning them.

M. Henry

Rank and riches are chains of gold, but still chains.
Ruffini

Wealth is not only what you have but it is also what you are.
Sterline W. Sill

To love means to commit oneself without guarantee, to give oneself completely in the hope that our love will produce love in the loved person. Love is an act of faith, and whoever is of little faith is also of little love.
Erich Fromm

Contentment, and indeed usefulness, comes as the infallible result of great acceptances, great humilities—of not trying to make ourselves this or that, but of surrendering ourselves to the fullness of life—of letting life flow through us. To be used—that is the sublimest thing we know.
David Grayson

The world is a great mirror. It reflects back to you what you are. If you are loving, if you are friendly, if you are helpful, the world will prove loving and friendly and helpful to you. The world is what you are.
Thomas Dreier

Happiness is determined by the number of persons one loves.
Dagobert D. Runes

The harvest of happiness is most often reaped by the hands of helpfulness.
Gilbert Hay

The moving finger writes, and, having writ,
Moves on; nor all your Piety nor Wit,
Shall lure it back to cancel half a line,
Nor all your Tears wash out a word of it.
Omar Khayyam

Honor, glory, praise, renown and fame—each is but an echo, a shade, a dream, a flower that is spoiled with every shower.
Torquato Tasso

I have learned that success is to be measured not so much by the position that one has reached in life as by the obstacles which he has overcome while trying to succeed.
Booker T. Washington

Happy the man who has broken the chains which hurt the mind and has given up worrying once and for all.

Ovid

Fame usually comes to those who are thinking about something else.

Oliver Wendell Holmes

The desire for fame is the last weakness wise men put off.

Tacitus

Fear less, hope more; eat less, chew more; whine less, breathe more; talk less, say more; hate less, love more; and all good things are yours.

Swedish proverb

True contentment does not depend on what we have. A tub was large enough for Diogenes, a world too little for Alexander.

C. C. Colton

He enjoys much who is thankful for little. A grateful mind is both a great and happy mind.

Thomas Secker

It is not in mortals to command success, but we will do more, we will deserve it.

Joseph Addison

Every person is responsible for all the good within the scope of his abilities, and for no more, and none can tell whose sphere is the largest.

Gail Hamilton

Not his job makes a man little or big, it is himself, his spirit, his character. If these be right, then his job will sooner or later reflect the fact. He will not forever be kept down when his merits entitle him to be raised up. The wait may be long. But it will not be heartbreaking. His inner consciousness of faithful effort will buoy him. Life's "failures" do not all wear rags; some of the most pitiable of them can write their names to seven-figure checks. The "successes" are not all recognizable on sight.

B. C. Forbes

The reward of a thing well done, is to have done it.

Ralph Waldo Emerson

Contentment lodges oftener in cottages than in palaces.

Thomas Fuller

A contented mind is the greatest blessing a man can enjoy in this world.

Joseph Addison

Success is full of promise till men get it, and then it is as a last year's nest, from which the bird has flown.

Henry Ward Beecher

Success is counted sweetest by those who ne'er succeed.

Emily Dickinson

For happiness must be tricked! She loves to see men at work. She loves sweat, weariness, self-sacrifice. She will be found not in palaces but lurking in cornfields and factories, and hovering over littered desks; she crowns the unconscious head of the busy child. If you look up suddenly from your work you will see her, but if you look too long she fades sorrowfully away.

David Grayson

Man is the kind of creature who cannot be whole except he be committed, because he cannot find himself without finding a center beyond himself. In short, the emancipation of the self requires committment.

Reinhold Niebuhr

Lack of desire is the greatest riches.

Seneca

I dread success. To have succeeded is to have finished one's business on earth. . . . I like a state of continual becoming . . . with a goal in front and not behind. Then too I like fighting successful people, attacking them, rousing them, trying their mettle, kicking down their sand castles so as to make them build stone ones and so on. It develops one's muscles. Besides one learns from it.

George Bernard Shaw

While one finds company in himself and his pursuits, he cannot feel old, no matter what his years may be.

Amos Bronson Alcott